BE YOUR OWN MENTOR

RANDOM HOUSE

NEW YORK

BE YOUR OWN MENTOR

STRATEGIES FROM TOP WOMEN ON THE SECRETS OF SUCCESS

Sheila Wellington
and Catalyst

WITH BETTY SPENCE

RANDOM HOUSE and colophon are registered trademarks of Random House, Inc.

Cataloging-in-Publication Data is available.
ISBN 0-375-50060-X

Printed in the United States of America on acid-free paper
Random House website address: www.atrandom.com

10 12 14 16 18 19 17 15 13 11

Book design by Victoria Wong

This book is dedicated to the mentors, friends,
and family of Catalyst . . .

Diane Allison · Jennifer Allyn · Raquel Arroyo · Patrick Block
· Barbara Bayeghems · Michelle Brown-Nevers · The Brunetti-
Huneke Family · André Canty-Swapp · Steven Chen · Wei Li
Chen · Jennifer Chi Ling Lam · Tony & Helen Combopiano ·
Evelyn Criswell · May Daniel · Dorothy Derr · Esmeralda Diaz
· Mary Baker Eddy · Robin Ely · Ruth Fanelli · Gillian Collins
Farrell · Edna Forbes · Jody Franklin · Monica Gallagher ·
Helen Estuar Gonzalez · Jill Gregerson · Jennette R. Gregory ·
Maria R. C. Guida · Catherine L. Harold · Howard Hayghe ·
Carol Hickey · Trudi Hoffman · Sarah Holland · Christine
Hospedales · Debra Hunsberger · Selma Hutchings · Brennan
James · Scott Kane · Doreen Elizabeth Kersey · Liz Kim · Jade
Kolb · Roger, Sara and Andrew Kropf · Elizabeth LaBella ·
Jacqueline LaBella · Esther Levine · Grace Leung · Steven M.
Levy · Chris Madell · Antonia Magliulo · Sarah Mahrer · Lilly
Ann Mattis · Chris McBride · Tacara McBride · Derrel
McDavid · Michele McKenley · Ann McManus · Helen
McManus · Manjula Mehta · Nandini Mehta · Bettie Moore ·
Carol Moore · Clara Moore · Motu · Angela Ossorio ·
Oluremi Adebisi Oyewole · Khristianna and Alix Randazzo ·
Natalie Rarick · Kathy Regan · Mary Regan · Carol Rex ·
Dayna Rittenberg · Julie Russell · Courtney Sexton · Norma
Shand · Eunice Shea · Buffy Summers · Ross Takahashi · Celia
Teller · Helen Collins Tobin · Katherine Tobin · Ka Yee Tom ·
Valerie & Barrington Tulley · Lynn Untz · Margaret Wade ·
Michaela Walsh · Lance Arthur Watson · Mary & Tennyson
Watson · Jo Weiss · Sharon Welle · Harry Wellington · John
Wilcha · Patricia Wilcha · Carol Winograd · Gladys Wolfe ·
Anna Wong · Michael Yip · Wan Tai Yip · Chui Wah Yu

Acknowledgments

This book is the product of Catalyst's work over the years with women and men in a myriad of organizations who have generously participated in interviews, focus groups, and surveys, some of which have been cited in this book.

Everyone at Catalyst is indebted to our Board of Directors and Board of Advisers for their dedication and wisdom, which continue to help us realize our mission of advancing women.

Thanks go to all the staff at Catalyst, past and present, whose collective knowledge, solid research, and dedication to the goal of advancing women have provided the foundation for this book. Special thanks to Betty Spence, whose name appears on the title page. We are also indebted to Carol Wheeler for her invaluable contribution. Our gratitude goes to Marcia Brumit Kropf and Mary Mattis, who were deeply involved in the project from its inception. Thanks also to the many current and former Catalyst staff who have written, reviewed, and edited numerous drafts or sections of this book, especially Nancy Guida, Donna Manning, Jamie Parilla, Merle Pollak, Rennie Roberts, Gayle Turk, and Jo Weiss. We would like to express special appreciation to Kate Medina, our editor at Random House, for her belief and support, and, for good and sufficient reason, to Jeremy Feigelson, Barbara Paul Robinson, and Mariana Vaidman-Stone of Debevoise & Plimpton.

Members of Catalyst's Communications Department provided invaluable editorial assistance: Jamie Parilla, Robin Madell, Sonia Ossorio, Debbie Zarlin, Daniela Brunetti-Huneke, and Cameal Phillips. Special thanks to Jill Gregerson, who provided painstaking work preparing the manuscript for the publisher.

We are grateful to Michele LaBella and the Information Center staff, including Jan Combopiano, Jacqueline Tyson, Michelle Bernard, and Ellen Savett for rapid turnaround of critical research information, and thanks to Rachel Gonzalez, Nicole Johnsen, Tammy Lilly, and Veera Pollard for their meticulous attention to verification of data. The following members of our research team were indispensable in providing issue expertise: Jennifer Allyn, Paulette Gerkovich, Katherine Giscombe, Nancy Kane, and Tara Levine. Thanks also to Frank Ricotta and Jennette Gregory for technical support and to Tayo Akinyemi for her last-minute assistance.

A heartfelt thank-you to Ann Patruno and Cherish Pratt for keeping Sheila Wellington's life organized.

Many thanks to the executive and career coaches who were interviewed for this book.

Finally, at the heart of this book you will find the words of women pioneers—from corporations, firms, nonprofits, and academia. The insight they provided during the interviews added enormous value to the final product. We thank them for their contributions and applaud their bravery.

Contents

BE YOUR
OWN
MENTOR

Introduction

In my experience, the single most important reason why—among the equally talented—men tend to rise higher than women is that most men have mentors and most women do not. My opinion is confirmed by more than thirty years of research on women and their work conducted by Catalyst, the organization I head, which is the nation's preeminent source of information on women in the workplace. Mentors are more important to career success than hard work, more important than talent, more important than intelligence. Why? Because you need to learn how to operate in the work world—whether in a corporation, a professional firm, a nonprofit, a university, or the public sector—and mentors can teach you how. The dictionary will tell you that a mentor is "an experienced and trusted counselor." At work, that translates into a person who can hook you up with the experiences and people you need to move ahead—and tell you how to handle them. Mentors can show you the ropes. And pull strings.

Mentoring in the work world has traditionally existed as an informal practice. An executive takes a liking to an up-and-comer and brings him under his wing. Often, he selects someone who reminds him of himself as he was when starting out. Athena, the goddess of wisdom, was the first mentor. In the *Odyssey* she took on the form of a man named Mentor in order to give Odysseus advice. She then guided Odysseus's son, Telemachus. Even nowadays, men are the traditional mentors. When women train their sights upward, they often see no one in senior management who looks like them. Even in organizations that have made women's advancement a priority, there aren't enough women mentors to go around. The few women near the top tell us that they mentor happily and often, but they just don't have time for everyone.

If you're a woman of color, the problem of finding a mentor is doubly difficult. Of the 2.9 million women holding managerial and administrative jobs in the private sector, only 14 percent are women of color (6.6 percent African American, 5.2 percent Hispanic, and 2.5 percent Asian/other). In Catalyst's survey *Women of Color in Corporate Management,*[1] women of color stress the critical importance of mentors to a career and report that a lack of mentoring has been a serious barrier to their advancement. They also make it clear, though, that it really isn't necessary to have a mentor who looks like you. Said one African-American manager who found a white male mentor, "I did it for selfish reasons. I know the world is white male, and so I had to think and do as the white male, so [I knew] he would help me."

These days, women need good advice from a trusted mentor more than ever. The number of women nearing senior management ranks increases yearly. In 1950, only a third of women worked outside the home. Women's wholesale entry into the workplace started in the late 1960s, when, new degrees in our briefcases—B.A.s, M.A.s, Ph.D.s, and, yes, MBAs—we forged a shift in workforce demographics. Today women make up nearly

47 percent of the workforce, and by last year, 60 percent of women were working.[2] For more than three decades, we have been storming the citadel of the American workplace. That should have been long enough for us to see some numbers approaching parity in executive suites, but when I look around, despite the occasional well-publicized example, I just don't see parity, and I doubt anyone else can either. The statistics speak for themselves: generally, in the American workforce, the higher the level, the fewer women are on it. In fact, women from all kinds of organizations tell me they keep hitting professional roadblocks. The thousands of women Catalyst has interviewed since its founding in 1962—ranging from the pioneers to Generation Z—have made it clear that they need more guidance. They need to know what to do to get where they want to go.

Be Your Own Mentor is a response to that need. With it, I hope to help you be your own Athena. As your guide, I will be presumptuous enough to act as an older, wiser adviser to whom you can turn with your questions about how you can move ahead. (My own experience has been informed and enhanced by Catalyst's body of knowledge on this subject, gained through research in the real world—with corporations, firms, nonprofits, academia, and women themselves.) I will help you map out your life and provision you with the skills and equipment to pull down the barriers you meet or circumvent them when that's the best approach. Whether you're a woman just starting out with fresh parchment in your pocket, one bent on a career change, or a manager doing well but wanting to do better, this book is for you.

Why a book specifically for women? Men face many of the same career roadblocks that women do, but women come at them from a different angle and need different advice. Traditionally, too, men have had better access to career guidance. It's still more comfortable for men in the know to offer their advice to other men, so we face some unique questions, such as: How can women develop credibility in a male environment? How can a woman land the kind of assignment or client that offers the experience she needs to move up? What kind of style will work best with the men in one's office environment? For a woman with a business and professional degree, what's better, working for a corporation or a firm? Other questions include these: What should you do when the men around you are advancing and you're not? How can you best respond to bias? How can you be more effective at getting promotions or an international assignment? How can you arrange to make your work schedule dovetail with your other responsibilities? Or, do you even want to work full-time (or at all) at this stage of your life and career?

Feel free to come sit in my virtual office whenever you need to; call on this book when you feel frustrated, puzzled, blocked, or ambitious and eager to make your next move.

You'll see that many leading women in today's workforce have taken the time to share their inside information with you here. Their own personal strategies are recommendations for the ways you can act. These "pioneer women" (they broke new ground for all of us) reveal how they made it to the highest ranks. Their profiles and career paths are recounted in the Appendix, "Pioneer Profiles." Their advice is also sprinkled liberally throughout the book.

You'll also find sections called "Women say," "Men say," and "CEOs say." These are the real thing: verbatims from Catalyst studies, conferences, research, surveys, focus groups, and interviews. The speakers remain anonymous, but what they say speaks volumes—the words will help define issues you'll be facing and may point to solutions that will work for you.

I hope to be able to clear up your misconceptions about the workplace, help you find or change jobs, diversify your experience, and build networks. You'll see how other women remain sane—and, yes, happy—as they work full tilt. In sum, *Be Your Own Mentor* teaches the basics of getting ahead in a work world still largely governed by men. Of course, a book cannot actually give you the nurturing support a live mentor might. So I also talk about finding temporary, if not full-time, flesh-and-blood advisers and supporters and where to look both inside and outside your organization for them.

With me as your desktop mentor, you won't be alone in navigating the waters of the work world. Like Athena with Telemachus, Catalyst and I will equip you for your voyage, help keep the wind at your back, and make your career odyssey a worthwhile adventure.

ABOUT CATALYST

Be Your Own Mentor comes from the nation's preeminent source of information on women in the workplace. Founded in 1962, Catalyst is a nonprofit organization working to advance women in business. It has a dual mission: to enable women in business and the professions to achieve their maximum potential and to assist employers in capitalizing on the talents of women. Catalyst conducts original research, advises corporations and firms on the recruitment, retention, and advancement of women, and educates the media and the public on workplace issues related to women. Our research-driven base and our singular focus on effectiveness afford substantial credibility not only among women executives, but also with corporate and professional leaders nationally.

The knowledge base increases daily as Catalyst experts advise organizations on women's advancement, conduct focus groups and interviews, assist in creating women's networks, help to place women on corporate boards, conduct conferences, speak about the issues, and hold the annual competition for the Catalyst Award. Catalyst knows what works for working women, and what works for the organizations women work for.

❧

Wise Up

JUST THE FACTS*

12.5% of corporate officers are women.

4.1% of top earners are women.

6.2% of top managers are women (chairman, vice chairman, CEO, president, chief operating officer, senior executive vice president, executive vice president); 154 women versus 2,488 men.

7.3% of "line"—revenue-generating—positions are held by women.

*2000 Catalyst Census of Women Corporate Officers and Top Earners of the Fortune 500 (New York: Catalyst, 2000).

I'd like to be able to tell you that the glass ceiling has cracked and fallen in shards on the floors of executive suites everywhere. Like you, I've noted in the national media something of a "been there, done that" attitude about women's advancement in business, government, the professions, and academia. Every time one woman makes it, whenever there's any good news on the gender front, there are those who rush to believe the problem's solved.

A 1999 lead editorial in *The New York Times* noted, "There is still institutional resistance to women at some companies. Until recently, few companies have had women in senior posts who could serve as role models and mentors for younger women."[1] If you look even closer at Fortune 500 companies, you find that women hold slightly more than 6 percent of the most senior executive positions (chair, vice chair, CEO, president, COO, SEVP, EVP) and occupy slightly over 11 percent of Fortune 500 corporate board seats; 1.9 percent of board directors and 1.3 percent of corporate officers are women of color. Check the masthead on the stationery at most law firms, management consulting firms, or securities firms, and you'll note few women partners.

A small number of women have reached positions of real authority in their organizations. These pioneers serve as role models, as heroes for striving executive women. I'm encouraged by the giant strides some women have made, but primogeniture prevails in business. Mostly, men in the top jobs continue to choose other men to succeed them. The invisible biases that keep women out of the top jobs—first dubbed the "glass ceiling" by *The Wall Street Journal* in 1987—are present in all areas of the work world. Yes, increasingly, there are panes that show a crack where women have slipped through. But in all too many organizations, the broken glass is replaced pronto. We need more deferred maintenance in the glass-ceiling department.

Women in our groundbreaking survey *Women in Corporate Leadership** had reached senior management positions in sev-

---

* *Women in Corporate Leadership: Progress and Prospects* surveyed more than 1,200 women and interviewed 20 women at the vice presidential level and above,

eral areas—human resources, public relations, finance, information management—yet the majority told Catalyst they often felt like outsiders, subject to stereotypes and excluded from the informal networks that operate in corporations. As they were coming up in the corporation, they couldn't do business over lunch or dinner at the clubs that remained male bastions throughout the sixties and seventies. Nor could they swing a club at 8 A.M. on the golf links with the COO, who might pass along a golf buddy's name to the CEO as candidate for managing an overseas operation (women weren't allowed to tee off until after noon at most country clubs where senior executives played golf).* Things are getting better, but if we aren't at TGIF with the guys, we miss both the grape and the grapevine about the exciting opening in marketing. And we sure miss what's going down in the men's room. Worse, sometimes we don't know what we're missing or even that we are missing anything at all.

THE TRUTH ABOUT THE WORKPLACE

As your mentor, I want to give the facts to you straight: Lots of us have been missing out. The level playing field is too often a myth. These days, women and men may start out at the same level, but a gap seems to open up between them as their careers develop. Women's experience in the work world is inevitably different from men's—something that is not very pleasant to hear. But take it from me, you can either delude yourself with false hopes or face reality and learn how to deal with it. It's hard to

---

most of whom were within two reports of the CEO and who had an average yearly salary of $250,000. From Fortune 1000 CEOs, we had a 33 percent response rate.

*New Jersey recently made illegal the practice of limiting women's tee times, but it remains a common practice in many states.

do both. The misconceptions that follow are all variations on a theme, but if you read each one, you may finally "get it."

Workplace Misconception 1: It won't matter that I'm a woman.

Fact: The question is not what's legal or what's right; it's a fact of life: gender by and large determines career experiences. Being female simply is different. How far you get, the jobs you land, the kinds of opportunities you're offered, the salary you receive . . . all of these will probably be different for you as a woman than they are for your male colleagues.

In 1962, when Catalyst was founded, it was widely believed that by the year 2000, gender would be inconsequential in the workplace. The 1990s showed otherwise. Catalyst's annual accounting of women board members, corporate officers, and top earners, along with our surveys of high-level corporate women and of chief executives in the Fortune 500, documents the existence of a glass ceiling, why it continues, and how entrenched it is. Outside the private sector, in nonprofits, institutions, and academia, women often find the same situation.

Among the small number of women who have made it to the highest tier of management, I occasionally hear one say that being a woman hasn't affected her progress. I smile and think that this accomplished, title-holding pioneer woman is terribly lucky and, for sure, most unusual. For every one of these fortunate women, hundreds say the opposite. Being a woman does matter. Only two women serve as chief executives of Fortune 500 companies (still not even *one* percent), with six more in the Fortune 501–1000. Men make up 93.2 percent of top management in America's leading corporations.

Women in Corporate Leadership included interviews of Fortune 1000 chief executives and of high-ranking women in their companies. The CEOs' responses to questions about women's progress revealed a lack of awareness of the glass ceiling and its causes. The women, though, saw it all too clearly. The women's ceiling is the CEO's carpeted floor. The survey asked, "What holds women back from the highest ranks?" Chief executives answered that women "lack line management [revenue-generating] experience" and "haven't been in the pipeline long enough." The women in the survey agreed that a lack of line experience did hold them back. But instead of listing this first, as the CEOs did, they listed it third. The top reasons they listed reveal why they lack that essential line experience.

The biggest barriers to women's advancement, women said, include being stereotyped by their male managers and being excluded from informal networks. It's the factors that are indiscernible to the chief executives—but glaringly obvious to women—that keep us from being assigned to key jobs and gaining the experience we need to advance. What gets in women's way are the unrecognized biases about abilities, commitment, availability, flexibility, assertiveness. And it's also about not having the right connections. Women of color especially stress that being outsiders is a key reason for their lack of progress.

The discrepancy between the chief executives' perspective and that of the most successful women at their companies exposes the extent of the problem. In fact, women were more than twice as likely as CEOs to consider factors in the culture of the job itself as barriers to advancement. The men at the top rarely see this; it hasn't been part of their experience. CEOs were more than twice as likely as the women to fault "time in the pipeline," meaning they think it's only a matter of time before women catch up. The women know from their own years of experience that time hasn't dislodged the barriers so far.

Although our study included corporate women only, all the research in other fields, such as academia and the nonprofit world (and I've read just about everything), strongly suggests that the situation is the same everywhere.

From the Pioneers: *Bias is an everyday reality.*
Patricia "Tosh" Barron (Clinical Associate Professor, Stern School of Business, New York University), whose successful managerial career at Xerox proved that women can succeed in positions previously held by men, says, "You're always, consciously or unconsciously, under a microscope as a woman. There's still the feeling that to really advance, you've got to be better than the men. Your challenge is to communicate how you're up to the tasks."

Judith Rodin (President, University of Pennsylvania, and first woman president of an Ivy League institution): "Clearly, there's still a glass ceiling in academia, although not in department chairmen so much as there used to be. Women leaders are still unusual in medicine, an area just beginning to be broken into."

I do see more and more organizations recognizing that their policies and practices hinder or exclude women, and they are starting to make important changes. Some are doing it because of legal pressure, some because it's right, and others because it's good business. Even though you'll certainly be better off working at one of these places (see Chapter 2 for how to find them), you'll still need to know what challenges you'll face—and what to do about them. The workplace is experiencing a slow evolution, not a revolution, toward gender blindness, and we have a long way to go.

Why? Because men designed the workplace, and they designed it to fit their own needs. That's only to be expected, and for a long time it worked well. It doesn't work as well, however, for the millions of women who have flowed into the workforce since the 1960s (and, by extension, since many men are deeply connected with those women, it's not working as well now for men either). Over and over, women of ambition, talent, and commitment have run into barriers that are apparently invisible to many men.

Although these barriers often result from unintended and un-examined assumptions by men about women, that doesn't make them any easier to circumvent. Maybe men didn't aim to keep women out when they set up the ways of doing business. I think the majority don't mean to exclude us now. But until women play a major role in revamping the business culture, we simply have to learn to contend with rules we did not make and that don't always make sense for us.

Workplace Misconception 2: Sure, there's a mythology about women, but it doesn't affect real women; it won't affect me.

Fact: No matter how competent, strong, talented, or smart you are, the myths about women can cloud your future when you least expect it. These myths can lurk anywhere—at law firms, accounting firms, management consulting firms, and banks, in corporations large and small, at not-for-profits in all shapes and sizes, in government agencies, and in academia. You cannot hide from others' preconceptions, but you can debunk them with reality.

Here are some common myths about women in the work-place:

- Women are less committed to their jobs than men are.
- Women can't or won't put in the hours that are required to get the job done.
- Women are not qualified or prepared for the job.
- Women are not aggressive enough.
- Women don't take risks.
- Women become pregnant and then stay home.
- Women won't relocate or can't travel for work.
- Women aren't rainmakers.
- Women don't need to work, because men support them.

On what are these myths founded? Some on fear and some on truth. Yes, it is true that women become pregnant, but not all of us and not for long. (And frankly, I never felt healthier than during my two pregnancies.) As one high-level woman put it to an appalled boss who did not want to lose her, "I'm not going to be pregnant forever." It is true that most new mothers want to take maternity leave, but most of them resume work as fully committed as ever; in 1995, 83 percent returned within six months after childbirth.[2]

It's true that some women don't want to relocate for personal or family reasons. But I know great numbers of women who gladly move for their work. Male managers often don't know this. If you sense that you're being denied opportunities simply because you're a woman, it's up to you to change things. Here's what you can do:

1. Bring up the subject.
2. Make it clear that you as an individual are open to relocation, travel, risks . . . whatever it takes to rise.
3. If nothing changes after a decent interval, remind your manager again.
4. If there's still no change, consider looking for a new job.

What I consider the most pernicious myth is that when women leave jobs, they go home to stay. Whenever I talk with the media, I try to quash this myth. How many women do you know who can afford such a luxury? The numbers from Catalyst's studies and the U.S. Bureau of Labor Statistics make it clear that women are in the workplace to stay.* When women leave an organization, it's often because they've hit impenetrable barriers. Many leave to start their own businesses, which women are doing at twice the rate of men.[3] Or they resurface at

*For more on this, see Chapter 7, "Making Your Life Work."

other organizations that have already tackled some of these issues and have implemented changes that afford an environment conducive to the retention and advancement of women.* If you are fortunate enough to find such an organization early in your work life, your career progress may match your expectations.

Workplace Misconception 3: As soon as I prove myself, they'll forget the gender thing.

Fact: Senior managers are still mostly men, and many male managers who haven't worked with many women tend to make generalizations about them.† If their wives don't work, they may think it's weird that you want to. If the women they know aren't assertive, they may doubt, for instance, whether any woman can nail down a new account. If they've lost one woman to maternity leave, they'll expect all other women to follow suit. If you have children, they may even suspect that you can't be a good mother if you're working. Obviously, these beliefs can make a manager deal differently with a woman than with a man. He might not offer a married woman an assignment that requires relocation, especially a woman with children, because he assumes she won't want (or be able) to move her family. Or he might assign a lucrative sales territory to a man with a macho style rather than to a service-oriented woman, even though her numbers show her style works.

At most organizations, managers deciding who gets an assignment naturally choose someone they know and trust. If they hang out at lunch or after work or on the golf course with the

---

*According to a 1998 Hewitt Associates study of U.S. employers, 77 percent offered alternative work arrangements, up from 60 percent in 1993. The need for such arrangements is gaining acceptance, but too often a stigma is still attached to their use.
†A woman might also have biases based on her personal experience as a woman or with women, although Catalyst finds that more and more women managers are supportive of their younger colleagues.

guys who work for them, it's these faces they'll think of when opportunities arise. The informal methods many organizations still use to decide who gets an assignment or a promotion leave a lot of room for ingrained bias. Some organizations do use job competencies and formal review processes, and some trend-setting professional firms review how assignments are made, but such methods are far from universal.

Women say:
Sales rep, transportation company: "My boss is male-oriented. He feels women belong at home. He's discussed career advancement with every one of the men but has yet to discuss it with me or the other women. He will never promote us; he'll never look for something for us to move to."

CFO, consumer products firm: "I have ups and downs all the time. The level of abuse you take on a nontraditional path doesn't stop. In fact, it accelerates as you go up because you're more and more threatening. It's constant, overt, in your face, behind your back. It's all the classical stuff: of a man they say, 'He's hard-charging; he takes command,' but when a woman acts the same way, she's 'pushy.' They're always diminishing your capabilities, finding ways not to acknowledge the breadth of your competency as a senior executive. It's the way it is. You've got to shut it off and go on."

Men say:
Manager, industrial products company: "I don't see how you can avoid the whole issue around child rearing—the problem of career interruption, the challenge of child care, the restricted travel. It has a subtle influence on women's promotability. You can't possibly hire a woman at the age of twenty-five who will look you in the eye and say, 'Trust me, I'm never going to have kids.'"

Catalyst's research also shows that managers tend to resist putting women into risky assignments. Studies show that managers hesitate to assign tasks to women who don't already have the precise experience needed for the job, whereas they readily assign them to men without such experience.

> **CEOs say:**
> **CEO, Fortune 1000 company:** "We use lack of specific training for a job as a reason not to open the jobs to women, when we are more ready to bring men into jobs for which they are not specifically trained. That kind of discrimination or stereotyping is difficult to get at."
>
> **CEO, Fortune 500 company:** "There's a certain amount of reluctance on the part of any manufacturing company to ask some young woman to move to a remote location and start working as a foreman. I think there's a reluctance on the part of women to do that."

Another reason you might not get a promotion is that your manager thinks men don't like reporting to women. In Catalyst studies in both the United States and Canada, women managers said they believe men have a difficult time being supervised by women.[4]

When managers withhold opportunities as a result of such generalized suppositions, it's hard to prove yourself. You miss out on critical developmental opportunities that would get you your shot at the top. These biases affect you more as you move up the ladder and the competition increases. Note the numbers: Women make up 49 percent of managerial and professional specialty positions but only 5 percent of the highest management positions.

It's up to you to counteract these myths early in your career. Assert yourself from day one in your relationship with your manager, so he knows your willingness and readiness to take on new responsibilities. You don't, however, want to come across as if you have a chip on your shoulder. Not all male managers carry these biases. If you have one who respects women's work, trusts their capabilities, and feels comfortable with their style, you'll know it. And you'll be lucky indeed.

Workplace Misconception 4: Time will solve my problems.

Fact: Time is just as likely to work against you. The glass ceiling may not affect you in your first few years in an organization. Glass being invisible, you might not notice it until you're in your thirties and ready to move out of middle management. Then you can crash into it and become permanently disabled by the concussion or suffer a tremendous pain in the neck figuring out what to do next.

Bosses are in the grip of this misconception, too. The top brass also misjudge the time factor by assuming that the pipeline will pump women into senior managerial positions in due time. Few CEOs are like the one whose words follow.

> **CEOs say:**
> **CEO, Fortune 500 company:** "The reason there are not many women in the senior ranks is not that women haven't been in the pipeline long enough to advance; it's what they've done while they are in the pipeline."

Take it as gospel: Time is not enough. You need to use your time to get the kinds of experience that lead to the top.

Workplace Misconception 5: Talent and hard work bring success.

Fact: Those two qualities, essential as they are, are definitely not enough. Most smart, capable women enter the workplace believing that their talent and hard work will carry them as far as they want to go. But few organizations have any apparatus in place that zeroes in on talent, then taps, develops, and rewards it. Talent alone will not necessarily win out in a business environment.

Most people who succeed work hard. The women interviewed for *Women in Corporate Leadership* said that "consistently exceeding performance expectations" was more important than anything else they had done—and more essential for women than for men. Successful women indicate that they have to "overperform" to prove their ability and to counter negative assumptions in a predominantly male environment.

Women say:
Senior manager, management consulting firm: "The starting position when a man becomes partner is 'Great, he's a partner.' With a woman it's 'We'll see what she can do.' To even be accepted, you've got to be twenty to twenty-five percent better."

Catalyst survey participant:* "I don't think it's just a matter of if you perform all right, everything will turn out, because we haven't progressed as rapidly as we would have liked."

CFO, consumer products company: "Just doing what's required on a day-to-day basis keeps you in the middle of the pack—even if you do it better than anyone else. Women have to stretch beyond that."

If your only strategy is working like a dog, you're likely to find the path to upper management blocked.

So what's the missing ingredient? Something elusive called style. The women who've reached executive levels today say that their success depended on developing a style with which men felt comfortable working. This style is as much a way of working as it is how you look or what you say. We cover style specifically in Chapter 4, but all its components are discussed throughout the book—it's all about your very way of being at work. Many women of color, especially African Americans, reported in *Women of Color in Corporate Management: Opportunities and*

---

*This designation indicates a write-in response on Catalyst surveys.

Barriers that they felt they had to change their style to fit into the corporate environment.*

OUTLOOK FOR THE FUTURE

Despite all the problems that remain, there is a rapidly growing contingent of women in management. Change is happening, and more is on the way. Among the pioneers quoted in this book, we found some who are optimists about women's future. Here are some encouraging words:

> **From the Pioneers: It's getting better all the time.**
> **Lois Juliber** (COO, Colgate-Palmolive): "I had to prove myself as a woman. I found there were standards and demands I had to achieve because I was a woman. But the world was different. Today I look at some parts of our company and find things very balanced, very normal, and the relationships between men and women are more natural now than fifteen or twenty years ago. Lunch with the guys used to be a big breakthrough, but now young women and men hang out together, talking about what thirty-year-olds talk about."
>
> **Nancy Karch** (Retired Director, McKinsey & Company): "[When I started at McKinsey] there were ten men and three women in my class. . . . Another woman up ahead of us didn't manage for five years. At the time, there was no mechanism for noticing this. . . . We saw that there was a question: Could a woman manage a McKinsey team and be a senior person with the client? They were concerned about the client side." But that's changed, she says. "That's the last time gender was an explicit concern. . . . Other women don't deal with this now. . . . Young women build credibility quickly now."

---

*Thirty-five percent of African-American women participants in our survey versus 25 percent of Asian-American and 20 percent of Latina women strongly agreed that women must adjust their styles to fit into the corporate environment. (*Women of Color in Corporate Management: Opportunities and Barriers* [New York: Catalyst, 1999].)

I, too, can be counted among the optimists. At Catalyst, we hear the buzz changing in corner offices and cubicles across the country. We've seen organizations realize how debilitating female turnover can be, then work to implement programs and policies to arrest it. I'm hearing from more CEOs and other top executives about how they've made recruitment, retention, and advancement of women top priorities. Some demonstrate true commitment, backing up what they say by linking compensation for managers to advancement of women and minorities. So just maybe the myths about women are on the wane. But don't bet your future on it. Your awareness of how things work will help you break down the barriers that continue to stand.

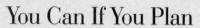

You Can If You Plan

How do you, a woman, find the kind of job that you can leverage into a fulfilling career? In today's world, you need to think of your career evolving as a series of related or even unrelated jobs. I don't mean you should rely on serendipity. You need to control your career, and that requires planning. Think: "How can I find the job that suits me now and will also lead to the next job that will suit me and, in fact, unfold into a meaningful career?" In other words, you should set your sights on mastering a succession of jobs that will allow you to grow, change, and succeed.

Twenty years ago, *The Managerial Woman,* a seminal work by Margaret Hennig and Ann Jardim on women in the workplace, concluded that women needed to shift their focus from how well they do their job to what job they have: Is it one with profit-and-loss responsibility? Is it one that diversifies their experience? Catalyst research confirms that women still haven't learned to do this, and many managers reinforce their error at performance review time. When reviewing men, they focus on positioning them for their next move; when reviewing women, they tend to focus on current performance.

Whether you're just looking for your first job or want to change what you're doing fast, don't make the mistake of being cavalier about the process. You'll spend more than half of your waking hours at your job. It's worth making a careful decision. There's a danger in thinking that all organizations are alike. Some companies, for example, make their employees feel uncomfortable about taking the family leave ensured by the law, while others go out of their way to provide flexibility. Some career paths have a low ceiling; eventually you'll find yourself unable to move up. Others have the potential to move you upward as you go along. It's worth taking the time to research various fields and choose wisely.

Have you researched career paths in your areas of interest? Do you know what the prerequisites are for the job you're seeking, what you'll do at that job, what it's worth in terms of compensation, and what could follow from it? Have you investigated your workplace of choice to find out its stance on women's advancement? Do you know what people who work there say about the place? (Later in this chapter, I'll give you some leads on how to get the inside scoop.)

If you're job-hunting, do your homework. The perfect job for you rarely falls into your lap. You must be prepared to *work* to find a new job—whether a first job or the next job or a midcareer change of direction—and particularly if you want it to lead to better jobs, with greater responsibility, autonomy, and income.

CONSIDER YOUR CAREER IN THE LARGER PERSPECTIVE OF YOUR LIFE

When I ask women between the ages of thirty and forty what they plan to be doing in five or ten years, they are often ambivalent or vague in their responses. Ask a man the same question, and he's likely to know the level he wants to reach at his current organization or another one, as well as what income he expects to be earning by a specific age. It's curious, because by and large these men went to the same schools we did, had the same kinds of parents, pushed away the same broccoli. Does this future-vision gene come with the Y chromosome? I don't think so. Of course, having a Y chromosome means never having to say, "May I take a maternity leave?"

We women, I've noticed, often have trouble moving from the abstract concept of what we want to the concrete reality of getting there. Those of us who have succeeded had to learn this on our own. In my generation, our mothers tended to be wives and at-home moms, fitting in with the plans of others rather than formulating long-term plans of their own. Our fathers often saw us as educable, perhaps, but not headed for the realm of work. We had few peer-mentors, such as the college buddy who takes you in hand and teaches you the ropes of succeeding on campus and later in business.

All this is changing, but perhaps not fast enough. I still speak with women of every age every day who have not laid out any long-term plans for themselves.

Long-term plans in the twenty-first century? Are they even worth the effort, with mergers, economic shifts, and globalization? Absolutely. Gone are the days when "good behavior" got you a job for life. These days, a long-term career plan is more important than ever. Still, you don't want to lose your flexibility. So how can you forge a path between rigidity and impulse shopping for a career?

Well, first listen to those who know. The pioneer women in this book generally believe that *some* kind of planning is essential. Many of these women didn't plan at first—because they couldn't. They told me that when they entered the workplace in the late 1960s and early 1970s, finding *any* job was lucky. They took what they could get—and made a success of their careers despite it all. Eight to ten years into their careers, with their fields selected and their paths more clear, they realized how important planning was. Nevertheless, they are against rigidly structured schemes. They advise you to remain open and flexible, so you can take advantage of opportunities that come along, but to keep track of your progress, work on moving up regularly, and give major importance to your own growth and satisfaction.

From the Pioneers: Position yourself for opportunities.

Marie Knowles (Executive Vice President and CFO, Atlantic Richfield): "Get a variety of skills and consider how that skill base can be applied in a variety of situations. A broad base of activities means they can't put you in a cubbyhole, which happens more with women than men. . . . [Planning is] evolutionary. I started as a chemical engineer and migrated from a career about things to one about people. There's no way I would have known to do that at twenty-two or at thirty-two. . . . I stepped back and looked at my résumé as if it were the balance sheet of a company: if you have only one product line or one customer, you're held hostage by that."

Lulu Wang (Partner and CEO, Tupelo Capital Management): "I always made five-year plans. I would write them out, put them in a drawer, and I always updated them at the end of each year. I knew when I was analyzing companies [as a securities analyst] that the best managements always had a view of where they wanted to take their company. I practiced the same disciplines I asked them to have for their companies. It was a way to make sure I was focused and stayed on track. . . . At an early stage, I learned to make choices and prioritize."

From the Pioneers: To thine own self be true.

Tosh Barron (Clinical Associate Professor, Stern School of Business, New York University): "Know yourself. Don't let the 'lemming effect' control you, going into jobs your friends go into that may not be right for you. A young person won't have perfect knowledge of herself, but you do have to take stock of what you like and what you think you'll be good at. . . . I didn't get so locked into something I couldn't try things. You need to be careful not to get stuck in a rut that won't serve you well as the company changes over time. And there's no need to think you're only going to have one career. Think in terms of four or five careers, not simultaneously. Have a sense of direction, but be open to opportunities."

From the Pioneers: Planning is an ongoing activity.
Carolee Friedlander (Founder, President, and CEO, Carolee Designs): "[A career plan] keeps you on the road. You might get off track, detours will take you off, and nothing is set in stone. You will change it, but you must change it consciously, or it will happen to you. Identify it, implement it, control it. That's how you will achieve the goals you have set."

CONNECTING YOUR WORK AND YOUR PASSION

Marcia Worthing, who does outplacement counseling for Mullin & Associates, and Sheryl Spanier, of the executive counseling agency Right Management Consultants, both urge you to find harmony between your work and what you care about before you begin planning. Can you match your career aspirations with your personal values? Worthing advises clients who aren't happy in their current job or career to figure out what their passion is. What job did you really love? Can you do that kind of thing again? You're a lot more likely to make it when you love what you're doing. If you can't work where your passion is, at least recognize what it is and try to incorporate elements of it elsewhere in your life.

Spanier emphasizes the "connection between doing and being, between who you are as a person and what you do in your work." She suggests that as you plan, you think about your temperament, your talents, your passions, and your resources: "Look at the themes and patterns of your life to date. What are the skills you have developed, and how can you put them to work so those skills match your personality?"

Why plan—and, maybe more important, how? The consultants say that planners succeed more often than drifters. Detailed plans with specific time frames help the most. Jean Otte of the national mentoring organization Women Unlimited advises: "Break it down into manageable pieces, with achievable goals and timelines. Make it practical, as in 'I want to do . . . whatever.' How am I going to do that? Who am I going to engage in this with me? What resources, what information, do I need?"

How can you do that? Spanier recommends what she calls the "self-developed" career plan, a totally individual plan that may or may not take into account traditional career paths, depending on your interests. A guide to putting together such a plan, based on a set of questions, follows. Above all, it allows for change and personal growth.

HOW TO CREATE A SELF-DEVELOPED CAREER PLAN

To gain structure and a feeling of control, you need to have both a long-term plan and a short-term plan. For starters, set aside an hour or so. Sit down at your desk (or wherever you're most comfortable) with a lined legal-size pad and a sharpened pencil (or, alternatively, a computer, on which you can change and correct your words even more easily), and get to work.

Start with your long-term vision. Three big questions will help refine your long-term vision; they are important to answer as you plan a satisfying career. Don't ponder these for too long. You just want to know what your vision is right now—that's why you're not using pen and ink.

- How much time do you want to devote to family, friends, community, leisure, anything outside your career?
- What do you want to be able to say you've accomplished in life?
- What kind of retirement lifestyle do you want?

Specific questions for framing a short-term plan. Once you get a fix on what matters to you in the long run, use your answers to guide your thinking about how to launch yourself and move forward toward your goals. With the aid of the following series of questions, you can refine your approach to different situations or time periods in your career life. (Sometimes answering these somewhat more specific questions will help you answer the three big ones above, too.) Ask yourself these questions at different points in your career.

When You're Starting Out

Early in your work career, consider the following:

- What are the issues, concerns, and ideas you've always cared about?
- Can you identify themes and patterns in your successes in work so far?
- What are your top motivations for working (money, power, fame, dedication to a cause, something else)?
- What do you do better than anyone else? List your work-related skills and compare these with what's required in the work you're thinking about.
- How do you see yourself functioning in the work world? (As a leader? An influencer? A team member?)
- What work have you done that you've enjoyed?
- What size organization do you want to work for?
- Is there a cause you'd like to promote, and is it feasible to work for an organization that supports that cause?
- How important is money to you—now and later?
- If you're involved in a long-term relationship, how will your goals be affected by your partner's income, career goals, and commitment?
- Would a change in marital status necessitate an alternate plan?

When You Have a Professional Degree
- Do you want to become a partner in a firm?
- Do you know the differing demands of firms and corporations? (See Chapter 10.)
- If you're already working at a firm, do you find you want greater flexibility? Have you considered a move to a corporation or nonprofit?
- If you're considering working for a firm, do you know what the seasonal demands are and how many billable hours are expected?
- How do you feel about travel on the job?
- Would you like client development as much as delivery?

If You're Considering Returning to School
- Is the degree you're thinking about necessary to your goal, and have you researched the career paths of graduates of the school you're considering?
- Will an advanced degree help you on your current career track?
- Do you need an advanced degree to change to a career track that interests you?
- Can you afford to stop working to earn the degree? Will your organization help pay for it?
- Will your organization take you back once you get your degree? If not, do you have another employer in mind?
- Will you get an appropriate return on your financial investment in your education? If not, how much does that matter?

Before You Change Jobs or Try for the Next Career Step
- Are you growing and learning at the rate you had hoped?
- Is your job on a career path you care about? If so, what are the next levels? Do you have the skills for the next level? If not, what can you do to get them?

If You're Wondering About Shifting Careers

- How do you define satisfaction, and is your career satisfying?
- Do you want to put time into something you believe in?
- Does a different industry or field beckon you? Are your skills transferable?
- Are you now able to take the time to acquire the skills for a new career? Do you want to add even more work to your schedule?
- What part does money play in this desire to make a shift?

Planning a Family While on the Job

- Do you want to return to your current job? How soon?
- Do you want to continue to work full-time after you have a child? Can you afford not to?
- Do you want to stay on the career path or partner track you're on? Have other women at your organization been able to do that?
- Does your spouse or partner have access to paternity or family leave?
- How flexible is your spouse's or partner's work schedule, and how much help can you expect at home?
- What personal resources do you have, in case you decide to extend your leave by taking time without pay? How long can your family manage with a reduced income?
- Do you know what the law requires of your employers, according to the Family and Medical Leave Act?
- What policies and programs (medical benefits, leave of absence benefits, phase-into-work arrangements) does your employer offer to support your maternity leave, and how do they work?
- At your organization, does the parental leave policy exist in theory but not reality? Do parents pay a career price for using policies that exist on the books but are not genuinely embraced by the organization?

• Are there women at your organization who have recently taken maternity leave? Is there a women's network, or are there women working with you who've taken leave and can advise you? (See Chapter 7, "Making Your Life Work," for questions to ask employers when you are thinking about taking maternity leave or about flexible work arrangements.)

These questions are just a beginning. Networking, research, and a fair amount of soul-searching will help you answer them—at the stage in your career when you need them. Return to them when you start having career doubts.

UNDERSTANDING CAREER PATHS

Most careers have clearly delineated paths that you can research and then follow. (See the appendix of Pioneer Profiles for the career paths of top women in their fields.) If you have chosen such a career, take the time to think about where you'd like to be in five years. Then fill in the steps to getting there and toward your overarching goals. Some career paths offer limited opportunities for vertical jumps. In these jobs, your challenge will be to accrue new and diverse experiences.

Planning will help you think in terms of laying down a foundation of the particular experiences you need to create a résumé to move you to senior management, if that's where you've set your sights. But planning is also crucial if you've made middle management your goal or, for example, if what you want is to become an expert. An organized approach will increase your chances of success at any level. Focus on competencies that are portable, as you're unlikely to stay in one organization. Many things play into a successful career path even if you do stay at one organization—including switching functions, moving from a division to headquarters, or gaining international experience. (See Chapters 3 and 4 for tips on this process.)

From the Pioneers: Build the foundation you need.

Carol Bartz (Chair, CEO, and President, Autodesk): "I have a whole theory of creating your career path as though you're building a pyramid. Concentrate on getting the right foundation pieces in. Mine were in sales and marketing, with a technical background, and I managed engineers and worked in customer service. I had done all the functions, so it was easier for me to ascend. You must be sure you don't have an unstable base."

Lulu Wang (Partner and CEO, Tupelo Capital Management): "I really thought my professional life should be a progression, and I worked with a view toward that. I thought with each new step, How does that build to the next level of excellence and achievement?" Wang described her strategy for gathering experience and skills so she could start her own securities firm. "I knew that having mastered research and portfolio management, and having dealt with and marketed to very senior clients, I then would have the skills I needed to start my own firm. . . . I started without an MBA. . . . In 1980, I enrolled in Columbia University's Executive Program to get my MBA while still working full-time. Having that MBA in addition to my degree from Wellesley has been an important plus in my career."

Barbara Paul Robinson (Partner, Debevoise & Plimpton): "Don't sit back and wait for the luck of the draw. If you want to be a good litigator, figure out what you should do at two years, at four years, at six years. Figure out if you're developing the skills you need, and figure out how to get them. It might not happen naturally. A woman should not just accept what the system gives her. Men are more likely to buck the system; not accepting what they're dealt comes easier for them. Women should reach out and grab what they want."

Be flexible. Never cast your career plan in stone. Once you've moved up a bit on a particular organization's ladder, you'll probably know more about what you ultimately want. You might want to change companies, industries, locations, even careers.

You may prefer variety and enjoy the challenge of new jobs in new organizations; or you may opt for stability, if you can get it. You may want to take some time out to have children or get another degree. You may find entrepreneurial outlets within your organization, or you may want to start your own business.

Above all, you want to grasp opportunities as they arise. Keep in mind that risk taking is a top recommendation by women achievers in Catalyst surveys and by woman after woman profiled here. When Catalyst first sought me out, not only was it a surprise (because I'd always worked in public health or education—never in the business of advancing women), it was also risky to take over an organization that was so identified with one woman, Felice Schwartz, who founded Catalyst and ran it for thirty years. What a great ride I've been having—because I reached out and grabbed the brass ring.

From the Pioneers:
Anne Mulcahy (President and COO, Xerox Corporation): "I would focus on succeeding and enjoying the current versus planning the future. I think so many men and women get obsessed with the next step that they don't optimize their current job and they miss the opportunities that aren't in this plan that they've built. I think this has two negative side effects. It distracts from what you should be doing [when you're] just focused on the end point. You absolutely don't see the opportunities that are passing you by that may not be the precise next step that you've designed. Those can be the most enriching, the ones that are off the beaten path that can add a lot more value."

Writing up a career plan is an exercise in goal orientation. Get as much advice on your plan as you can. Talk to people in your field of interest; the more inside scoop you can get, the better. Talk to career coaches to get their take on how to get where you're going. Talk to people in your network about their planning experiences. The more input you get, the surer you will be of your direction. Plus, you might encounter someone who can help make your plan real. Having clear goals makes you more aware of the opportunities around you.

But a career plan is only on paper; it is not your life. Keep your plan fluid. View your working life as a journey. There are places you may stop because the price (read *pay*) is right. Others may turn you on intellectually, or the challenge may excite you. Or they may afford the independence you need at the time. Some stops may be totally delightful, while at others you might feel as if you're doing time. (Keep your plan in your bottom-right desk drawer [in an unmarked file?] for periodic reviews.) Scratch in revisions, make corrections, be amused at a diversionary course you've taken, or inspire yourself to get back on track. But whatever you do, take the basic concept of your career plan and career decisions seriously. Define yourself, or you will be defined.

AFTER THE PLAN, THE EXECUTION

Once you've created a career plan and you have an idea of the steps you need to take to reach your goal, more questions are in order:

Should I choose a woman-friendly organization? Why not? Even some of the most traditionally male organizations have begun to recognize that if they don't attract women, they can't always get or keep the best talent. So they are working to make their organizations places where women may succeed as quickly as men. Catalyst now advises organizations in many fields, including those in which it has traditionally been difficult for women to get ahead. And it's certainly more pleasant to work in an organization where your gender is not a barrier.

From the Pioneers:
Ellen Hancock (Chair and CEO, Exodus Communications): "If you're graduating today, you can find an organization that sup-

ports women's advancement. If they don't have women corporate officers, don't go there, or you'll spend too much of your life fighting. You can't change a whole company. You want to be working on your own style and your own skills, not on fighting the culture."

What is a woman-friendly organization, and how can I find one? If you choose to work in the corporate world, you may fare better in certain industries or at certain companies. I'm defining as "woman-friendly" a company that has made a point of women's advancement. Catalyst's research shows that the more women directors there are at a company, the greater the number of women in officer positions.* That may or may not reflect cause and effect, but at the very least, good numbers do reveal the organizations where advancement opportunities exist for women. For more information, or for organizations outside the Fortune 1000, you can examine annual reports, go on the Internet, talk to career counselors and executive search firms. Some observers believe that newer or smaller companies will prove better for women than the companies Catalyst has studied. I personally think the jury is still out on that one. But explore for yourself as new industries and new organizations emerge.

*It's a statistically significant correlation.

IS THE E-WORLD A BETTER WORLD FOR WOMEN?

With high-tech business growing at an exponential pace, the demand for talent is so intense that it tends to level the playing field. "I could get a Martian hired if I tried" was the way the woman head of a technology search firm put it in *The New York Times* in March 2000. Many women in high positions in business seem to be defecting to the tech world, and in 1999, women held high management posts in 45 percent of Internet start-ups. Seven percent in that category had women chief executives.[1] All this contrasts quite favorably with the situation at Fortune 500 companies, as reported in Catalyst's annual surveys. But, are the data accurate and, anyway, how is working at these companies? There are varying reports—some focus on the "guy culture" aspect, others on the increasing presence of women, which is tending toward a critical mass. Frankly, the industries and the companies are changing so fast, it's hard to generalize, but Ellen Hancock, a former top Apple executive who now heads Exodus Communications, certainly is worth listening to. She was recently quoted in the *Los Angeles Times* as calling the technology industry "one of the better gender-blind industries." Hancock added, "I think we are building a strong network of women helping women and we will continue to do so."

It's probably important to remember that whatever dot-com companies are like, they are most often also corporations (witness their initial public offerings, which a lot of investors want some of) and, as time goes on, they may behave more and more like one.

Lists of good companies are published annually by various magazines, including *Working Mother*'s list of the "100 Best Companies for Working Mothers," and *Fortune*'s "100 Best Companies to Work for in America," among others. Although these lists are based on the companies' own reports, they are good jumping-off points for further research. Merely wanting to be on such a list indicates an interest in gender issues—or at least a concern about their images in this area.

SEARCHING THE WEB

By now, we all know about the job listings on the Internet—most big-newspaper classified sections, for example, are there, or you can go to a portmanteau site such as Head-hunter.net, where you'll find 140,000 listings worldwide. More interesting are the newest additions to e-search, sites such as WetFeet.com, where you can get the lowdown on companies and industries, learning about their history and their culture as well as their pay scale, who they're hiring and in what field, and their approach to diversity. Look up Avon, for example, and you'll learn that it won Working Mother's Leadership Award seven years in a row as a "Best Company for Women to Work For," as well as being on Fortune's list of "America's 50 Best Companies for Minorities."

When you interview for a position, look around you. Do you see women in the corner offices? Try to arrange a meeting with potential colleagues. If they seem friendly and accessible, consider asking them about the environment for women (but only after you receive an offer). Once you have received an offer, here are some questions to ask before accepting it:

The Woman-Friendly Test

- How many women are there in senior management, and at what levels?
- At a firm: How many partners are there, and how many are women?
- What is the career path for this job (what would be the next position up)?
- What are the opportunities to move from line to staff and back again?
- How are work assignments made? Do supervisors ad-lib them or is there a formal process that management uses to make decisions?

- What is the success profile here—for the job and for the company?
- What is the work culture like (client-driven, face-time-focused, etc.)?
- Is there a formal mentoring program? How does it work?
- Is there a women's network? What does it do?
- What kind of training and development is offered?
- Is there a formal process for performance appraisal?
- What flexible work arrangements are available? Do people use them?
- How much control would someone at my level have over her own schedule?

A barrage of such questions may not be the wisest approach. But you should find a way to work them in, especially if you're having a series of interviews with different people and talking to potential colleagues, who will also probably know a lot of the answers and may even talk about them if you're discreet in bringing them up. You can also get some of this information from publicly available documents and from your own network of friends and colleagues. (Doesn't someone you went to school with have a friend who works at the organization?)

Should you take a job at an organization that's not woman-friendly? All things being equal, probably not. But in nontraditional fields for women, such as the sciences, engineering, and heavy industry, you may find advantages in being a pioneer. Some of these organizations, now eager for the best talent, have begun avid recruitment of women. Opportunities for advancement may exist because you are the only woman or one of a few. If you decide on such a workplace, you'll find much of the advice throughout this book doubly essential as you wend your way beyond the male corridors of power into (almost wholly) male laboratories, control rooms, and factory floors.

THE JOB SEARCH

Career counselors estimate that people entering the job market today are likely to change employers at least six times in their lives.

Plan on a minimum of several months or more for any job search. If you are already fairly senior, your hunt could take up to a year. Landing a serious job requires serious interviews, probably several of them, often stretching out over many weeks or months. And then there's the research you need to do.

Conventional wisdom is right; often the best time to look for a job is while you have one. It's certainly not impossible to find a job when you're unemployed, and you do have more free time to do it, but most experts concur that you're coming from a position of strength if you're already in a job.

Get the details in writing going in. Don't delude yourself into thinking you'll be able to renegotiate what you do—or what you earn—once the job starts. That almost never happens. If you're promised a raise at a certain time in the future, see if you can get the promise in writing before you sign on the dotted line. If the promise of a fast promotion tempts you to take a job, again, try to get the promise in writing, up front, before you sign up. You don't want to push anyone into a discomfort zone doing this, but if you can, it's good to cover yourself: What if your boss is transferred, quits, gets amnesia? Since every job lays the groundwork for jobs to come, beware of settling just to get in the door. The job you take should be one that will be instrumental in helping you move up where you are or in helping you move laterally to another organization. If you've taken the time to do the right research, you'll know what you want, and you can ask for it. And remember: You do have to ask. The interviewer (or your new boss) is not a mind reader.

Self-respect is key to success. One of the fundamental rules of the work world is that you must take yourself seriously before others will. If you must compromise and take a job that's less than ideal, take care that you have a professional attitude about it. Live up to your own highest standards, even if the organization's standards disappoint you. Even if you're pretty sure that this job is temporary, that you're going to go back to school or take a year off in Tahiti, present yourself seriously—*take* yourself seriously—from the get-go.

> **Women say:**
> **Financial authority, Fortune 500 board member:** "If you believe and have a vision that you're going to succeed at whatever goal you set yourself, you're really unstoppable. You become what you think you are. If you think you're a success in a given field, you certainly can achieve it."

Monitor your career progress. As the months and years go by, remain vigilant regarding your advancement. Not only do many women neglect long-term thinking about their careers, they don't keep their goal in focus. This certainly gives men—and the women who do so—a competitive advantage. Update your résumé regularly. Even if you don't send it out, it will give you something to review.

Marcia Worthing emphasizes the importance of assessing your strengths and accomplishments continually, both in order to reinforce what you're learning and so that you understand what knowledge you've gained. "Keep asking yourself, 'Am I obtaining the skills I need to move to the next career phase?' " says Worthing.

Worthing counsels viewing yourself in terms of the marketplace, too. "Be sure you keep track of how you fit in the bigger picture outside your organization," she advises. "Understand how your skills fit in, so you know how marketable you are." This includes knowing how your salary compares to those of others doing similar work outside your organization. That's not always easy to determine, but you can check with professional organizations and associations in your area of interest and talk to people in your networks to get as much information as you can. *Working Woman,* among other magazines, publishes an annual salary issue.

Such knowledge will prepare you for a change of company, whether chosen or forced. Worthing finds that women neglect this "marketability self-assessment" more often than men. With the uncertainty workers face today, such vigilance will mean that if and when you're thrown for a loop, you will land on your feet.

What is a successful career? Success in the most profound sense is personal. We may choose to measure success by how far we have advanced, how much money we make, or how others view us. Or we may measure success by such internal standards as how much we have learned, how much we have contributed to the world around us, how good we feel. When you ask men how they measure success, the majority answer, "Money, power, position." Women, when asked, tend not to mention money. More women today than a generation ago may mention power and position, but women often ask, "Do I make a difference?" You can make a difference if you find the right job for you, be it in the for-profit or nonprofit sector. If you haven't found such a position and "making a difference" matters for you, I urge you to seek it. But don't undervalue the importance of money. Your income now will contribute to your long-term financial security and that of your family. A lack of attention to the financial aspect of work may be one reason why women are 70 percent more likely to spend their retirement in poverty than men.[2] Yet it is important to note that your definitions of success, and your choices about what type of success to pursue, can change over time. The decisions that you make today about where to focus your energies can evolve into different choices tomorrow, next month, or next year depending on your specific career interests and current family situation. At one phase of your life, you might care more about money and position; at another phase, about making a difference in the community. Or a time may come where you decide to work part-time or not work at all. Women should embrace whichever choices they make and not waste time feeling guilty about their decisions.

Jean Otte suggests that you think in terms of "How would I define success if there were no perceived limits to where I could be, who I could be, what I could do?" It's good advice because it encourages you to have vision, which is often key to achievement. Ann Pauker, another career counselor, suggests that women redefine success throughout their careers as "a balance of several aspects of their lives: professional life, learning, fitness, and family. When women take over the business world," she says with a laugh, "it will be like that."

Until that happens, you are most likely to succeed if you control your career. The chapters that follow focus on how you can do that.

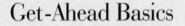

CHAPTER 3

Get-Ahead Basics

From the Pioneers: Meet the challenge.
Cathleen Black (President, Hearst Magazines): "When women are faced with a barrier—and it doesn't matter whether we're talking about the old-boys' network or backlash from your visibility—the way to react is not to simply complain, it's to plan your attack. Success is the ability to use your leverage to get where you want to be. It's the ability to use all your tools. It's keeping your head out and up. It's the willingness to take the risk, to step up to the opportunity."

Yes, there's still a glass ceiling, but that's no reason to feel boxed in. To break through glass, all you need is determination, discipline, persistence, smarts, courage, and a winning strategy. You obviously have the first five things, or you wouldn't be reading this book. The winning strategy is what we'll work on here.

YOU ARE RESPONSIBLE FOR YOUR OWN ADVANCEMENT

People—women *and* men—make or break their own careers. Others may show an interest in you, may lend a hand, may even mentor you, offering advice and guidance. Some companies really are there for you with commitment and real programs, not paper policies, and accountability, not lip service. But I advise you not to completely count on any one person, company, or even book. **You need to pursue effective career management strategies on your own if you want to advance.** Only you can ultimately imagine, shape, and move your own career forward.

For one of our surveys, Catalyst asked men at the top of the career ladder what women need to do to succeed. One summed it up as "Acquire skills and credibility, take charge, do the same things that men do." Let's think about what that means: "The same things that men do." Remember former Texas governor Ann Richards at the 1988 Democratic Convention, referring to Ginger Rogers's skill: "She danced all the steps Fred Astaire did, but she did it backward and in high heels." Like Rogers, we're caught in a man's choreography, in a workplace created by men. But her strategy worked. When we do what men do, we don't get the same response. When we're assertive, we're often called unfeminine or bitchy;* when we're less in-your-face, we're often ignored. Indeed, we may dance divinely, but men see us as different and we're always aware that we are.

But being different doesn't have to be bad. In your career, you will have to be acquiring credibility and skills, taking charge and moving yourself forward. To accomplish this, you might decide to trade in your high heels for tougher footwear.

*See Chapter 4, "Style Matters."

AXIOMS FOR ADVANCEMENT

An axiom, according to the *American Heritage Dictionary*, is a universally recognized truth. Our Axioms for Advancement are basic truths recognized by most successful people as being essential to getting ahead. Some are clearly workplace common sense. Some you may already have learned from colleagues, peers, friends, or bosses. I find, though, that many women unknowingly omit some of these crucial tactics in striving for success, when they need them all.

These eight advancement axioms are truths for which I can vouch. They have emerged from my own time-tested experience, from women my colleagues have worked with doing research, from the women pioneers in this book, and from other women Catalyst has interviewed who have been down the road you're traveling. They're not always easy to abide by—change is never easy—but none requires that you change who you are. (I don't believe the answer to advancing women in the workplace is to "fix the women.")

Axiom 1. The best isn't good enough. Successful women tell Catalyst over and over, "Perform beyond expectations." Performance is bottom line, no matter where you work, no matter what your field—for men and women alike. You've got to deliver on the expectations of your boss, and then some.

Gender bias occasionally works to your advantage, especially when coupled with hard work. Male colleagues apparently had such low expectations of one pioneer woman executive's ability to perform that they were surprised by results of any kind. When she performed really well, people took notice. You'll still find this to be the case in many organizations, certainly in those where you're one of just a few women.

Deliver results on time or ahead of time. Deliver more than people expect. Impress them over and over again. This is how you build a track record that will serve you well both with your immediate boss and with the organization at large. This is how you counter the "competency barrier" that women tell us they face when working with men. Results take time to accumulate, so recognition might not come overnight. Be patient (but not too patient).

From the Pioneers: Performance comes first.
Rebecca McDonald (Chair and CEO, Enron Asia-Pacific, Africa, and China): "Performance counts. Talent notwithstanding, education notwithstanding, day in and day out, that's what gets people's respect."

CEOs say:
CEO, Fortune 500 company: "The single most important thing is to perform well in those jobs that display the characteristics important for people who are going to be successful in line management jobs. But it's not just a matter of performing all right and everything will turn out, because companies haven't progressed as rapidly as we would have liked in advancing women."

NEEDED: TRUE GRIT AND TIME MANAGEMENT

This is a good time to confirm your suspicions with a crucial fact: The demanding work schedules required for professional success require real physical stamina. You need a particularly strong commitment to hard work and the kind of grit that allows you to survive, even thrive, under some pretty intense stress. Do you manage time well? If not, you'll have to learn how. Start by really using that datebook. Or if you're comfortable with the technology, use a personal digital assistant (PDA). Your back and shoulders will thank you—those crammed datebooks can be a pain—and you'll have plenty of room in your tote bag for papers or even a laptop computer. Try to think ahead so you can plan a week in advance, but use a pencil (if not a cursor) for flexibility. When changes happen, as they inevitably will, update your book. Your life, I promise you, will almost instantly become better organized.

Axiom 2. Time is of the essence. Some studies have shown women progressing at the same speed as men when they don't take breaks or leaves. But women with families often must take leave, or use flexible work schedules, and they can find the time commitment demanded by success exacts a pretty high price.

Women intent on succeeding manage to fit work in with family, though. Some executive women we've talked to describe workdays that begin at 5 A.M. with predawn reading before their children awaken. Or there are late-night phone calls and faxes at home, as well as travel schedules and after-hours business obligations that may keep them out several evenings weekly. Technology helps make this work, but the double edge of the technosword is that not only do you have access to your office, it has access to you—all the time. Telecommuting, a great aid to flexibility, can increase stress as well as productivity.

I do want to point out that women who succeed at work often repeat that success at home. Necessity being the mother of efficiency, efficient working mothers soon mutate into great time managers in both milieus. Let me make this clear: Despite the demands on them, most of the executive-level women we work with are happy with their jobs. And with their lives. They've made conscious choices that have worked for them and have brought them the professional, monetary, and personal rewards they hoped for. Fulfillment comes in different guises. For some it's work, for some it's family, for some it's a combination. For some women, taking time out while their children are small brings great joy; for others, being at home doesn't help them or their kids. Knowing you've made the choice that's right for you and believing in it are essential.*

From the Pioneers: Working works for women.
Roberta Gutman (Corporate Vice President and Director of Global Diversity, Motorola): "I'm living proof that you can have a successful career and a successful family and love every minute of it."

Barbara Paul Robinson (Partner, Debevoise & Plimpton): "Not being home full-time is a plus. Then you're not living entirely through your kids, so when they become teenagers and want to be independent, you say, 'Go!' There's not a lot of tension when you're all rooting for the same thing."

Joan Leiman (Executive Deputy Vice President for the Health Sciences and Clinical Professor of Public Health, Columbia University) looks back to the early days of her career and notes, "There's no magic way to balance work and personal life. When one has small children, it's very difficult. When I saw my colleagues at the Budget Bureau moving up to be assistants to the mayor, I sort of wanted to do it, but I couldn't. That was just the life I had at that time. Being at the beck and call of the mayor and having small children wouldn't really work. . . . I eventually did it when they were older when I felt I could manage it."

Be a myth breaker. As we said in Chapter 1, the mythology is that women are immovable objects—that our children or husbands, or our future children or husbands, preclude our being mobile or taking on last-minute tasks. So don't wait for your boss to ask you to relocate; initiate the conversation on your own. Or should you be offered an opportunity you must turn down because the timing doesn't work for you, make it clear you'd like another bite of that apple and indicate just when.

*See Chapter 7, "Making Your Life Work."

Here's where planning can be crucial. There'll be periods in your life when you can curtail your outside activities and focus totally on your job. But when life intervenes, you'll need to find ways to work that will not consume most of your energy. Try to anticipate the times when you're going to be most flexible—your first years on the job, when the kids start spending a full day in school, before you become responsible for aging parents, and so on—and use these times to make your major career efforts.

Axiom 3. If you don't blow your horn, nobody else will. False modesty and timid reticence have no place in an ambitious woman's office tool kit. Again and again, I hear how men keep their managers informed about their progress on a project, while women work on it quietly, leave it on their managers' desks, and walk away. When you're involved in an assignment, keep those you're working for posted so that they know what's happening.

- If you're making good progress and you're excited about it, don't hesitate to make your enthusiasm known to your boss.
- If you have questions about a project, don't be afraid to ask. That's what the guys do. That way your boss knows you're keeping on top of it, and that he or she can trust you.
- When you've completed the work, be sure your boss knows the results—and if they're good, don't hesitate to crow a little.

Subtlety is good, but recognition is better. Don't sit around and wait to be noticed. Some say self-advertisement is not a woman's forte, but you can learn it. Successful work deserves public recognition—inside as well as outside your organization.

- Make sure that your boss, above all, knows what you've done.
- Meet with your mentor, if you have one, when you have something to brag about, describe what you've done, and ask for input. Who better to talk you up?

- In your daily dealings with people you work with, on your teams, on task forces, with colleagues, find a way (discreetly, if that's more comfortable) to let everyone know what you've accomplished.
- Don't rely on your performance review. Yes, you want your success to be documented. But remember, the people making assignments don't necessarily see those documents. The goal is to get people bragging about you in public.

In your life outside work, do the same. If you serve on a committee, volunteer for a cause, or get involved in the community, let people there know what you've been doing at work—the successful product launch you spearheaded, the amazing acquisition you made, the grant you were just awarded. One way is to call on these people for advice, thus letting them know the kinds of projects you're involved in, how you think, the choices you've made, and the fact that you know the right questions to ask. They'll know who you are later, when you may need them—and even if you'll never need their help, you'll get some good practice.*

From the Pioneers: Spread the word about yourself.
Ellen Hancock (Chair and CEO, Exodus Communications): "Women aren't getting the credit. It's because women don't share with other people the fact that they're making those decisions and taking those risks. Men do that more. Women aren't as political. We tend to say, 'These are my roles and responsibilities,' and just take care of those. You've got to blow your own horn: it's part of the management process to share with people."

Axiom 4. Expertise impresses. If you develop an expertise in a unique, relevant specialty, people will turn to you for that expertise and your reputation will be much enhanced.

*See Chapter 6, "Your Number One Success Strategy: Networking."

To decide what specialty you want to develop, look around your organization and assess what information or expertise might be lacking. You might concentrate on certain new issues that affect your job area or subject matter; you could develop cross-industry or cross-subject expertise that others don't have; you could become the liaison with others in your field. Once you've identified an area or focus that no one seems to command, you can develop it for yourself: research it at the library, go on the Internet, interview experts at other companies or in comparable fields. You want to arrange things so that people will come to depend on you. This is not an overnight task, but you could make yourself indispensable—a highly desirable result.

Women say:

Corporate controller, consumer products company: "You have to have a specialty—and you have to do it better than anybody else can conceivably know how to do it. And therefore, when the general manager needs help on that specialty, you're the expert, the only one who can handle that problem."

CFO, petroleum company: "My advanced degree in chemical engineering gave me a differential capability. Everyone knew how difficult it was to achieve in my academic field, so with that degree they couldn't diminish my intellect. That ticket forced them to accept me. It's very specific, but it's a credibility chip."

From the Pioneers: Prove yourself continually.

Judith Rodin (President, University of Pennsylvania): "I was often the first woman in my department. I felt the need to demonstrate that I was good over and over again, probably to a greater extent than any of my male colleagues."

Lulu Wang (Partner and CEO, Tupelo Capital Management) says when she started out with a degree in English literature, she didn't plan on being a securities analyst, but she had a plan: "I realized that the only way to make a real entrance in a field was to develop expertise that no one else has developed. I learned the art of differentiation very early, which is key to making a spot for yourself and getting the foundation."

Make sure your expertise doesn't lock you into a single area if you want to advance to senior management. Think of having sequential specialties, so that after ten or fifteen years, you have a varied portfolio. And keep in mind that, if they're women, even experts have to prove themselves over and over again.

Credibility comes with results. When you're just starting out, it is essential to develop listening skills. As your experience increases and you establish yourself, you will earn trust. Success breeds success. Once you have certain achievements under your belt, once you've earned money or garnered a reputation for your organization, your reputation will grow and greater opportunities will come your way. Equally important, you will have more latitude for risk taking, and you'll be forgiven for ventures that don't pan out.

From the Pioneers: There are many ways to build credibility.
Linda Alvarado (President and CEO, Alvarado Construction): "I'm always dealing with the credibility gap: 'Would you trust a woman?' I have to sell credibility and confidence in me as a leader; I don't sell pictures of high-rises. Men don't have to do that." In fact, she says, she signed everything "LG" in the beginning "so they didn't know I was a woman and wouldn't judge a bid before they met me and the people in my organization. We were invited to a final selection interview on one project, and I walked in with the male engineer and a male Alvarado project manager. The selection committee ignored me completely, directing all the questions to the two guys, even on revising the price, which was of course my decision. As we left, we heard one man say, 'Oh, my gosh. Alvarado is a girl!' Nevertheless, we got the work."

Over time, Alvarado was able to turn her uniqueness into an advantage. "My being a Hispanic woman meant that people remembered us. It raised our profile in ways other construction companies couldn't match: 'that woman-owned firm.' "

Andrea Jung (President and CEO, Avon): "As a newcomer, I developed good listening skills, to learn and to understand. Developing listening skills is part of credibility. Then results matter. Results speak for themselves. Credibility is about developing a track record."

Ellen Hancock (Chair and CEO, Exodus Communications) emphasizes that she built her credibility by "working hard. People that you've worked with in the past know that you're working hard. And from that we build credibility."

Think before you speak. As you build up your credibility, you must also always protect it. Don't allow yourself to get caught up in situations, meetings, or arguments in which you cannot counter challenges to your expertise. This takes judgment, knowing when to talk and when not to, which fights are worth the effort and which should be allowed to pass.

Don't let anyone see your confidence be shaken, as when people who know less than you (but think they know more) challenge you in front of others. Just take it all calmly, even if you're seething inside. I make sure I'm thoroughly prepared for such encounters—in the old days I even practiced them with my husband—because I know they can spring up anytime from any quarter. That way I can stay calm and counter even the most aggressive challenges.

Credentials ratchet up your credibility. Education lays the foundation for your career, helping you to develop problem-solving skills and/or technical expertise. But a specialty degree in your particular field not only will increase your knowledge, it will also make you stand out from the pack. A myth women still fight is that they don't hold the credentials. But human resources records often reveal that women hold more degrees than men do. Once you get a degree—or any professional credentials—be sure everyone knows it.

Should you get an MBA? The fact is, certain companies will not even look at you if you don't have one. Some top companies won't look at you if your MBA isn't from one of the top schools, as indicated in the 2000 Catalyst study *Women and the MBA: Gateway to Opportunity*, details of which are available at www.catalystwomen.org.

Most chief executives today see the MBA as a practical and potent means of gaining access to the highest echelons in the corporate universe. Some recruit by offering those with high potential paid tuition to earn their MBAs.

The MBA can open up a whole new way of looking at things. One of our pioneers, Betty Beene, President and CEO of United Way of America, recommends it to women who want to advance in the nonprofit sector, as well as in the private sector. "It changes the way you think about the world," she says. "It gives you a common language for dealing with business leaders; it provides a vocabulary for what you intuitively know."

Both our pioneers and Fortune 1000 CEOs note that the value of an MBA depends upon your field. Dot coms and other start-ups probably couldn't care less. But that could change: lately, as much as a third of the class in top business schools has moved directly into start-ups. That might eventually make the MBA desirable there, too.

From the Pioneers: The MBA can help.
Maureen Kempston Darkes (President and General Manager, General Motors of Canada): "[Education was] the basis of my future opportunities. I knew that whatever I got in life, I would have to learn, and education was the first step."

Judy Sprieser (CEO, Transora): "Getting an MBA if you want to succeed in business is a wise thing to do. But a general liberal arts undergraduate degree is also important, leading to broad-based thinking. Women and men who pursue technical training from high school on have a more narrow focus."

Women say:
Vice president, airline: "Had I not had the MBA, I clearly wouldn't be in the position I'm in. Certainly I could have ac-

quired a lot of the knowledge base and financial skills on my own, but it really helps having the staff respect you because you have the same ticket to entry that they did."

Corporate controller, consumer products company: "Education is terribly important. Women have to credential themselves even more than men. It's important to get certain notches on the belt and to make them visible."

Axiom 5. Nothing comes to she who waits. Many male bosses expect men to take charge; they may assume that women don't take that approach. Men don't wait to be asked to do things. They just do them, often bluffing their way through when they don't know how. Women rarely consider behaving this way, and if they do, they often feel uncomfortable about it. Nevertheless, my advice is to try it. When you see a task in the offing that you know you'd be good at, don't just hope you'll be tapped for it. Muster up your courage, square your shoulders, walk into your boss's office, and tell him or her your plans for dealing with the job. And then do it.

Taking the initiative is critical to getting ahead. It's where you express your originality and your vision, as well as your strength. You need to be a self-starter if you want to move upward. As a woman, you may meet resistance when you start things moving. There's that catch-22 again: when women are assertive, they face negative reactions, but when they're not assertive, they can't advance. This occurs most often in an area where one is the first woman or one of a few. Men don't have to contend with this, and they usually look at you as if you're nuts when you tell them about it. The women pioneers recommend that you keep your sense of humor as you figure out how to take the initiative without scaring anyone.*

*See Chapter 4, "Style Matters."

From the Pioneers: Ask for what you want.
Judy Sprieser (CEO, Transora): "[Women make a mistake expecting] opportunities to be handed to them. It's not going to happen. You can't just say, 'Give me more responsibility, please.' " Her career parallels her childhood, when "rather than be told no when I asked to do something, I preferred to face punishment for something I didn't do well. I act like it's mine, rather than ask and have it given. If you're a woman, you have to work harder and you have to grab it for yourself."

Barbara Paul Robinson (Partner, Debevoise & Plimpton) knew early on to ask for what she wanted. Pregnant in 1967, she says, "I liked my job and didn't want to leave. Not knowing any better, I asked the partners if I could go on a regular schedule [five days per week]." The firm had women who'd dropped out to have families, but this was a new one. They took a while to decide, then agreed—if she would shift from litigation to trust and estates. After her second child, she worked three days per week, then realized, "If I'm ever going to be partner, I've got to come back full-time. I surprised the partners again when I asked to be considered for partnership."

Ellen Hancock (Chair and CEO, Exodus Communications): "Men are good at saying, 'Here's what I want,' and women need to do the same thing." But she advises not showing your ambition too early. "Don't get too far out of bounds in the discussion with your boss; don't go five or six steps past where you are. Think two jobs out. If you're a director, you can ask about becoming a vice president. Say, 'Here's what I want, and I'm ready for it,' or ask what you need to do to be ready. There's nothing wrong with putting it on the table. Women assume the system will take care of them, and that's a failing. Men assume they have to take care of themselves and they tell the system what they want."

Axiom 6: It's not just corporations that need to diversify. To succeed, you have to diversify your experience. If you're aiming for the upper ranks, you need to think in terms of gaining broad experience in many aspects of running an organization. You need to learn how things work. It's like learning how to fix a clock—you start by taking it apart to see how it works. You must get inside and fiddle with all the parts. From the time you take your first position at an organization, in whatever position, you should be scoping out the other areas where you'll need to work.

Be sure you learn the business of the business. At most organizations, to move to the most senior positions you need experience that includes bottom-line responsibility. I cover this in detail in Chapter 9, but for now, let me underscore that almost no one ever makes it to a corner office without having experience related to bringing in the bucks, the business of the business—in, say, planning, operations, and marketing.

Another thing you may need to do is move laterally—and in some cases downward—in order to get the diverse experience you need. Don't automatically reject these moves. Weigh them carefully. They may seem like side steps while they're actually stepping-stones—to build the résumé you need for further advancement.

Does your company have formal career-track policies? Men learn how essential diverse experience is from their mentors and bosses. That's one reason why men who start out as women's peers seem to keep moving up, while women are stuck in the same position, performing superbly, and finding themselves looking up at the guys at the top.

That's why we suggest you should find out if an organization has formal career-track policies *before* you take a job. Such practices usually include detailed career tracks and ways of identifying high-potential employees for those tracks, as well as cross-functional job rotations. Large organizations are more likely than small ones to have implemented such practices, but there are many nonprofits and new organizations that have enforced them from their inception.

More and more organizations have created structured succession-planning processes, too, with systems for identifying and developing high-potential managerial talent. They might have structured job rotation. They might have executive mentoring programs with clearly defined developmental expectations. Yet one of the biggest stumbling blocks for these practices is getting news of them to everyone who needs to know. Take it upon yourself to find out if these exist. Remember, you have to ask. As a woman, you're unlikely to be handed the chance to diversify your experience. Managers may assume that you can't or won't make a geographic move, or they just don't think of you when risky, paradigm-changing assignments come along.

DIVERSE ASSIGNMENTS: HOW TO MAKE THEM HAPPEN

Dealing with your boss might be the hardest part. Try these tactics:

- Set up a meeting with your boss to find out what's available and how you can land such assignments.
- Create a relationship with him or her in order to be informed when things come up.
- Let your boss know you want to learn about many aspects of the organization. If your boss feels threatened by your ambition and won't offer you the opportunities you want, gain the experience you need while working for him or her and move out.
- Sometimes women become too good for their own good. If your boss has come to really rely on you and wants to keep you, you may find yourself in a bind. You should nonetheless make your desires known. Perhaps you can convince your boss that you're a better employee when you're happy, and you'll be happier and more effective if you're upwardly mobile. Or perhaps you can convince him or her of the ben-

efits from successfully developing staff (you), who will then become part of a network of your boss's alumni, spread throughout the company.

- Make connections with colleagues in the new areas you have targeted. The more people you know, the better your opportunities to diversify and to use this diversification to propel yourself upward. It's also a strategy that could help you find sponsors other than your boss to help you with an upward or lateral move.
- Keep your eyes open for opportunities wherever you are: Watch for job postings and look on the intranet. Keep an ear open to the rumor mill.
- If your organization does not post jobs, work with other women and human resources to make that happen.
- If your organization has a women's network, you can get that on the agenda. Use the relationships you develop in your network as a chance to learn informally about other jobs.
- Sign up for in-house leadership training opportunities. Inquire about the existence of special courses and programs. These can build your familiarity with what's needed to advance and widen the spectrum of people you know in your office.

Axiom 7. Fortune favors the brave. Performing well at what you've done before will not move you ahead. You need to demonstrate your readiness for the new, the bold, the daring. You need to take risks. Stretch assignments offer you the chance to cultivate new abilities and show them off, often in a challenging or difficult situation—a new product launch or the rescue of a failing unit, for example. A stretch assignment means you're doing new things in a place where you don't naturally fit. Stretch assignments can be found—or created—at every level. You don't know exactly what to do, but your confidence in the face of the unknown proves your executive potential. CEOs get to their positions by making one stretch after another.

Stretch assignments are not usually offered to women because women aren't in the high-visibility positions. You may need to create your own. Use your imagination to assess what needs to be done (often what no one else wants to do because it's too risky or just too hard). Then figure out who you need to convince that you're the person for the job. A "turnaround" offers the greatest stretch opportunity of all: you take a product or project that's not doing well and make it a success. That draws attention to your multiple skills, your willingness to take risks, and your ability to move the organization forward. Several of our pioneers made it just that way.

From the Pioneers: How to handle risks.

Carly Fiorina (Chair and CEO, Hewlett-Packard) says what you need to learn to take risks is instinct and judgment, and "these come out of the general skills you've built up, and from having sufficient knowledge of your industry and the capabilities of your company. I've always believed I needed to know what I don't know. And it's important to acknowledge both for the sake of realism and for the sake of motivation that failure is a real possibility. That's been the case in every job I've ever taken, and it's the case with everyone. There are worse things in life than failure. Failure as a possibility doesn't intimidate me. It motivates me." She offers advice for picking yourself up after a flop: "Acknowledge it publicly and privately and then make it right. You can't stop to figure out what the perfect decision is or get paralyzed by a mistake. You have to react, redirect, learn, but you gotta keep moving. In business and in life, forward momentum is everything. Acknowledge the failure, then say what has to happen to keep the business—or you— moving forward."

Women say:

Former senior vice president, technology: "Many times my company pushed me ahead of where I thought I was ready to be. I can identify the exact points where they knew that they were taking a risk and were encouraging me to do something I might not have done on my own. They were great that way."

From the Pioneers: Success requires taking risks.
Judith Rodin (President, University of Pennsylvania): "From freshmen to Ph.D. candidates, women are less willing to take risks to put their ideas out there and have them shot down. Even the smartest. But the more they are able to do that, the more successful I've seen them become in academia and outside."

Risk Taking Made Easy

You have to let go of your perfectionism. Try to practice the "80/20 principle": You can be "perfect" only 80 percent of the time. You need to identify where, when, and to what the 20 percent applies. Obviously, you don't want to be "less than perfect" for an important presentation. But you don't want to let your perfectionism hold you back and keep you from taking risks. Try these paths to risk:

- If you hear of a tough job, get in there and grab it.
- Ask around, learn what's available and what new directions the organization may be heading in.
- Take on a new venture for the company.
- Let your boss know you want an international assignment (if you're at an organization where globalization looms large). Or you might consider working on international projects at home; that also can stretch your muscles.

Stretches and risks come in many different guises. One woman stepped out of R and D for a year to accept a corporate assignment from the chairman of the board—in other words, out of the dead end and onto the fast track. "I wanted the chairman to think of me not just as a scientist but as a business person dealing with an issue that was policy-oriented and very strategic," she explained. It turned out to be an excellent career move, giving her high-level visibility and leading to a promotion at the end of the assignment. Stretch assignments can be frightening, but they are often defining moments in careers.

Axiom 8. Money matters. Many women, especially when they're starting out, believe that money doesn't matter. Later, usually too late, they find out that it does. In general, men do not embrace this philosophy. The Bureau of Labor Statistics' much-publicized gap between men's and women's salaries is real. For every dollar earned by men, women earn 77 cents.[1] Among private-sector managers and professionals, men and women start out with relatively even salaries, but as their careers progress, men pull ahead of women. For every dollar earned by white male managers, white women managers earn 59 cents and women of color managers earn 57 cents.[2]

Women and minorities have been dubbed "managerial bargains." One study found that because women tend to accept or reject an offer outright and rarely ask for more money, they often begin at lower salary levels than those who negotiate (read: men).[3] So not only do women's salaries start out lower than men's, they fall further behind year by year, and by retirement the career-long salary gap makes women's retirement earnings pale by comparison to men's. I frequently hear women say they feared to negotiate when offered their first position. But even women who are firmly entrenched and recognized for their achievements continue to take new positions without negotiating.

From the Pioneers: Get paid what you're worth.
Joan Leiman (Executive Deputy Vice President for the Health Sciences, Columbia University): "Women are managerial bargains because we expect to be rewarded. That's how we grew up: we did good work in school, we got an A." In the workplace, she says, "even when your work is very good, even

Ratio of Managers' Earning by Gender, Race, and Ethnicity

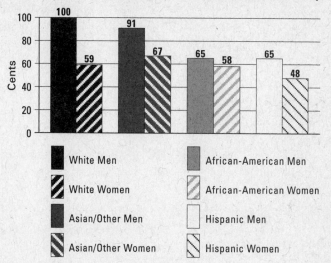

SOURCE: *Women of Color in Corporate Management: A Statistical Picture* (New York: Catalyst, 1997).

when you're working for excellent people, they're not going to adjust your salary voluntarily." She had an unusual catalyst inspire her trip into her boss's office: "A member of my staff told me, with some bitterness, 'You're not aggressive enough about your salary, so the rest of us are being held down. It's not fair,' he said. I decided he was right and went in to the dean and gave him a proposal that he accepted."

Who's at fault here? Well, of course, it's unjust when women do not receive equal pay for equal work. But Utopia is far down the road. Most bosses will pay you as little as they can get away with; their responsibility is to their bottom line. I advise you to take your compensation into your own hands. First, start with the right salary. Your potential employer is not going to help you out here. You—and only you—can make it clear what salary you'll accept when you're applying for a job.

From the Pioneers: Beware of the perception of your needs.
Yvonne M. Curl (Vice President and Chief Marketing Officer, Avaya Communication): "[The bias is] subtle, but there's still a perception that if you make good money, that's enough because you're not the head of the household. Pay equity issues persist."

Women say:
Catalyst focus group participant: "A lot of times you go in to negotiate your salary, women don't know they can say, 'No, I want this. I want more.' They just wait for an offer. We don't know our market value."

How do you know what salary to ask for? Here's where research is crucial—and worth the time and effort involved. Check with executive recruiting firms, which often share databases of salary information; check the Internet; call companies advertising jobs similar to the one you're considering and ask what the salary range is. Human resources at the organization to which you're applying should give salary ranges for positions you're considering. Talk to former or current employees who might have information on what others earn (though probably they won't talk about their own salaries).

Don't raise specific compensation requests until the final interview stages, when a company is ready to make an offer. And when it does, assume you're being offered a low salary in the salary range for a position. Don't accept it. Bargain. A lot hangs in the balance here: you won't get a chance to make up for a mistake unless you change employers.[4]

Make this your mantra: Never accept the first offer. Know what you deserve and demand it. If for some reason you can't get more money, negotiate for perks such as time off or flexible work hours. It might help to keep this in mind: the worst that can happen is that if you really want the job, you'll have to fall back to the employer's original offer.

NEGOTIATING A SALARY INCREASE

Career counselor Sheryl Spanier works with women about how to negotiate salary increases. "For men," she says, "negotiating a raise is not a matter of self-worth nor whether they deserve it. This is what they have to do. Pull your ego and self-worth out of it." She offers some basic tips to women for negotiating salary:

- Expect what you're worth. "Don't go in thinking you're going to be gifted—or shafted," says Spanier. "Attitude makes all the difference."
- View the negotiation as a game. Spanier suggests you practice with a friend or relative and "start by asking for a million-dollar raise. It's just a number. Then ask for a five-dollar raise. Make it abstract, and get into the game mode. By the time you work around to the number you want, your comfort level will have increased."
- Specify your value to the organization. Demonstrate what you've brought it and if you've expanded your position. Think retention-cost issues and make your boss realize the cost of losing you. Bring along any data that will back you up. Include nothing personal. Spanier recommends holding this thought during the negotiations: "I've enjoyed it here because you value my worth. I need to know that you see the business benefit of my continuing."
- Ask clear questions. "Be direct," advises Spanier. "Ask, 'What do you mean? I don't see how you can rate this less than . . .' and so on. Bosses generally appreciate your honesty."
- Decide your break point in advance. Spanier says, "Know when you'll walk. In order to really negotiate anything, you need to be willing not to have it. If you need it, you can't negotiate, and don't feel obliged to do so; there's no shame in that. If you're not prepared to counter, don't negotiate."

- Have a backup plan. "Know what you're willing to give for what you're willing to get," suggests Spanier. Determining where you'll compromise before you enter the room will give you the confidence you need.
- And when you get the raise, say the right thing. Spanier recommends something along the lines of "I really appreciate that I'm valued."

You're not going to get what you want every time you ask, but you'll find that negotiation will come more easily each time you do it. A salary negotiation is a test of nerve, like serious poker. These days I'm a tough negotiator when it comes to raises, but I learned the hard way. Getting my first professional job in 1968, I hesitated to ask about salary. After I had said yes, my new boss said to me, "How does $12,000 a year sound to you?" With a graduate degree and a very good record, I demurred. He responded, "I could get anyone at your level for $10,000 a year and a hot meal." I took the job and the salary. Where was this book when I needed it?

Look elsewhere if you don't get what you need. Consider other offers seriously. Then, when you're really interested in one, discuss it with your boss. You may find this your best negotiating tool: the very real possibility of your leaving.

From the Pioneers: Use offers to increase your worth.
Judith Rodin (President, University of Pennsylvania) received many offers during her academic career. One she received while at Yale, following which she spoke with the president. "I indicated I was considering another position of leadership, but that what I wanted was a position of leadership at Yale." That (and her ability) earned her the chairmanship of her department "with the thought that I would then be a candidate for the most important deanship—dean of the graduate school, which led to the provost position." She advises, "Use your offers to

better your position if you want to stay where you are. Women
are reluctant to do that; men do it often and with a great degree
of comfort. You can't be shy about it. I learned that from male
mentors."

When your workload increases, ask for more pay. Among
men, it is understood that more work calls for more money and
a better title. Women hope that once they've done the additional
work, manna will drop out of heaven on them in the form of a
raise and promotion. Not bloody likely. Don't let your assets—
your efficiency and productivity—turn you into an overbur-
dened, underpaid sucker. Your resentment could build up inside
you. Surprise your boss, who expects women to say yes to more
work. Just because he expects your acquiescence doesn't mean
that's the only avenue open to you.

Choose your moment carefully. Bad timing has killed many a
woman's raise or promotion. Get your boss when you're most
needed. A good moment is when new business comes in and he
needs someone to handle the account. Don't wait until you're
staying late and working weekends. Certainly don't wait until
you're handing the work over. The best time to ask is before you
accept new responsibilities. And when you ask for a raise, ask
for a better title, too.

SEXUAL HARASSMENT:
WHAT IT IS AND HOW TO HANDLE IT

No book on women in the workplace would be complete without a discussion of sexual harassment.

Title VII of the Civil Rights Act of 1964 defines sexual harassment as "unwelcome sexually related behavior that creates
an intimidating, hostile and offensive work environment." As
this definition makes clear, sexual harassment is not limited to
cases in which an employer or employee seeks to coerce someone into sexual acts (known as "quid pro quo" harassment), but

also includes the existence of a hostile work environment, defined as regular and repeated actions or things displayed around the workplace that produce unreasonable interference with job performance and that create an intimidating or offensive work environment.

All companies, regardless of size, should have a specific policy defining sexual harassment, articulating the company's strong disapproval of it, giving examples of illegal behavior, and outlining penalties. In fact, it is a company's legal responsibility to have zero tolerance for sexual harassment in the workplace since the courts have ruled that (1) an employer can be held responsible for sexual harassment by its supervisors if it knew or should have known about the conduct but did nothing to correct it; and (2) a work environment can be considered hostile even if it does not affect the worker's well-being.

Progressive organizations provide advice to their employees on how to deal with this behavior. Knowing your own company's policy is essential to being prepared to deal with such issues.

Now that you know what sexual harassment is, what can you do to avoid having to deal with this debilitating issue in your career? For starters, your best defense is in finding out a prospective employer's commitment to a zero tolerance policy on sexual harassment. Companies with the best practices related to sexual harassment

- have sexual harassment policies that are widely publicized, explain the prohibited conduct, and make clear that corrective actions will be taken when illegal or inappropriate behaviors occur and are confirmed.
- provide sensitivity training for employees as part of new-hire orientation and at regular intervals thereafter.
- provide supervisor training that emphasizes both the kinds of behavior to avoid and affirmative responsibilities for follow-

ing up when inappropriate or illegal behavior is observed, even if no employee has filed a complaint.

• have a complaint process that is widely communicated and accessible; that includes gender diversity in points of access for making a complaint; that allows employees to bypass anyone in their supervisory chain of command; that provides confidentiality and due process; and that includes a wide range of corrective actions.

• use a diverse committee to investigate allegations.

• include corrective actions that have teeth.

Why so much emphasis on finding an employer who is in the forefront on this issue? Because in too many situations women don't really win when they are put in a position of suing a company over the behavior of an employee or because of a hostile work environment. Though the Civil Rights Act of 1991 allowed targets of sexual harassment to sue for compensatory and punitive damages up to $300,000 plus back pay, plaintiffs lose about half of the cases that are decided by trial courts.[5] When they win, they usually get small awards. In contrast, the emotional and psychological costs to women can be immense and the damage to their careers is often irreparable. So I advise that you make sure you choose a company that will be on your side should you have the unfortunate experience of sexual harassment on the job.

But be aware that no matter how good your organization's policy is, making a charge of harassment might have a negative impact. And once you make a complaint to your supervisor, he or she has no choice but to pass it on, because companies are liable if they allow such behavior to continue. So be careful to weigh various factors. Ask yourself:

• Is reporting this worth the possibility of jeopardizing my career, or can I handle it some other way?

- If I say nothing, will some other woman suffer similarly in the future?

Obviously, the most threatening cases are those in which the harasser has power over his victim. You may still be able to deal with such behavior short of making a formal complaint—if you decide that this is the way you want to go. Sometimes harassment can be deflected with humor. If it persists, you can often straighten it out by talking to the offending party himself. Something along the lines of, "I don't know if you realize what you're doing, but . . ." may work, since more and more men are aware of the pitfalls they face as a result of such behavior. Quite a few women have told Catalyst that they handled harassment by switching functions, departments, or even jobs.

It's important to realize that different industries and different functions have different levels of acceptable behavior. In sales, for instance, where Catalyst did a major study, more than a few women said they were expected to accept a certain sexual undercurrent and a lot of kidding on a gender-related basis. Many women have found that consulting with a trusted female colleague can be a helpful first step—not only to get her assessment of the seriousness of the problem but also to have a witness to their experience should they decide to make a complaint at a later time. What if your company doesn't have an effective sexual harassment policy or process? This is an excellent issue for a women's network to tackle, since there is safety in numbers.

Finally, if you are a woman in a company that does not have an effective sexual harassment policy or process and you are being harassed, never, ever blame yourself. Women frequently think, "It must have been something I said or did." Changing your style isn't the solution to sexual harassment. And you probably can't solve the problem on your own. Nor should you be expected to. In fact, doing so may lead to charges that you tolerated or even encouraged the behavior, or may put you in harm's way. Catalyst's extensive experience conducting post-departure interviews for companies shows that women who find themselves in this situation do one of three things: they accept the situation because they cannot afford to leave or lose their jobs, they leave their jobs without telling anyone about their experience or lodging a formal complaint, or they take their employer to court. None of these solutions is a win-win for you or your career. But you should never forget that sexual harassment is not only inappropriate, it is illegal.

All that said, let's not forget that the brave women who have litigated this issue have made the workplace a better place for all of us. Thanks to them, you may never face this repellent behavior.

≫

CHAPTER 4

Style Matters

In Catalyst's studies of women near the top in business in the United States and Canada,[1] successful women reported that "finding a style with which men are comfortable" was an important success strategy, second only to "exceeding performance expectations." Style matters. This has always been the case, but in today's competitive environment, where almost everyone at your level has comparable skills and credentials, your style sets you apart. How you are perceived by those with whom you work can make or break your career. Controlling that perception could be your most compelling success strategy.

Women Catalyst talks to every day say that they have personally crafted the style that has worked toward their advancement, and that involves altering behavior that makes others—men included—uncomfortable. The women pioneers in the workplace created theirs by trial and error—mostly through their own mistakes and triumphs. Today you can deliberately use what has worked for those pioneers and what is working now for other women above you, by asking for and heeding their advice.

Those whose jobs entail daily "face time"—that's most of us—are under constant observation. Nevertheless, most of us prepare on autopilot, dressing between bites of toast and getting the kids off, the dog out, the fish fed. Some do a terrific job on their physical appearance. But even the most artfully presented women seldom pay much attention to crafting the other critical aspect of style: *how we interact as we get things done.* (This is the kind of style that's germane even to those whose work can be done at home in casual clothes. And even most telecommuters have to show up in an office occasionally.)

Most of us do things at work, as elsewhere, with little thought for how we appear as we do them. Who has the time? In fact, those who are most successful seem to *make* the time. They develop elements of style that serve to further their advancement. And if they notice that their style isn't working for their colleagues, reports, and bosses, they take steps to change it.

An effective style doesn't leap full-blown from our heads, like Athena from the head of Zeus. There are people with a natural affinity for the workplace, whose personalities both blend in with their office culture and promote their uniqueness. I find, though, that these people are pretty rare. Even the naturals need to tweak their style, refine it as they work for changing goals in order to succeed. Common sense will tell you that what works for a new employee is bound to change as she climbs the organizational ladder. But most of us, no matter how gracious, aren't office naturals, so you'd be well advised to give attention to your style at work, honing it often so it serves you well.

From the Pioneers: Pay attention to your style.
Ellen Hancock (Chair and CEO, Exodus Communications), who worked her way to senior management at IBM, says, "Women

must be careful about style; they must know what's expected of them, because it really makes a difference in how you fit in." Using appearance as an example, she explains, "The IBM culture cared about our audience and how you looked to them. For years I wore what the guys wore: navy blue suit, white blouse, blue shoes." She tells how "only when I got comfortable with my persona did I add color." And today, is it different running a hot Internet company? "I buy outfits with blouse, jacket, skirt, and pants: I wear the skirt on the East Coast. On the West Coast, you must be casual. When I moved out to California, the press started asking if I was capable of wearing jeans. I said, 'Hey, I can do this.'" She stresses, "Style questions seem trivial, but they're really important."

Yvonne M. Curl (Vice President and Chief Marketing Officer, Avaya Communication): "Ask yourself, 'Is my style effective? Does it get the results I want?' Watch and learn what effect your style is making. I believe there are issues with understanding styles and that sometimes women's styles are perceived as something they're not. So you should be aware of what's going on around you. Ask for feedback."

Zoë Baird (President, The Markle Foundation): "Women need to understand how they're perceived by others. I've seen style issues used against women in performance reviews, and the way they were talked about shouldn't be seen as acceptable language."

First, there's your physical appearance. Everyone has an image, and whether we like it or not, a lot of it stems from our appearance. People judge us by what they see; nearly everyone everywhere appraises you on your appearance. Meg Armstrong of the Leadership Group asserts that when you're in a new situation, business or personal, you have five seconds to make the right impression. She says that "people make almost 85 to 90 percent of their decisions about you on what they see with their eyes in the first five seconds. Your voice counts, too."

First impressions matter as much in the workplace as they do on first dates. Once you're perceived badly in your organization, you're marked for failure, and it may be almost impossible to recover. It may not be fair, it may not be right, and it's probably not smart, but it happens. You can't take the risk that "they'll learn to love me when they get to know me." You want to have the right style so they'll love you straight from the start.

Style includes behavior. Your style is the sum total of your self-presentation. It consists of how you look and how you act. It is a series of habits that include not only the sartorial—that's really the easy part—but also your carriage, your attitude, and the way you do things. It is the way you speak, the subliminal messages you send, the way you manage your workload, contribute to meetings, arrive in a room, interact with colleagues, bosses, and staff, and respond to jokes. When you're a manager in particular (or on your way to becoming one), these are work skills. Like your work, they convey your ability to perform well.

Clothes, alas, do make the woman. The concept of "dressing for success" did not die in the 1980s, although what "success" clothes are has changed. Office clothing became a uniform for men many years ago, although there are nuances there, too, that we may not be as aware of as men are. Nevertheless, communications researcher Deborah Tannen says that a woman's clothing, hair, and shoes are "marked" in a way that men's are not, so that "everything she wears is fodder for interpretation of character."[2] Even so, who among us envies the necktie? At least in most offices we have some leeway for self-expression.

But you can get into trouble if you express yourself too much in workplaces where sartorial flair goes against the preferred style. Ellen Snee, who counsels women in the workplace environment, advises conservatism. According to Snee, "There are dress codes in every industry. Women should know what they are; the men all do. And the higher you get, the fewer the people who are different, and the more the dominant style reigns. If you're different, you're going to make people uncomfortable."

Snee's word choice echoes Catalyst's findings: The comfort of others around us must be considered if we are to succeed. What you wear must make others feel comfortable. At the office, if you're serious about success, you're not dressing for yourself, you're dressing so others will accept you as one of them. You need to understand what attire is appropriate for your particular line of work.

If you're new to a particular industry or field (read: culture), start out by dressing conservatively. You can't go far wrong with a tailored suit and simple jewelry (unless you're working in a dot-com business, in which case you might look a little over-dressed). Then watch and wait. If you're sensitive to what's going on around you, it shouldn't take long for you to determine the permissible, and the preferred, style of dress.

Women still stick out in the business environment. It's a fact of life. Because women still hold only 12.5 percent of top corporate jobs, whenever you enter a top management meeting, you're going to be noticed. You'll be seen as different, and most men will respond to you differently than they do to others at the table. It's not just the corporate jobs; women are also not well represented in other workplaces. In 1998, women accounted for 15.7 percent of partners in law firms ("Women's Numbers Rise at the Bigger Law Firms," *National Law Journal,* December 14, 1998). In 1999, women represented over 10 percent of the partners in the nation's largest accounting firms.[3] A study conducted in 1999 by Wall Street's major trade association, the Securities Industry Association (SIA), showed that women held only 12.2 percent of the high-paying broker positions.[4] In the nonprofit sector women are better represented: women account for 49.9 percent of CEO positions and 67.7 percent of program officer positions in foundations and corporation foundations/giving programs (Council on Foundations, 1998 Salary Report). In academia, male full professors outnumber female full professors by almost 5 to 1; at the assistant professor rank, the percentage of male and female professors is almost equal (AAUP, Doing Better: The Annual Report on the Economic Status of the Profession, 1997–98). In the government, women in the top jobs (statewide elected officials, state legislators, highest court justices, department heads, and governor's office top advisers) constitute approximately 25 percent of the officials (1998 Women's Leadership Profile Compendium Report, Center for Women in Government).

Be aware that in work settings where you're still the minority, your style may be assessed and criticized and could be used against you. Meg Armstrong worked with a CEO whose mentor took him aside many years ago following his first lunch with senior management and "told him never to wear white socks again, then told him exactly what to wear, how to sit, when not to interrupt at the table." Then he admitted to Armstrong, "[I'd] never have told a young woman this." So you're probably not going to get much helpful style advice from men, although just observing the successful women in your office or out in the world can make them your mentors in spite of themselves. Most of the women pioneers in this book had to feel their way with what they wore and how they acted, with no women mentors to advise them and no women higher-ups to copy. But you don't have to. Look around. Remember Yogi Berra's words: "You can see a lot by watching."

Here's what some top women have to say about how they've been perceived:

From the Pioneers: Women are treated differently.

Barbara Paul Robinson (Partner, Debevoise & Plimpton): "The band of tolerable types of women is narrower than for men in my field [the law] in both looks and style, although it's improving with more women in positions of success. Women partners in my firm are good-looking and dress well. They're not too quiet, although their style is quiet. . . . A woman may be too quiet, while a man can be a ghost and it's fine."

Women say:

General counsel, high-tech company: "I'm the only woman, and the first meeting I walked into was like going into a locker room where everybody all of a sudden shuts up. It took nearly an hour of talking through the issues with them, giving examples of how I approach different intellectual property issues, before they began to relax and open up."

Senior-level Asian-American executive: "There are certain stereotypes associated with being Asian and being a woman. With Asian women, there sometimes is the 'China doll syndrome.' But it's even a problem that I don't fit that image. I'm aggressive and have a big mouth, and it's like shattering an image, although that image is wrong. You shatter their illusion of what you should be like."

Senior-level African-American manager: "From seven in the morning until seven at night, we became an extension of white America. Then we'd go home, and Friday night until Sunday night, we're black again. On Monday morning when the alarm goes off, we become white again. In terms of [my company] appreciating African-American culture, they don't have a clue. . . . It's a bit like, 'Here's our corporate culture, and you fit or you don't fit.' "

No matter where you work, you will probably deal with people who still hold notions about what women can and can't do and how women should and shouldn't behave. There's a whole array of other questions that might pass through your male colleagues' and bosses' minds: "I haven't worked with many women. Will she do the task as well as a man? Will she get emotional under stress? Will I be too attracted to her when we're here late at night? What will my wife think when we travel together? How will the clients respond? Is she strong enough to carry the presentation materials?" Absurd, maybe, but all these may play into their silent assessment of you the first time they meet you and inform their every interaction with you—at least until they discover you have a style with which they're comfortable.

TEN TIPS FOR DEVELOPING YOUR OWN SUCCESSFUL STYLE

1. Make others comfortable. Be aware of the comfort zones of your peers and superiors. You'll still be a woman, and men have to live with that. But many won't be comfortable until they know they can depend on you and even to some extent anticipate your responses—just as they would be able to with another man. People—especially those in senior management—don't like to be taken by surprise. You can put them at ease with your style: your way of speaking, your manner of dress, your humor, your ease, your confidence.

From the Pioneers: Make those you work with comfortable.
Marie Knowles (Executive Vice President and CFO, Atlantic Richfield): "The key on the style issue is having one that engenders trust. That's why people hire someone just like them: they think they've got a level of predictability; they know how that person will react in certain situations. This is the core of the difficulty organizations have in assimilating diversity. When things are different cross-culturally, you've got a certain amount of unpredictability."

Carolee Friedlander (Founder, President, and CEO, Carolee Designs): "If you've placed yourself in an environment that holds certain concepts dear to you, then being able to clearly communicate them is very important. That's figuring out what the rules are for that environment and what's going to make you successful there. In my business, there are certain buzzwords which give the perception that we know what we are doing and where we are going. If there are things I need from a retail group, I must find out what makes them successful, what will make them want Carolee products." One key way to make sure everyone feels comfortable is to know what issues are important to the group you are meeting with. Friedlander tells of a keynote speech she delivered at the Harvard Business School where women admitted that "if they [the women] couldn't communicate freely to a new client, and if they don't know what will turn them on, what makes them tick, then they won't be able to play the game. If I'm walking blind, I won't succeed."

2. Get past other people's assumptions. You'll need to find your own ways to deal with people's assumptions and prejudices, but here's some guidance. Most important, be aware of them. Don't let yourself be fazed by boorishness, sexism, or stupid comments, and don't be surprised at how pernicious the myths are about your skills and commitment. In most workplaces, you're going to meet discrimination, whether conscious or unconscious, at some point—maybe sooner, maybe later. Most women have met it by the time they're ready to move out of middle management.

Regarding the physical trappings, career counselor Sheryl Spanier suggests that women "be aware of the reaction you're raising in men." Is it paternalistic? Or sexual? We can't do anything about the fact that these guys have a perception of women that preceded us. That's a reality. If we're aware of their reaction, we can do something about managing our own reaction to their assumptions. We can ignore them, parry them, laugh them off, overturn them, shut them off, and transcend it—if we are prepared.

My advice is that you accept two things. One is that you can't stop their hormonal reaction to you, but most of the time you can manage it with style. The smartest organizations, those that mandate behavior change, still can't control their employees' thinking.

3. Develop the right look. When working on your style, first think about how you look: your clothes, your hair, your makeup. Women have found the equivalent of the man's office uniform in the well-styled suit, but even so, our greater flexibility in attire requires the use of some pretty perceptive radar to keep from going wrong. Silk blouse or T-shirt under the jacket? How low the neckline, how high the hem? How casual is casual? You need to ask, "What are other women wearing? Do I look good in that? If not, how much can I vary the style without going too far? How can I conform and yet be myself?"

Yes, there are nonconformists. If being one matters to you, go ahead and do it. But if that's the choice you make, you may have to compensate in some other area in order to get ahead in your organization.

If possible, spend some money on how you look. This includes both what you wear and how you groom yourself. Most career counselors devote time with a client to assessing clothes and general appearance and making decisions about appropriate adjustments. To start with, you can't go wrong with a couple of well-made suits and a good haircut. Getting attention because of your appearance can be a good thing in the office, so long as it's the kind of attention you want. Look contemporary, and you'll seem well informed. Look sexy, and you'll distract from work matters. Look too casual or at all sloppy, and you'll give the impression that your work or your thinking might also be sloppy.

When I moved to New York to take my job at Catalyst, I made adjustments in my work wear. Academic tweeds seemed out of place in an organization that deals with corporate types so frequently. Even I—hardly a style leader, as my mother often lamented—got the point.

Don't fail to pay attention to the question of formal versus informal wear. You need to dress at the appropriate level, even on dress-down days. Some women make the mistake of dressing *too* casually on "casual Fridays," undercutting the intelligent, businesslike image they project during the rest of the week. Career counselor Jean Otte observes that "even if casual dress-down is the style of your organization, you could still be the best casually dressed person in the office and get noticed. You want to get noticed." Noticed, though, for your fine tailoring, not for your inappropriate ensembles.

4. Develop your room radar. Start by being alert to what's going on around you in a meeting room. Make a practice of "reading" whatever room you enter, assessing the people there and the ways they're interacting. Some people do this intuitively. Others need to learn how. Knowing some psychology helps, but you can also wing it. Start with the basics, and once you get good at it, the nuances will follow. Who's in the power seat? Who's next to that person? Who's holding forth? Who's holding back? Who's nervous and who's not, and why? Who's really running the meeting? To whom does everyone defer? Are there any undercurrents? Then decide who in the room you need to influence with your ideas and how you can adjust your style to accomplish that. If you concentrate on this kind of analysis, you won't have time to be nervous about the meeting or your performance.

5. Sell to your audience. Once you've psyched out the power structure and the undercurrents, Meg Armstrong recommends that you view those present as your customers, to whom you're going to sell your ideas. If you're making a presentation, or if you have an idea you want people to buy into, you must convince your "customers" that it's a good one. Now you can tailor your approach to the individuals you want to influence by doing what's called "selling to type." You know which person or people in the room are the most important to sell to. What does their type need in order to buy in? Does one person want the data first, with no beating around the bush? Maybe another person prefers to hear ideas first and data second. A third might want conclusions first and then the deductions that went into them. Is there someone who needs to establish a relationship with you before you launch into data and ideas?

If you've worked with the people in the room before, you will have a basic idea of what they need before you even arrive at the meeting. However, every room, every meeting, is different and warrants a radar reading each and every time. The balance of power can change. Change your selling style—your presentation—accordingly. The appropriate pitch will hit home, the others will buy your ideas, and you'll have won the day. Once you've sold them one idea, they'll become comfortable with the process, and your next sale will be much easier.

This technique need not be confined to group meetings. You'll also find it useful in one-on-one negotiations with your boss, as well as with those you're managing. You must be flexible, ready to change as the tenor of a meeting changes. A rigid style, believing there's only one way to be—such as direct, wily, conservative, or sharklike—is not your best tool. A successful style adapter does not change who she is; she only makes modifications to get to her goal.

6. Eschew emotion. Certain behaviors work against you in the workplace, and you need to avoid them. Emoting about anything, be it your own screwup, frustration at yet another photocopier jam, work poorly presented by your staff, or losing a salary negotiation, is one surefire way to make others uncomfortable in the workplace. Keep your cool; emotionalism makes you look unreliable and unsteady and reinforces the stereotypes about women that men already hold.

That said, clearly everyone becomes emotional from time to time, men and women alike. How you handle your emotions will determine how effective your style has become: Does it offer the protection of self-control? Career counselor Sheryl Spanier finds that many among her clientele fall into the trap of personalizing events in the office, a situation that brings out emotion and leads to behaviors and interactions that are counterproductive. "I hear men say 'Get over it' behind a woman's back," she says.

If you can't put problems and slights into perspective quickly—and many of us can't—at least don't talk about them at work. You can learn to control what comes out of your mouth and how you behave while you're on the premises. A few deep breaths, a walk around the block, a long heart-to-heart with your spouse, partner, best friend—these should calm you and restore the rationality you'd clearly prefer to project.

7. Develop "executive presence." Probably the most essential style element for success is what Meg Armstrong calls "executive presence." It includes the presentation that you aced at the big meeting, as well as your day-to-day ability to handle everything from a subordinate's goofing off to a rude remark from a colleague. Your organization wants to know that it can send you anywhere in the world on any assignment or to solve any problem, that you will project the right image anywhere, that you will demonstrate poise, and that you will never embarrass it. If you don't know the local protocol, the company wants to be sure you'll be able to find it out.

What elements should you put together to achieve executive presence? Women in Catalyst's research listed some of them: maintaining an energetic, positive attitude; being a team player; not taking things too seriously; picking your battles prudently; conveying confidence by the way you carry yourself and the way you communicate; maintaining a sense of humor; combining problem-solving and people management skills in your daily work. One woman laid out a concise, gender-neutral description of the style of a successful senior executive:

> **General counsel:** "I believe it's important in many organizations to develop a reputation as someone who can provide sound advice but also solve problems; move the ball forward, work effectively with other people, manage projects, manage people, bring people together, facilitate the reconciliation of conflicting viewpoints."

Executive presence makes you stand out above others, even those who have the same brainpower and technical skill. You can acquire it, and the more you use it, the better it will be.

8. Radiate confidence. This means exuding self-assurance and carrying things off with aplomb. Confident individuals take slights with a grain of salt. They let negative comments slide. When someone razzes them, they don't take the bait easily. They keep things in perspective. That's easier said than done, maybe, if you're the kind of woman in a hurry who's intensely focused on getting ahead, but it's crucially important. Try to look at yourself from a little way off, from a distance, to see if you might be coming across as off-puttingly intense. Then take a couple of breaths and think: It'll all be the same in a hundred years (or whatever works for you as a breather). You won't always feel confident, but that doesn't mean you can't act that way. Bluffing has long been part of the art of getting ahead, and you, too, can practice it.

> *From the Pioneers: Style emerges from your strength and your humor.*
> **Zoë Baird** (President, The Markle Foundation): "From my own experience and from observing and working with other women, particularly younger women developing their careers, being confident comes through and creates comfort in others. If you're going to be a leader, you need to understand who you are yourself and then to lead through strength and confidence."

> *Women say:*
> **Fellow, IBM:** "Women have to have complete confidence in themselves. We have to believe that we are dead right and pursue our goals with that inner assurance. We are often not going to get that confidence from the environment."

9. Learn the art of the humorous comeback. Women who've succeeded stress again and again the importance of the quick response that shows you can take things lightly. You should go a step beyond the invaluable assets of laughing at situations and at yourself. You can learn the art of the funny story and the snappy comeback.

"Oh, but I'm not funny," you may say. Yes, humor is a gift. But don't you spend time and effort on picking out the perfect gift for a person you care about? I recommend you put some time and effort into developing your sense of humor so you can laugh and make others laugh. Meg Armstrong calls humor "a learned gift." She tells how at a senior-level seminar for a major company, executives wondered how some guys always have the right comeback. A member of the board laid it out: "You don't have to invent anything. When you hear a story, get out your pen and ask them to say that again slowly." Armstrong elucidates, "Guys sit around sharing great one-liners they 'came up with,' when most of the time they just have a list. They memorize these things!" So go ahead, write down punch lines. Or if you have trouble remembering a story itself, write the whole thing down. You probably don't remember jokes because you haven't con-sidered them important. Take it from me: They are.

But a sense of humor isn't only about jokes. Use your intelli-gence on this one; you don't have much trouble learning any other skills you need. Pay attention to what's funny around you and to what others find funny. Listen to how funny people de-liver lines. Copy their timing. To be funny requires taking risks, but we know you're a risk taker if you're on the fast track any-way. Practice humor by taking risks with the supermarket check-out guy first. Then take risks at being funny with friends. Then dare to try it at your office, starting with your closest and most trusted colleagues. Before long, you may try it in your depart-ment meetings. There's nothing like getting a laugh, and you'll love what it does for your image.

10. **Be seen as a team player.** Another aspect of our tendency to shun the limelight is that women are often not recognized as effective members of a team. I find that most women really are team players. The difference is that we seldom draw attention to the work we've done. Women generally join a team, participate in the planning, get their assigned tasks, go off and do a bang-up

job on them, and move on. Men on the team tend to talk about what they have to do, talk about what they're doing, and then talk about what they've done. If you don't do the same, few people will be aware of what you've done. Doing so will head off the charge that you're not a team player, plus you'll get credit for what you've done.

COMMUNICATING EFFECTIVELY WITH MEN

From the Pioneers: The communication issue is paramount for women.
Zoë Baird (President, The Markle Foundation): "I believe the single most important issue facing women at work is language: how people talk about women, the way they listen to women and are they listened to."

We hear from women that they sometimes miss or don't understand certain unspoken signals from men. It goes the other way, too—sometimes men don't quite get what women are trying to tell them. We hear women express frustration about their style of speech being misconstrued.

Too tentative. Some of the problems arise from the childhood conditioning to which many of us were (and are) subjected—for example, a tendency to be tentative or diffident in presenting ourselves and our ideas, adding phrases such as "I think" or "I'm sorry" to sentences we speak in which we're actually very sure of ourselves or not at all sorry.* Other women understand such conventions, whereas men in the office might consider them an indication that you don't know what you're talking about. Your credibility and the accuracy of what you're saying may be called into question if your presentation style is too self-effacing.

---

*See Chapter 5, "Become Known."

Again, I advise you to watch and listen. Observe what the people who are highly regarded as communicators do. See what styles work. Learn them.

Too acquiescent. Many women don't realize until they've moved a few rungs up the workplace ladder that men sometimes simply ignore what women say. If you haven't experienced this yet, you may be shocked the first time it happens to you. In fact, it can still be a surprise to me (although luckily it doesn't happen very often anymore). The story we hear over and over is that a women offers an idea in a meeting and no one responds. The meeting proceeds as if she hadn't spoken. Later in the meeting, a man at the table rephrases the woman's idea, people grab at it, and it takes off. The man, of course, gets the kudos. This happens more frequently than you may imagine, which will offer small comfort when it happens to you. In any case, you must find a way to deal with it.

Two Strategies for Being Heard

- Take the direct approach—right there and then. Repeat what you said. Or say that you're glad your point was responded to so positively by Mr. Smith-Jones (the one who stole your idea). Or you can address a friend at the table directly, someone you expect will take up the concept. It's not a bad idea to plan such a scenario with a colleague in advance. Women of color tell Catalyst they need to be straightforward in confronting others as a means of dispelling negative preconceptions about them, but they counsel tact.

- Wait until after the meeting and then actively pursue those who have ignored you, so that they will hear your point and you can work with them to change their behavior. Private confrontations may be more likely to work in your favor than public ones, at least until you have polished your executive presence to a high gloss.

Too verbose. In Catalyst's focus groups and interviews with men in various industries, we hear one criticism of women's communication style over and over again: women spend too much time getting to the point. There's too much clutter in our remarks. Clearly, we need to work on being concise, on delivering a message directly.

Too polite. Don't wait to speak up at meetings. You can't influence others if you keep your mouth shut. Women are sometimes too democratic—they wait for others to speak, thereby losing the opening. Or because they fear appearing pushy, many women hold back until later, when they may offer their ideas one-on-one to the appropriate individual. This does nothing to establish you as a confident, competent individual at the meeting table.

Put it into writing. Whatever happens, since women's voices aren't always heard, it's an effective tactic to put the ideas you've voiced at a meeting in writing and zap them off to those you want to influence.

From the Pioneers: Don't let them ignore you.

Geraldine Laybourne (Founder, Chair, and CEO, Oxygen Media) found her points ignored in meetings and worked with a female colleague to change this. "We had this understanding," she says, "that when she'd say something and nobody was giving her credit and two minutes later a guy would repeat what she said, I'd say, 'You're right! Sarah's idea is really right!' Or if they didn't hear it, I'd say, 'Did you hear her?' And she did the same: 'Did you guys hear Gerry?' Our messages are so important for the guys to hear that we have to help each other." Laybourne attributes her success at MTV to this strategy, as well: "I think that's a secret of why MTV Networks was such a big success."

Rita Wilson (President, Allstate Indemnity Company): "Sure, I've been ignored. Especially when your comments/opinions come from a totally different perspective, pointing out other possibilities or solutions. I initiate contact; I seek the opposition out. That's startling to people; they figure the case was closed. I won't let them ignore me."

Work on your communications skills.* You can always improve these, even if you're already articulate and poised, but there are certain elements to focus on if you're finding that you're not being heard.

Hispanic women tell Catalyst that they find others discounting what they say or that even their accents are mocked. Communications issues for women of color are compounded if they speak with an accent, they say. Asian-American women voice concern at being passed over for managerial positions because they're soft-spoken and are stereotyped as shy and self-effacing. They report that working on their communications skills helps a lot.

For example:

- Learn how to pace your speaking. Women sometimes speak too fast. Breathe deeply, which slows you down and allows for more deliberate speech.
- Lower the pitch of your voice. A lower voice commands more attention and respect.
- Do not allow yourself to be interrupted. If someone is interrupting, say, "Just give me a minute to finish and then I do want to hear your point of view." Remember, say this calmly and firmly, without rancor.

Is women's language different? Some of the pioneers quoted in this book emphasize that it is, and I don't dispute their experience, although I believe it may be more extreme in certain fields than in others. One of the pioneers, a veteran of Wall Street, posits that the workplace can be a foreign country for women

---

*See Chapter 5, "Become Known," for more on communications and training.

and that it's important for women to work with men to develop an effective communications style. She counsels getting male feedback about what has occurred at meetings and about your ways of articulating ideas.

From the Pioneers: Learn how to communicate.

Janet Hanson (Founder, President, and CEO, Milestone Capital Management): "I believe that language is one of the biggest challenges facing women and men in the financial industry. . . . I've seen a lot of miscommunications because women frequently misinterpret verbal cues from men and can miss non-verbal messages altogether. In malespeak, men get right to the point, and women often don't. Many women—myself included—have no problem communicating with clients or others outside of the organization who are male, but the disconnect still occurs when dealing with male employees, peers, and bosses. Learning how to speak someone else's language starts with being able to see things from their, not your own, perspective. While mentors can be helpful with this to a point, you really can't give this job to anybody else—you have to consciously figure it out for yourself."

Lynn Forester (Founder and Co-chair, FirstMark Communications International): "I am able to convey a vision or the terms of a deal to men on the other side in a way that's easier than if [my male partner] were doing it. I can ask for things that my partner can't. I get deals men are astonished by. When I come in, it's less threatening, and it works if it's smart. . . . [I'm] straightforward. I don't ask for things in a shy way. I make it clear that the best interest for the venture is if I am free to do those things I know I do better than other people. We have to ask for what we want."

What's your office culture? Every industry and every workplace—perhaps every department in every company (but you don't want to get so provincial that you wouldn't fit in anywhere in your organization)—has its own culture. You would probably be well advised to match yours to it. Again, your powers of observation come into play. How do people dress? With casual dress the latest trend, there's more variation than ever. These days, a giant law firm might look as casual as a dot com, but watch it: if superiors are still addressed by title—Mr. or Ms.— you can bet that the culture is still formal in major respects. What do people talk about? Is it all business or is it more personal? If the CEO writes about his family for the intranet, you can probably assume there's more leeway for self-expression. But don't rely on only one sign. Be an amateur anthropologist and figure out just how the tribe works. Until you do, err on the side of conservatism in dress, speech, and style. (Also remember: every business has its own language, and it is incumbent upon anyone entering it to learn the vernacular.)

> **From the Pioneers: Modify your behavior.**
> **Carol Bartz** (Chair, CEO, and President, Autodesk): "When creating your style, never sit there with a hair shirt on. And don't try to conquer every mountain. How many mountains can you climb over before you're the dead one? Pick your battles. . . . If you really don't fit in, let it go or try to find a different place to work."
>
> **Marie Knowles** (Executive Vice President and CFO, Atlantic Richfield): "You've got to get feedback. Male feedback is good. You don't know what's working if people don't help you."
>
> **Nancy Karch** (Retired Director, McKinsey & Company): "Early in my career I was too willing to speak my mind quickly. . . . I spoke out without getting input and didn't realize I was insulting people. An organization is like an anthill: there's an order you have to think about, and in hindsight I see I didn't understand that. I would have been more influential faster if I hadn't been so feisty."

Make changes, not war. If you're just starting out, or if you've been working for some time and are confronting some gender-related style issues for the first time, recognize that having to adjust your style is just part of the game. The rules are changing and will continue to change as more and more women reach top positions. And, remember, when you're the one at the top, work to fix the organization so women don't have to do all the adjusting.

Let me take a moment to talk directly to those readers who are thirty years old and younger. Those of you who have had the good fortune to attend colleges and universities where the playing field for women and men has become relatively level may have a hard time with what I'm pushing for here. Some of you have expressed distaste at any expectation that you should tinker with your style. You tell us you get angry when facing obstacles to advancement that men don't face. This is just not smart behavior if you hope to get anywhere but gone. Alas, the workplace can throw a dash of cold water in your face if you expect too much. Yes, some of the newer start-ups, dot coms in particular, look more like where you went to school. But don't kid yourself: those offices are usually overwhelmingly male, too, and they'll require similar adjustments. Most workplaces— corporate, professional firm, nonprofit, academic—despite the pace of change, remain antediluvian, at least in some ways.

Women say:
Vice president, automotive company: "I think it was important I didn't carry a chip on my shoulder as a woman. I have seen women who do that, and it's just awful."

Vice president, R and D: "You knew there was a hostile environment out there. But just developing survival skills and ignoring as much of it as possible was what worked best."

CEO, biotechnology firm: "The answer is always taking charge and being responsible for your destiny. Never whining, never complaining that there's a glass ceiling, just getting through it."

IS THERE ONE "RIGHT" STYLE FOR WOMEN?

I sometimes wonder how much of the style reshaping engaged in by the first generations of women in the workplace was imposed by the workplace and those in it and how much was self-imposed by women concerned about fitting in. Did women worry about it more than they had to? Don't go too far: if you have an individual style that works for you, just work on tweaking it here and there. None of this means you have to force yourself into an organizational mold that fits like the corsets of times past. The pioneers agree that there's no advantage to being a clone.

> *From the Pioneers: Be yourself.*
> **Roberta Gutman** (Corporate Vice President and Director of Global Diversity, Motorola): "We waste time being chameleons, who we think we should be in a given situation, instead of melding who we are, not changing who we are. We try to blend into norms that make us behave less than the way we really are so we lose who we really are—in behaviors, in priorities." She stayed her course when "counseled by middle management in every single place I've worked that 'women don't curse,' that 'sometimes you're too direct,' or 'there's too much levity.' This wasn't coming from the people who ran the place, however, and so I didn't change what I felt was working."
>
> **Rita Wilson** (President, Allstate Indemnity Company): "Don't play games. Stay very true to yourself, true to what makes you unique—as an individual and a woman in the workplace. You don't shed your perspectives, your passions, and your beliefs regardless of where you are. You'll have to make adjustments and some concessions to achieve your goals. Everybody does. Pick your battles carefully, but don't leave pieces of yourself along the way. It's virtually impossible to go back and recoup them."

Is there a female management style? I've read all the literature and heard all the anecdotes. My opinion is that there is not one definitive "female" management style. Some say women are better leaders and managers by virtue of their "female" management style, their superior team-building skills, their ability to nurture and groom other employees, even perhaps their "feminine intuition." However, I have also worked with nurturing male managers and with tyrannical women, and I don't believe these are the exceptions that prove the rule. I'd like to see women resist being typecast for any purpose, because we are multifarious, wonderful beings. Do you know a woman who is a consensus builder? I know one who is a control freak. I bet I can match your narcissist with my nurturer.

How you manage emerges from your personality. Certain approaches work for some women, and other approaches work for others. Besides observing others you need to be very aware of yourself and who you are in order to develop the management style that allows you to excel. Don't feel you have to conform to somebody else's definition of the right style, whether it is nurturing or aggressive or somewhere in between. You need to define your own management style as you create your own workplace style.

The more you work on your style so you're seen as an "insider," the more others will trust you and listen to you. Yes, sometimes, to get recognition for your ideas you have to go on the offensive rather than backing off, but that doesn't mean you should do it angrily; it is possible to go on the offensive calmly and even with humor.

Most of all, your main focus must be on producing results for the organization. Your image should be one *you* can live with, as well as one the organization is comfortable with. Pick your battles carefully. And sometimes, as we'll see, it's a good idea to plan a strategic exit—on your terms, not theirs.

≈

CHAPTER 5

Become Known

Many women are reluctant, even afraid, to stand out. From the time we were young girls, many of us were trained *not* to stand out. In school, we learned to raise our hands and wait to be recognized (often in the very same classrooms where boys blurted out the answers). Boys were learning to speak up and stand out, while we received accolades for our manners. Even in the grown-up world, a man who gains prominence is seldom seen as a show-off, whereas a woman often is.

Nevertheless, standing out, becoming visible, is what you need to do. Chief executives stress the importance of visibility to advancement. You need to showcase your talent and accomplishments so that the people with power to make decisions know about you and will think of you for opportunities.

If attention getting is to work as an advancement strategy for women, it requires technique and savvy. If you're visible, you're vulnerable. You can be the object of jealousy. Jealousy can erode office camaraderie, which is of concern to women as much as to men, since camaraderie promotes good morale and productivity. You don't want jealousy to lead to a serious loss of support. Deal with it as you would any other aspect of office politics: It's part of the game. If you've gotten a great write-up in an internal or external publication and some guy at the office says to you, "How does it feel to be important?" just say something like "Pretty good." Then take everyone out for a drink.

The women pioneers whose words follow emphasize the importance of maintaining your relationships at the same time as you're gaining exposure for your accomplishments.

From the Pioneers: Deal with criticism.
Carole St. Mark (Founder and President, Growth Management): "I'm not an extrovert," and so, she says, she walked carefully to make visibility work for her. "It's a two-edged sword. It's a tremendous opportunity, but you must be careful because your mistakes will be broadcast to the world. It's important to get exposed to decision makers, like division heads, the vice president of human resources, the head of a line operation. But getting the CEO's attention could irritate the rest of the operation. Don't underestimate the need to have good relationships with peers, subordinates, and superiors. You can have too much publicity, turning people off. If you build up resentment, they're anxious to trip you up."

Maureen Kempston Darkes (President and General Manager, General Motors of Canada): "As you grow in your job and gain confidence, you'll find visibility is easier to deal with. Getting publicity goes with the job, but the visibility I get is a reflection of the team I work with. I never see an interview as focusing on me. It's a chance to talk about the business and the team I'm working with."

Marie Knowles (Executive Vice President and CFO, Atlantic Richfield): "I don't duck interviews. It's important to have visibility. Doing them is good for the company, it's good for women, and it's good for people to see role models and make judgments, to learn something from it. My chairman has been happy with the publicity; he feels it's been good for the firm. My peers haven't been as comfortable. I've tried to keep those that matter in touch with why I'm getting covered."

Ask yourself, "Am I able to talk about what I've done? Am I able to do it where the people who matter will hear it?" If you can get the word out yourself, that's the way to go. If your mentors and other fans are talking about you and your latest accomplishments, that's a great start.

However, there's much more you can do. Good internal publicity will help you advance. Visibility in the community won't hurt either, and the experience you garner in working for it will help you in other ways, too.

HOW TO INCREASE YOUR VISIBILITY

Join associations and/or professional organizations. This kind of exposure is one of the best tickets to moving to senior management in your field. But don't just join, work at it!

- Most organizations are eager for new leaders; accept an officership in your local chapter.
- Circulate at national conventions and trade shows.
- Join panel discussions. Being viewed as a contributor to your profession can be a major asset to your career.
- Seek out public speaking opportunities in your organization and at industry and trade conferences. Although public speaking may terrify you (it's Americans' greatest fear, according to recent polls, so you're not alone), it's a talent you can acquire. You can get training, either on your own or through your communications department. Start small by
  - Speaking at meetings
  - Asking questions at conferences

- Spearheading discussions at staff workshops
- Hosting customer relations seminars
- Get your name in print, starting with small steps:
  - Suggest a topic to the editor of your in-house newsletter.
  - Write a short piece for your community newspaper.
  - If you can be published in a trade journal on your technical specialty, it will go a long way toward building your credibility.
- Volunteer for the visible assignments you know you can do. If you've been building your reputation, you may just get the go-ahead. And when that assignment results in a resounding success, your own visibility will skyrocket.

PLANNING FOR PRESS COVERAGE

If you're a new manager or in early middle management, keep the advice that follows in the bottom drawer of your desk until you're ready. But once you're approaching senior management and need to break through to the next level, most of the pioneers in this book advise judicious press coverage as a success strategy.

Use your communications department. If you find a receptive ear, make sure that the individual understands your goals and objectives. Do you want to be seen as an expert? Do you want to write papers? Do you want to be quoted? Do you want to talk about women's issues, or do you never want to do this? Do you want to talk about the company as a company, or do you want to talk only about your particular area? If you want to be a company spokesperson, say so. Many organizations are delighted when you volunteer, since having an articulate, prepared, personable spokesperson shows the company to best advantage. And the press knows that quoting only men doesn't look good anymore.

Be sure to pay attention to the relationship you're developing with the individual in your PR department. This is the person who can get you out in front—or not. One of our pioneers, Carole St. Mark, successfully worked with her communications department as a senior executive. During her last ten years at Pitney Bowes, she not only had media training, she also had a personal public relations person on staff who reported to her, prepared her press releases, screened all media representatives, helped with message points for interviews, and was present when she did interviews.

So go in and ask for what you want. Once people in your PR department have worked with you, offered you training, and come to trust your loyalty and articulation, they're likely to consider your talking to the press an asset.

You say your communications department doesn't offer the time or interest you want? Give some thought to hiring a public relations consultant. It may seem like a big step, but many successful men and women have. They tell Catalyst but keep others from knowing. Or another option: In some instances, a group of women have teamed up to hire a single publicist. Or the women's workplace network gets one or gives training to its members.

Men do interviews; women often do not. Not long ago, Catalyst heard from an Associated Press business reporter that nine out of ten men say yes when called for a business-related interview, while nine out of ten women say no. Using corporate communications to further a career is a male formula, it seems. You should help change this.

If it's your goal to change organizations once you reach senior management, you will find that good press can give you the competitive edge. One of the reasons most frequently cited by CEOs for women's exclusion from the higher ranks of management is that they don't know that qualified women are out there, who they are, or where to find them. You can correct this by getting yourself known.

From the Pioneers: Visibility offers high payoffs.
Rebecca McDonald (Chair and CEO, Enron Asia-Pacific, Africa, and China): "[I've] not had much in the way of negative reaction from coworkers to my press. A lot of the people I've worked with have been proud that the company's getting kudos for having one of the few women in the industry."

Dorrit Bern (Chair, CEO, and President of Charming Shoppes): "Do media interviews. Women have to be aggressive with everything, taking risks with tough jobs, big moves, and putting themselves out front in situations where you could be hurt in reputation if you didn't say the right things."

Carly Fiorina (Chair and CEO, Hewlett-Packard) describes her experience at AT&T when she spearheaded the launch of Lucent Technologies as "the most visible experience I'd had. It's very important that people know what you're doing. That's how they know what you're capable of. I found out—and so did others—that I can learn a whole bunch of new things in a hurry."

Carole St. Mark (Founder and President, Growth Management): "If the job you hold doesn't lend itself to being visible, find a role where what you do is noticed by people at the top. It doesn't have to be part of your job but could be running something else important to your company, like the United Way campaign or another volunteer project. Visibility is important." For St. Mark, a profile in *Fortune* led to her joining the board at Supervalu.

Rebecca McDonald: "There were things I said in a *Fortune* article that resonated with a man who was looking. The publicity captured part of my business personality so they knew important things before they met me." Publicity also brought her to the attention of the executive search firm that led to her joining the board of directors of Granite Construction.

> **From the Pioneers: In top management, you must deal with the press.**
> **Maureen Kempston Darkes** (President and General Manager, General Motors of Canada): "Negative press and positive press go with the territory. Some issues are difficult to deal with, but there's an interest in them and you have to understand it. It's part of the job, so you must deal with them fairly. . . . Just be honest; just be yourself."

What kind of publicity do you want? Stories on successful businesswomen, believe it or not, used to appear only in the society pages as recently as the late 1980s. We can count on this anomalous status changing, albeit slowly, as we're now among a growing mass of working women. Now stories on women appear in magazines such as *Business Week* and *Fortune;* and Carly Fiorina made the cover of *Forbes* and *Business Week* shortly after being named CEO of Hewlett-Packard. However, you also must resist being the token woman on women's issues. That will do you little good in the long run.

> **From the Pioneers: Overcome the woman's story for the business angle.**
> **Lynn Forester** (Founder and Co-chair, FirstMark Communications International): "I was contacted for an interview on 'powerful women and their hair.' "[1]

> **Ellen Hancock** (Chair and CEO, Exodus Communications): "I have found it very hard to get accepted as a business spokesperson for the firm instead of my describing my personal life, my relationship with my husband, what I like to do with my spare time. Until we aren't asked those questions, we will not have arrived. When we arrive, they're going to ask us how our business is doing. Those are the questions the men get. And if the men refuse to answer questions about their personal lives, the media continues with the rest of the interview. I have had interviews canceled because there was no rest of the interview."[2]

MAKING THE MEDIA WORK FOR YOU

Once you've decided you're ready for, senior enough for, and game for press coverage, how do you make the contacts, establish mutually productive relationships, and get the kind of exposure you want?

- Position yourself as a credible source. You need the expertise, and you need to be ready to explain it. You can write for trade publications. Reporters are always looking there for names of the up-and-coming, or they call friends in the trades to get referrals.
- Build personal relationships with the media, starting by being a source of background information, which can lead to increased on-the-record coverage and greater visibility. Begin by contacting reporters and editors in your field of expertise to establish relationships that will lead to future stories. Kathleen Pender of the *San Francisco Chronicle* said at Catalyst's San Francisco conference, "If you're interested in cultivating a relationship with the media, meet reporters, call them up. If you see something in a story that you're interested in or if they're covering your industry, call them up and introduce yourself. Say, 'This is what I do, and I'm willing to talk to you.' "
- Be prepared to go on the record. A lot of women don't want to be quoted, but you need to get over that because that will only result in the men having their names in lights and you, the source of the neon, remaining invisible. In the meantime, keep your PR department posted.
- Be accessible and available, especially early on, because sometimes the interviewer needs someone who'll show up on short notice. A great way to get started is by filling in for someone else. The stand-in gets a big break.
- Don't let your guard down even with women reporters. They're writing an article, they want to get the story, and they have a deadline. Even if you've built up a relationship that has become a friendship, remember that she has a job

to do, too, and prepare what you say carefully. Carol Jenkins, news anchor, talk show host, reporter, and producer, reminded women at a Catalyst/IWMF* conference in June 1996 in New York that "media interviews are a high risk for everybody. Some people think that the relationship between . . . people giving interviews and the media should be a cozy, friendly one, but it's not."[3] At all times, be careful about what you say.

- Decide what you want to see in print, because no matter what question is asked, you can eventually bring the answer around to what you want to see.
- Be proactive in making contacts. Identify and monitor reporters covering your field. Respond to their articles and stories through letters to the editor and op-eds.
- Learn the language of the media and the difference between comments "for attribution," "on/off the record," and "for background." Clearly communicate your position to a reporter before an interview begins. If you're uneasy about a particular reporter, test the waters with a few comments on a nonattribution basis. If the reporter truly protects you, the next time he or she calls, you can talk more freely.
- Decline interviews outside your area of expertise, and do not limit yourself to soft news or strictly women's issues. Accept appropriate interviews and be prepared to talk on the record.
- Make yourself accessible to reporters, and above all, respect reporters' deadlines. Delaying interviews can mean losing them to the clock, as well as losing your usefulness to the writer.
- To be newsworthy, it helps if
  - You're a recognized authority on a subject
  - You've done something highly unusual
  - You've won an award
  - You participated in or witnessed an important event
  - You have an offbeat job or hobby.

* International Women's Media Foundation

Should you get media training? Yes. I think it will really help with your comfort level. It's important that you be relaxed when you're interviewed, and it's important that you be prepared. Media training can help you learn how to speak in sound bites and how to give a good quote. If you're thinking about television interviews, media trainers will advise you on what to wear and give you feedback on your body language. Media trainers coach you on responding to difficult questions and about what to do if you start feeling uncomfortable. Training affords a venue for practice. Ideally, media training will not teach you anything artificial; indeed, it will teach you how to be yourself during interviews. Dee Dee Myers, cohost of *Equal Time* on CNBC and former presidential press secretary, said, "Women need to know how the game is played in order to feel comfortable giving the kind of useful information that reporters are interested in."[4] If your organization doesn't offer media training, you can find it externally on your own.

If you have a bad experience with the media, don't become discouraged. The more media coverage you get, the more likely it is that something will happen you don't like. One of the pioneers in this book found that despite a terrific story on her in one business publication, the photo they selected to use "was the one where I looked like I'd eat your children for lunch." Profit by your mistakes.

TO BE OR NOT TO BE SEEN

I counsel visibility tempered to fit the structure you're in. Take your cues from others, both men and women, who are managing visibility well. Find the balance that works in your office culture. Paul Critchlow, Senior Vice President, Marketing and Communications, Merrill Lynch, said at the Catalyst/IWMF conference, "Visibility is good for anybody if it's tied to your area of expertise." Weigh that against the advice given there by Ann Fudge, Executive Vice President, Kraft Foods: "There is a very fine line between visibility and overexposure. Even the best photographs can be ruined if they are overexposed." To the women who have succeeded with and by media coverage, other women in the workplace owe a debt, as they have helped further the cause of women's advancement in general, as well as their own. You can, too.

> **From the Pioneers: It's a historic moment.**
> **Linda Alvarado** (President and CEO, Alvarado Construction): "Women should consider taking the opportunity to respond as opinion leaders when papers want a quote from a business leader. Otherwise it's all men. There should be a sense of strategic interactions that demonstrate to your industry that women are doing things, and you can be a part of that."

Hearst Magazines president Cathleen Black said in her keynote speech at the Catalyst/IWMF event: "We all know the statistics: women's income up thirty percent in a decade, more than thirty-five percent of MBAs going to women, over forty percent of new CPAs going to women, women-owned businesses growing fifty percent faster than those owned by men. Where are these people? Where are their voices, their quotes, their stories?"

You have it in your power to help fill in the blanks in public perception. If you do it right, you'll be helping yourself and women in business everywhere.

〜

CHAPTER 6

Your Number One Success
Strategy: Networking

When I started working, I was determined to make it "on my own." My parents tried to connect me with different kinds of people, with successful friends, with friends of friends, but I thought accepting help would diminish my accomplishment. My own friends came up with angles to reach contacts they knew in fields I was interested in, but I declined their help. I even politely said no to professors who offered their connections. I didn't doubt for a second that I'd be recognized for my talent and hired where I wanted to work. What I didn't know was the way of the world. No one told me the work world doesn't seek you out and find just the right spot for your brains to work. It took many years to admit I had lost real opportunities because I hadn't met with my father's buddy, the head of XYZ Company or looked up the friend of the friend in my new city, or had missed my school reunions. I wore my independence like epaulets and marched alone. I was wrong.

It's not that you can't get anywhere alone. Good credentials and experience can and often will land you a good job, and if you follow the advice in Chapter 3, you'll advance. But the way will be easier and you may do a lot better if you seek out people and accept the help you're offered. People who need people are all the people in the world of work. It is people who link us with other people, and those people know of job openings, new directions, new job leads, ideas, hot tips. And just as important, helpful people encourage us when we're on a roll and offer perspective and support when the going gets tough. Most successful people take help anywhere they can get it; both women and men tell Catalyst about it in virtually all the research we do. What I in my naïveté saw as charity they call networking, a concept that without exaggeration could earn the title of the number one success strategy for women.

INFORMAL NETWORKING IS ESSENTIAL

There are two kinds of networks: the informal ones composed of everyone you know and everyone they know and so on, and the formal workplace networks set up to supplement the ones you've built up over the years. We'll talk about the latter later. For now, consider this: "Exclusion from informal networks" stands as one of the top barriers to success reported by women at or near the top in Catalyst's *Women in Corporate Leadership*[1] survey and in Catalyst's study of corporate and professional women in Canada.[2] Women of color emphasized a lack of informal networking as the second-biggest barrier to their advancement.[3]

We women watch men leave together for lunch as we bolt down a cup of yogurt at our desks. Then at day's end, we see men heading out together for drinks and more talk, while we go pick up the kids, pick up dinner, pick up the dry cleaning, pick up the house. If you can find the time to join the men, you won't miss out on talk about office issues, business leads, and job opportunities. But chances are you're not hearing any of that, and neither are most of the other women at your office. Incidentally, if you saw the football game last night on TV, it's a lot easier to banter with the boys at the morning meeting table. (On the other hand, if watching sports on television feels like a major betrayal of who you are, don't do it. Frankly, I don't. Never have. Nonetheless, it really can help smooth your way.)

During these informal networking sessions, men are building their lifelong contact base. Too many women are getting the job done at the office and at home but missing out on the good stuff. I have a friend who says it's not what you do from nine to five that counts; it's what you do from five to nine.

Even women who conscientiously set out to build their network at work may face a real problem doing so. You may have luck finding entry-level and midlevel women at your workplace, but Catalyst knows of a lot of companies where even this may present a challenge. The challenge will increase when you look at the executive level and end up having to search organization-wide to find a female colleague you can have lunch with. Most of your women colleagues won't be well connected, and you'll be lucky if you find anyone plugged into the real power. It's hard to put together a network from such slim pickings. You can see why finding a way to bond (an awful word but a very useful concept) with your male colleagues is nearly essential. Just an openness to friendly conversation and perhaps a quick lunch can lead to an informal networking session.

I can't think of a single facet of your work life that couldn't profit from the insights, help, and connections that come through networking. If you focus on creating and maintaining a wide-reaching network, you'll find a real treasure trove of information. People in your network may be able to tell you whether a particular job is a good job, if you should go after it, and how to go about it. They may even make the introduction for you.

They can offer some very practical assistance to you while you're in a particular job, such as pointers on how to close a deal, negotiate a raise, handle a looming disaster. You can get support and advice on how to deal with problem colleagues, advancement barriers, child care issues. You can exchange information about your specialty, your industry, the economy, where to acquire your next business. You'll become known as you get to know others.

From the Pioneers: Network, network!

Carly Fiorina (Chair and CEO, Hewlett-Packard) advises that networks be not just of women or of peers, but of people who have a point of view that can educate you, who can help an idea be disseminated and accepted, and who can give advice. "Networking is not about a club, not about seeking out people like you, or about people who agree with you. Find people who disagree with you strenuously. That helps you know you have the right perspective."

Yvonne M. Curl (Vice President and Chief Marketing Officer, Avaya Communication): "It's good to talk to people that have similar experiences so you don't think you're just crazy sometimes. It's helpful in putting biases into perspective. [Networking is] a learning process. You learn new ways of approaching things and new things about the business. The 'old boys' network' is a forum to share information. Information is power. You need to know what's going on when you're in meetings, and you find this out by networking."

Nancy Karch (Retired Director, McKinsey & Company): "[There's an] unfriendly environment, like the team sporting events, or when you're in a small town on business and the guys like to go out and eat late. Lots of people feel you have to be there, but you don't have to go." She also seeks ways "to gather women together to do things, sometimes gender-neutral. I didn't always go to the sports events the team went to. The guys went barhopping with the client, while a colleague and I and the client [a woman] went out for brunch and shopping. I did it my way."

Betty Beene (President and CEO, United Way of America): "I never make a call with key volunteers without asking for feedback. I ask them to tell me what I could have done better. Sometimes they hesitate, but I work best when someone challenges my judgment. So I ask them to think, 'If hindsight is twenty-twenty, what could I do to make what I did better?' You have to be the initiator to be sure you're getting the coaching and feedback you need."

Networking means making long-term contacts. Networks can serve as insurance for your professional longevity. When you're considering a change, contacts can connect you with your next job and your next. Career counselor Sheryl Spanier of Right Management Consultants stresses networking as a critical factor in making moves that will forward your career. She says, "Those who make good transitions are the women who have generated and nurtured relationships with men and women over a long period of time. Women in their fifties who are sought after have been really effective at building networks and have an existing and integral group of individuals—friends, colleagues, professional and personal mentors—who are there for them over time and for whom they are available, too." Some of the women pioneers used their networks during career shifts:

From the Pioneers: Networking leads to new jobs.
Rebecca McDonald (Chair and CEO, Enron Asia-Pacific, Africa, and China) discovered how important networks can be after a takeover at her company: "It was a female network that raised to Enron's attention that I was leaving my job." She tells it like this: a lawyer connected her to a consulting firm, which connected her to a woman attorney at Enron, who called the CEO, who called her. She finds that "networks are getting so much more mature, and more people know one another. It was not

just women helping women: this network extends into the whole company, including a relationship with the guy at the top."

Betty Beene (President and CEO, United Way of America): "Every time I moved to a new organization it was because I was recommended by someone in my former organization. Each time a search firm called me or each time I was asked to apply for a new position, they'd heard from people I worked with."

WHO'S IN A NETWORK?

Men say:
Catalyst focus group participant: "A lot of my friends from college, from boarding school, ended up going to one particular firm, so I met all the people there. Now they're at ten different firms, so I have contacts everywhere. I've been developing my Rolodex since the age of twelve."

The "old-boys' network" within which men in business operate—the informal buddy system that connects them with jobs and new business and other opportunities—has evolved from people the men have known through the years, from going through school, then working, changing jobs, making new connections through those old connections, and so on.

Women haven't thought in terms of connecting in ways that will help them professionally for as long as men have. Even so, everyone has a network, even if you don't call it by that name. No matter who you are, where you work, or where you went to school, you have contacts in probably more areas than you know, and should you begin to connect with them once again, you'll find your network's connections extending in many directions.

A network grows exponentially. The best personal network forms a river of people into which more and more helpful people flow from various tributaries all the time. Your river's original source is a natural lake fed by springs of personal friends, the ones you grew up with, went to school with, or live near. You may already think of them as dependable resources you can call on for support. They may have helped you or made connections for you, and you may have done the same for them. As this pool of friends flows out, the friends you make at work and the people you meet socially join it, and you have the beginning of a river.

For those of you who are forty or younger, the river probably runs particularly strong; you have been part of the vast influx of women into the workplace from the beginning. Your women friends from college probably went right to work, and they have probably introduced you to others, increasing your river's strength. You also may know alumnae who feel an affinity with you and want to help the younger versions of themselves move ahead. Many of you doubtless keep contact with men friends from college, and since they may be connected with the "old boys," you may have a connection there, if you'll use it. If you're over forty and, like many of us, raised families and now work outside the home, you might think about reestablishing college contacts, going to reunions, and contacting your alumni association. I've noticed that many such women now are playing catch-up with the "old boys," who have had a long lead time at doing this.

Colleagues form another tributary of helpful friends. Though they may not necessarily be social friends outside the office, you'll find them a great help, even if they're only in your work life. If you're at a firm, clients might become friends. Professionals have a running start on these relationships as a result of the socializing that's done with clients as part of new-business generation and business as usual. Friends and fellow networkers also develop through your membership in professional associations, volunteer work, women's organizations, and other outside organizations.

The river is now rushing along, sweeping up people you meet through these people: friends of your old friends, of your new friends at the office, and of your extracurricular and association friends. Technically they're acquaintances, but I suggest you see them as friends in your widening network river. A personal network can contain hundreds of them across the nation.

Equally important, a network can include people both above and below you at work. Bosses and former bosses, mentors past and present, and those for whom you have worked or who work for you now can stand by you forever, if you've been a good worker, good protégée, good boss, good friend.

From the Pioneers:
Carly Fiorina (Chair and CEO, Hewlett-Packard): "[Networking is] information, contacts, insight, advice, challenge from people from whom you can learn something." She finds it important to meet other CEOs, but also stresses the importance of networking with all levels, saying, "The worst thing a CEO can do is get disconnected from reality, from the rank and file."

How good is your current network? You may be surprised to find you actually have a pretty substantial network right now, even if you haven't consciously worked at it yet. Add up the helpful people from all the various areas of your life by asking yourself the following questions:

- Who do I know now? What do they do and with whom are they connected?
- Who have I relied on in the past year, and what for?
- How many of my colleagues are friends?
- Do I have alumnae contacts?
- What professional organizations do I belong to that have led to new acquaintances?
- Do I know people at clubs I belong to, and with whom they are connected?

This assessment probably reveals that you have different types of networking going for you already—some business, some personal. Let me assure you that even if your networking river is still just a trickle, you can build up its current with some work right now. It's never too soon or too late to start.

Just consider networking a part of life. Catalyst finds that most women tend to focus on their tasks and not pay enough attention to the people around them. According to career counselor Sheryl Spanier, "If women make one mistake in their career, not networking is it."

You should be building your network while you're looking for your first job, your next job, your tenth job, and you should network starting at entry level. Let people introduce you around. Any one of your new contacts might turn something up for you. Plus, you'll identify the people who may be able to help you later, if not now. The sooner people get to know you, the better.

Never stop. Continue to do your networking as you're advancing. As you're working toward partner at a firm or moving through middle management, build your network. It will matter to you in quite practical ways during these years, as you'll appreciate the insights of women who've had kids and continued to work, with or without a wrinkle in their business lives. You'll need lots of help and support if and when you decide to make the push for senior management and must deal with glass-ceiling issues. As you near partnership or senior management, a time when critical appraisal of your performance will probably increase, your network will matter more than ever. You must ask your helpful people for tough feedback about what you're doing right and what you need to improve, and how and where you need to burnish your image so you're perceived as you want and hope to be.

When you're working to develop your network, keep your career direction in mind. If you're going to remain in one field—law, for instance—will you remain at the same firm or will you want to move into the public sector or a nonprofit position later? Perhaps you'll want to try your hand at a corporation? Who do you know now, and who can you get to know in these areas? They'll be helping when the time comes, so you'll want to keep in touch. Or suppose you're an engineer or a writer at a company and you want to keep moving up for the time being but are thinking about a future shift to consulting. Who might help you when you need them, and how can you begin associating with them now? Someday you might want to start your own business. Figure out how you can get to know people in the area you're considering. Where can you find them and join in their activities?

Think in terms of two different types of helpful people: those who can be helpful in getting you where you're going and those who can be helpful later, should you consider a change in your job or in your career direction. Build relationships over time.

Once you're in senior management, you need to network ever more vigorously to stay on top of what's happening in your office, in your field, in the community, in the national and international economy, in government. Your networks can give you real information, not bluff, not PR. And if you're at a firm or own your own business, it goes without saying that it's contacts, contacts, contacts that bring in more business. Consider participating in community task forces and in various civic endeavors, as these will not only increase your client roster but enhance your reputation and that of your business.

From the Pioneers: Networking is vital to senior women and entrepreneurs.
Maureen Kempston Darkes (President and General Manager, General Motors of Canada): "The more senior you are in the business, and the more you deal in competitive businesses, the more important it is to know about the external environment. You need to understand what's going on beyond your day-to-day base. Just having broader contact with people

gives you an added base of knowledge to utilize. . . . So I chat with another CEO about the economy and trends, with some focus on a particular decision."

Dorrit Bern (Chair, CEO, and President, Charming Shoppes): "Women have to do a much better job of networking than they do. That's how you learn, how you gain the ability to call people, women and men, how you learn to ask questions, how you get introduced to someone in the business. Networking is critical, even in the lower levels of the organization it helps you identify the people in the company who will help you. If they know your face, if they like you, they'll help you. Women tend to sustain their own world, working. Men are playing golf, having drinks after work. That's the game, and it's got to be played. You aren't going to change it."

Linda Alvarado (President and CEO, Alvarado Construction): "It's people that make decisions," so you need to cultivate them. Her networks include industry associations, chambers of commerce, women's business organizations, Hispanic chambers, the Colorado Building and Industry Council, and the Associated General Contractors. If this looks like it takes time, you're right. And Alvarado emphasizes that joining isn't enough, "you've got to assume leadership positions. It's there you meet peers and are able not only to become more visible, but more likely to make senior decision-makers know you." She's been involved in task forces to analyze state procurement and in civic and philanthropic endeavors, and these not only led to additional clients, but also added to her reputation for civic responsibility. "I want the company to be known for our ability to build and contribute in cities where we do business. It's important for image and civic commitment."

Joan Leiman (Executive Deputy Vice President for the Health Sciences, Columbia University) is "a member of the Health Care Executive Forum, a small network of senior people in the field. Now I can pick up a phone if I need to find out something, or if I need to deal with someone at another hospital—someone will have a friend there I can call to get it done. I can do the same with people in government and other areas. I'm doing more networking now than ever before. Sometimes it leads to interesting projects I wouldn't otherwise be involved in."

Janet Hanson (Founder, President, and CEO, Milestone Capital Management): "Actively managing a complex network of internal and external relationships is critical to your success as a professional and a manager in virtually every type of business. As a former employee of Goldman Sachs, I reconnected with other women who had worked at the firm and formed '85Broads.com. This Internet-based, global network of women at every career and life stage provides a diverse base of recruiting, mentoring, entrepreneurial, educational, philanthropic, and lifestyle resources. Most important, it allows us to stay connected with other women who share a common background, language, and standard of excellence in all aspects of our lives."

NETWORKING HOW-TOS

I now suggest you pull out your career plan (see Chapter 2), and if you haven't yet added "networking" as a task to accomplish, do so now. Make networking as important as your business or financial plan, and attend to it frequently. Many women, hard at work, may never wander as far as other halls in their office. It's true that making these kinds of connections usually takes work. Fortunately, some of it is fun.

Look around your office, consider who you know, and start chatting with them about work-related matters. Start connecting the dots from them to people in the areas you're thinking of moving into or learning about. In *Six Degrees of Separation*, playwright John Guare theorizes that you can meet anyone in the world by going through a maximum of five other people; you are "six degrees of separation" away from the Dalai Lama, for example. It can't be that hard to meet the general manager of your plant or the partner of a client you'd like to work for. Who can connect you with these people? What can you do to meet them?

Office Networking Pathways

- Seek high-visibility assignments. They lead to advancement; they also expand the number and kinds of people you know.
- Volunteer for cross-organizational projects that will give you access to a large cross section of people.
- Seek out people in other departments with whom you have common ground, such as the same school, a recent maternity leave, and so on.
- Call someone whose work you've heard about and ask to talk about it.
- Attend training programs and presentations and connect with your fellow participants.
- If your organization has community projects such as Race for the Cure or Habitat for Humanity, join them in their work.
- Start chatting with people in the cafeteria line.
- And you can always try the coffeemaker in another department.

Network externally. As you advance, you're going to need information about what's going on outside your organization to see the larger business picture. You're going to need to know what opportunities are available or who's available for jobs you need to fill as a manager. You need to know lots of people in different places—in similar organizations, in the government, in finance. You need to go places to meet new clients. You want contacts to help you become known.

You can make this interesting, fun, and valuable for yourself if you choose activities and organizations that feed you personally as well as interest you professionally. Ask yourself two types of questions: (1) What can you volunteer for outside your organization where you'll enjoy the work? Or what professional or civic organizations can you join where you can learn new skills and develop current ones? and (2) Do these organizations include different types of people who might be helpful to you? Also, don't forget your alumni organization, where you already have something in common with people who might help you. Find alumni events that interest you and go for cocktails. Or if the events don't interest you, work with the group to instigate the types of events that will stimulate you and others.

When you're ready, join advisory boards, nonprofit boards, government boards, or commissions. Try for corporate boards, the ultimate networks. Many women begin board work at their volunteer organization of choice. Nonprofits make an excellent training ground and stepping-stone for future work on corporate boards. Consider hospital or bank boards. Not only will you make connections through this work, you'll enhance your visibility in the community, which can lead to recognition at work.

One of my colleagues knows a female executive at a Fortune 500 company who was involved with a fund-raiser for a local hospital. In fact, she ran the whole show, which broke all records for money raised. The morning after the event, the CEO of her company was golfing with a friend who happened to be on the hospital board, who told her boss about the fund-raiser and praised her on a job well done. She received a promotion not long after and was identified as a comer with high potential. That's how networking can work for you.

From the Pioneers: Reach beyond your organization.
Nancy Karch (Retired Director, McKinsey & Company): "I'm known as a preeminent adviser to retail business in the U.S. Lots of people know me, so I have entry. I did my networking around competence, not around social activity. I tell women that if they don't feel as secure as guys do walking through a fifty-four-year-old client's door, or if they don't see community leadership or golf clubs as the way to meet people, [they]

should meet people by competence. By making speeches, by participating at conferences. Then people know you have something valuable to say."

Judy Sprieser (CEO, Transora): "Achieving notoriety in the right circles has worked for me, like speaking at seminars, writing, and establishing myself as a technical expert. Word got out about me not through a social type of networking but through proving myself to be good or noteworthy." She also recommends "trying to be written up in executive magazines or trying to get female achiever awards. It's a self-promotion thing, and it works to expand whom you know."

Maureen Kempston Darkes (President and General Manager, General Motors of Canada): "I trained for a half marathon with women, sharing thoughts and ideas with them. Knowing people outside your industry is very important."

From the Pioneers: Decisions get made on the golf course.
Ellen Hancock (Chair and CEO, Exodus Communications), whose career spans conservative East Coast IBM to the wild and woolly Internet, recommends golf. "If I were in school now, I'd learn it; not learning it was my biggest mistake. Maybe I still will." Why? "It's a game with quiet time where people can talk about things. It's not like tennis, which I play and isn't helpful. Guys do a fair amount of work on the golf course. Women need to be where decisions are being made, and like it or not, some are made on the golf course. It's not unusual to ask someone, 'Have you talked to so-and-so recently?' and he says, 'I played golf with him Saturday.' So I say, learn it and don't make it a negative. Make it part of the portfolio."

What about golf and games? Golf continues as a key networking activity for men, and more and more women have learned the game for its career benefit, if not for pleasure. In our *Women in Corporate Leadership* study, Catalyst found that women played golf more than they participated in any other outside activity.

If you enjoy golf, go play it. Who knows, maybe the magic will kick in. Or maybe a deal you clinch or an opportunity you hear about on the course will be your payoff. Ask the guys directly if you can join them when they play. Talk to your boss about the game, and have him connect you with his golfing buddies or with someone in his network who plays.

Don't make excuses. I've heard many reasons given by women for not networking. Some believe that setting out to accrue helpful friends for your own ends makes one an "operator," an appellation most women run from. But frankly, it's how the game is played, and you need to play by the rules. You can be strategic in choosing your helpful people, but only if you don't help them back could you be accused of "operating." Don't feel that you shouldn't rely on your network friends. You absolutely should. That's one of the things friends are for, as long as you let them rely on you in return.

Women also tell Catalyst they're afraid of rejection or they're worried they're imposing. I've found you don't need to worry about either of these, because most women today—and, indeed, most men—welcome the chance to give insight, guidance, support. Timing and approach are everything.

I find that women particularly demur at approaching those above them. We seem to take more naturally to being friends with peers and subordinates than with those higher in the hierarchy. Perhaps we feel it's too obvious that we're looking for help and that somehow that's wrong. It's not; it's career-smart.

Then there's the truest excuse of all: "I don't have the time." Many women never hang out with women colleagues during or after work, let alone with men. We believe that's social, that we'd be goofing off. Wrong. It's working—maybe not on a task at hand but for your career goals. Women who succeed make the time for the strategies that will work. Make a schedule now that includes one networking activity. Start by having one lunch a week with someone at work. Join just one organization and attend one event a month. Build it from there.

But if you simply cannot give attention to networking now, keep it in mind for when you can. At a different stage of your career, you'll have more time and energy to devote to adding to your contacts on a regular basis—and you can decide what "regular" means. The successful women in *Women in Corporate Leadership* and many of the pioneers in this book combine outside-work activities with parenting.

AN EFFECTIVE SOLUTION: WOMEN'S NETWORKS

Because of women's historical exclusion from spontaneous, work-related networks, women at some organizations—and the organizations themselves—have created internal women's networks. These networks can be more or less formal and may include a handful of women or hundreds. They provide a venue for women to meet, to get to know one another, to help one another, and frequently to make changes for women at their organizations. Many hold regular networking sessions for members. They set up mentoring programs, hold speaker series, offer career development activities and training. Some have become strong enough and visible enough to hold high-profile national events for members and nonmembers, both women and men.

Catalyst works with many of these internal women's networks, and we've found across the board that they are a win-win activity, benefiting both the women involved and their organization. I've seen them help women with professional development and with making connections with others around the organization. I've seen them help the organization by serving as a resource and adviser to leadership on gender-related issues. Women who have participated in such networks say that not only do they end their isolation and bring them into the general workplace conversation, they also often further women's advancement at the organization.

How formal networks help women. Catalyst has monitored women's workplace networks over the years, and we find that they're proliferating rapidly. More than a third of Fortune 500 companies have such women's networks.* Most were created by senior women who recognized a need. The best of these networks have already made important differences for women at their organizations. Many such networks have addressed important issues women deal with in their particular workplaces, including the following:

- Myths about women's potential and commitment
- Women's difficulty in getting access to business information
- Lack of mentoring/career advice and support for women
- Career development—both their own and that of women to come
- Flexible work arrangements
- How the organization can further women's advancement
- Creating a better workplace for women

If there isn't a network where you work, think about forming one. It's women like you who start formal women's networks. I know of networks started by a single senior-level woman who was concerned about the environment and advancement issues for women. I know of networks that began at the grassroots level, where a few women begin informally by meeting to talk about what's happening at work.

With the growing number of women at work and the steady, though slow, increase in the number of women moving into senior management, women in many organizations no longer fear reprisals for organizing women's networks.

Finally, remember that to be an effective networker, you must give as much as you get. Indeed, networking assumes a quid pro

---

*The following partial list shows the pervasiveness of such networks: Ford, IBM, Hewlett-Packard, Procter & Gamble, Motorola, Merck Dow Chemical, American Stores, Xerox, 3M, Eastman Kodak, Texas Instruments, Bankers Trust, McDonald's, Kraft, McGraw-Hill.

quo. Career counselor Sheryl Spanier reports that the most successful networkers "have generated and nurtured relationships with men and women over a long period of time through mutual giving." Do things for others. Whenever you're privy to an opportunity that might be right for someone you know, pass the information along. Forward an article that's relevant to someone's work or life. When you learn something (unclassified) that might be important for someone in another department, let her or him know. Recommend office friends to your boss or other senior managers for assignments. Invite people to do things with you. Connect your office friends with appropriate individuals in your external network. The more you do, the more you'll get back.

CHAPTER 7

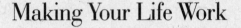

Making Your Life Work

Have you had your fill of images of the executive woman with no social life whose single-minded fury sweeps colleagues and civility from her path? "Ambition isn't feminine," "Work makes women bitches," they seem to be saying. Are you fed up with portrayals of the executive mother with a weeping child clinging to her leg as she leaves for the office? Images that say, "You're failing as a mother. You're failing as a wife. You're failing society." There you are, working to put food into your mouth and a roof over your head and you must contend with backlash to boot.

If you're like most women today, you expect to work—if not for your entire adult life, at least for parts of it. If you're like most working mothers, your children expect you to work. If you're married, as a nationally representative Catalyst study demonstrated, your husband is glad you work. Catalyst learned this in its study of dual-career marriages, where overwhelming evidence demonstrated that both husband and wife embrace having two jobs and two incomes for its positive effect on their lives.

I believe it's time to change the discourse about women working—and, for that matter, about women who have decided *not* to work at any given point in time. I'd like to see us doff the mantle of guilt dropped on our shoulders. Catalyst knows scores of successful women who work full-time and have full, satisfying personal lives. Catalyst also knows from its longitudinal study on flexible work arrangements that many women who work part-time are satisfied with making career trade-offs to gain better work/life balance. Women are building life strategies with a range of choices, customizing the amount of energy and focus that they give to their careers at different points in their life cycle—and that's okay. I'm not saying it's easy. We all get stressed out when the pressures of work or the pressures of family build up steam. We must all deal with caregiver issues, whether taking an elderly mother to the doctor or meeting with a child's teacher. We all grapple with how to meet with colleagues, clients, mentors, and important contacts to do the work outside the office that will pull us ahead. We all drop activities we'd love to do—dinner with friends, vacations, the evening's concert—because work cannot wait. How can we work ten hours at the office, run six miles, consume five servings of fruit and vegetables, quiz the kids on spelling or volunteer for a favorite cause, keep our spouses or partners delighted, meditate, and not drop dead from one single day of this pace? Life's exigencies catch up with all of us from time to time.

But we must cease chastising ourselves for circumstances beyond our control, circumstances that, in the long run, we not only manage to get through but often triumph over. How? We figure out solutions. My years at Catalyst have confirmed my faith in women's ingenuity. When we have to, we work things out on our own. When we can, we get help. We're exposing the myths that hold women back at work, and if we can't fix one workplace, we move on to a better one. We're fighting off yesterday's social expectations and resisting those who would dictate our choices. When I recall my first job interview, I realize how much things have changed. The man who interviewed me asked whether I was going to get pregnant. I said I had no plans to. He persisted: "Will you commit to not getting pregnant for two years?" I said yes. I meant it. (I got pregnant two and a half years later.)

Rather than feeling guilty, we're giving one another hearty pats on the back, accolades for our accomplishments. Our issues have moved to the workplace center stage, thanks to our drawing attention to them: extreme time demands in too many jobs, the business case for flexible work arrangements, women's and men's increasing clamor for a personal life. We're pushing organizations to change. And although this transition period has followed a rough road, we see progress, progress, in fact, for men as well as women.

That's why I want to change the discourse. It's time for us, the press, the entire society, to look forward to what women can accomplish and not back at the false paradise lost of the working father, stay-at-home mother, two children, and a cat and a dog in the picket-fenced yard. This chapter extols women's working and having a life. I'll talk about what's being done and what you can do. And most important, women with lives they enjoy, families they adore, and careers that are flourishing relate how they're doing it and offer suggestions as to how you can do it, too.

WOMEN IN A PERIOD OF SOCIAL TRANSITION

From the Pioneers:

Lynn Forester (Founder and Co-chair, FirstMark Communications International): "Women have to stop thinking they have to give up work when they have children. I think that guilt is both a natural thing and one of the most insidious things women do to each other. I remember knowing that mothers were talking about me when I traveled, saying, 'How can she leave town like that?' When I sold my first company, I said, 'I have enough money to not work again, so the first thing I'll do is fire the nanny and be with my children.' When I told the children at dinner, they cracked up laughing. I work, and I am a devoted mother, with my children a total priority in my life. The horrible part is what others are saying. The wonderful part is knowing that my children are proud of me."

Judy Sprieser (CEO, Transora): "Working makes me happy; it's what I want to do and need to do. The woman with kids around her ankle looks sad about it. Sure, I feel occasional guilt, but that's not very productive. I touch base with my kids from time to time to ask them, 'How do you feel about me working?' "

Zoë Baird (President, The Markle Foundation): "The first time my first child cried, I asked myself if I was making a mistake. But my pediatrician pointed out that any child cries when you're leaving the house, whether it's for the grocery store or for your work. You have to decide if it's a onetime thing or if you're making a miserable child. They adjust."

When I decided to go back to school before entering the work-place, I had no role models for working, let alone for simultane-ously raising a family, so I played it by ear. I went to graduate school—something ivy-covered wives rarely did decades ago—and the courses I elected had one thing in common: they all ended by 2:30. That was so I could be there when my sons got home from grammar school.

Why did I decide I had to work in the first place? Because one afternoon when I telephoned an older faculty wife I admired to ask her about something, her slurred speech made only one con-clusion possible: she was sitting at home alone, drinking. Oh my God, I thought, when the kids are gone, could that be me? I began to think about my future in a new way—and a working wife and mother began to take shape.

Likewise, the women pioneers in this book invented new ways of living to accompany their working. They have worked hard, and, according to their needs and desires, some spent time with friends, some dated, some got married, some did charitable work. Those who chose to had children, raised them, and sent them off into the world. With no social infrastructure estab-lished for child care, we working moms hired baby-sitters and nannies if we could afford them or enlisted relatives if we had them. Many of us who worked full-time came home to do what our mothers had done: shop and clean and cook and get the kids fed and through their homework and off to sports events, play dates, or guitar lessons.

We acted our part in the major societal transition (not com-pleted yet) as two decades of women flooded the workplace. We worked our way into leadership positions and have increasingly garnered recognition for our accomplishments. At the time I was completing college, most of my cohort began work as secretaries or assistants, rarely as peers of men. Now such women com-monly start out as professionals and executives. During my working lifetime, I've witnessed the stay-at-home mom transforming herself into the executive mother. Unfortunately, this transformation is hard for some in our society to accept. Women who broke the mold often faced censure. Some would still run the executive woman—and particularly the executive mother—out of town on a rail, and the media can be tough on us. It is hard to abandon the image of Mom baking cookies for happy children. Undeniably, from time to time, the backlash can get to us. We may wonder, "Am I succeeding professionally at the cost of failing personally?" Even the most successful pioneers in this book mention guilt, if only to denounce it or call it unproductive.

Every day I hear women expressing guilt about working, although in the same breath they say they love their jobs, need the income, and lead healthy and happy lives, many with children. But I've read every major study ever done on this issue and there's never been one that says the children of working mothers suffer because of it. As long as these mothers ensure that their children receive high-quality child care and have a loving relationship with the caregiving adult, children of working mothers do not suffer.

If a woman chooses to stay home rather than enter the workforce, that's an excellent choice as well. But the fact is that the majority of women are neither staying home nor returning home. Catalyst continually counters media stories in which, statistics to the contrary notwithstanding, reporters say that women are leaving the workplace in droves to stay home. One of the most significant of these journalistic controversies arose from a 1994 story claiming that labor statistics indicated that "women of child-bearing age are flocking back home. The trend line is sharpest among women 20 to 24."[1] The story took off as others spread this erroneous interpretation of data. Catalyst countered the story along with an economist at the U.S. Bureau of Labor Statistics, Howard Hayghe, who wrote, "The data clearly show that today's married mothers are not only more likely to work, but they are also far more likely to do so on a year-round full-time basis than their predecessors of 20 years ago." The real trend is that women enter the workplace and stay—year after year.[2]

JUST THE FACTS: WOMEN IN THE LABOR FORCE

WOMEN:*

Nearly 65 million women over age sixteen work today, a labor force participation rate of 60%.
39.5% of women in the labor force are mothers.
Among working mothers, 72.2% have children under eighteen years of age and nearly 64.8% have children under six years.

DUAL-EARNER FAMILIES:†

Among married couples, 60% have two careers.
Members of dual-earner families make up 45% of the U.S. workforce. In Canada, the majority of households are headed by two earners.

*Bureau of Labor Statistics Current Population Survey, U.S. Department of Labor, 1999.
†*Two Careers, One Marriage* (New York: Catalyst, 1998).

Anti–working woman hype particularly offends because it fails to take into account how many women play the role of top breadwinner or sole breadwinner in the household. It shows no cognizance of why women work. We work so we can afford good housing, good schools, and a college education for our children. Women work whether single, married, or divorced, with or without children. Surveys of girls and young women consistently demonstrate their intention to have careers. With or without families, we continue working. Women work to earn a living and to make a contribution to our world. We work because we want to, because we like to, and because we're good at it. Listen to some of the pioneers talk about the rewards of work.

From the Pioneers: We like to work.

Linda Alvarado (President and CEO, Alvarado Construction): "The rewarding experience of success, pride in accomplishment, and the economic benefit of providing for your family and of proving yourself: this is why we work. A husband was out there meeting interesting people and making deals and conducting business in various environments, and this made him a better, well-rounded father who can provide perspective on the world to his family. For many generations women missed the opportunity for this type of intellectual stimulation and interaction with others. Now women are contributing to the economy and achieving satisfaction in demonstrating their talent and achieving their personal goals. It's important that we have the same satisfaction that men have achieved!"

Zoë Baird (President, The Markle Foundation): "Work contributes to the person I am. I believe people must do what's satisfying to them. Each life is important."

Carolee Friedlander (Founder, President, and CEO, Carolee Designs): "I work to fulfill my natural and creative abilities. Work is one of the keys to feel we've achieved our potential as human beings with the gifts we have."

From the Pioneers: Kids respond positively.

Tosh Barron (Clinical Associate Professor, Stern School of Business, New York University): "My sons have been immensely proud of my work, amazingly so. One of them was very surprised when I retired [from Xerox]. He said, 'I like the fact that you work.' "

Dorrit Bern (Chair, CEO, and President, Charming Shoppes): "I have three extraordinary sons who believe there isn't anything a woman can't do. They're terribly independent. They can do things for themselves. They can organize their time. They had to learn how to do it, and I see that as a positive."

THE TIME-DEMAND ISSUE

Women say:
Partner, law firm: "What's really making women walk out the door, the straw that breaks the camel's back, is the effort that's required, the amount of hours, the inability to successfully work part-time and combine a family with a career. What finally causes you to hit the ground is when you say, 'I can't keep working sixty hours a week and do what I need to do with my life.' "

Men say:
Partner, management consulting firm: "The reason women don't make it is because they leave. That's not my fault."

That said, let's address the time-demand issue, which is not in any sense a small one. You indeed face many challenges to having a fulfilling career and a fulfilling personal life simultaneously. Men face such challenges, too,* but as a woman your challenge is compounded, since you continue to bear most of the weight of home and child care. It hasn't helped matters that during the last decades, the time crunch has increased as work demands burgeon in many fields, especially at firms. Women tell us that "everybody ought to have a wife."

Many organizations are coming to terms with the prevalence

---

*Catalyst's dual-career study showed a noteworthy number of both men and women who want more flexibility in their jobs. Seventy-two percent of women and 65 percent of men in dual-career marriages would choose the option to customize their career pace if they knew they could do it with impunity. It's a sign of the times that both men and women now want more of a personal life than many workplaces afford their employees today. (*Two Careers, One Marriage* [New York: Catalyst, 1998].)

of dual-career couples and with women in their workplace, as more and more of us enter the managerial ranks. They're finding that a flexible environment helps them retain valuable employees and attract the best new ones. They're also learning that offering alternative work arrangements to employees increases employees' loyalty to the organization.

STRATEGIES FOR MAKING YOUR LIFE WORK

Women often speak of "juggling" and "balancing," the terms of the hour for how to manage your work and your personal life. I'd like to see that language doctored as part of the change in discourse on women working. I like to call what women do "organizing"—it sounds more like the management skill that it is. The women Catalyst talks with have found solutions that work for them, thanks to an ability to plan, to create order, to coordinate, to orchestrate, to sort things out—in short, to organize. Like all of us, they've had their ups and downs, but they've been saved by their superb time management skills.

I want to stress that the women whose advice I incorporate here—women from our research studies, our focus groups, our interviews—uniformly emphasize their love of their jobs, their total commitment, and their hard work. When asked, they delineate the complicated issues they're dealing with, but they do not regret their choices. Again, I emphasize that they like their lives, as I do mine. So now let's look at how they made it to top management still satisfied with their choices. I have compiled their recommendations and Catalyst's into a list of eight Life Strategies. Further on in the chapter, you'll find an additional seven Working Mom Life Strategies.

Life Strategy 1. Get help. Hiring domestic help holds the title of most frequently voiced strategy for balancing career and personal life. We found this in *Women in Corporate Leadership*, in *Closing the Gap: Women's Advancement in Corporate and Professional Canada*, and in our advisory work inside companies and firms. As for working mothers, most avail themselves of child care services.* This commonsense approach works, if you can afford it. You can't do everything. I remember the first time I hesitantly hired someone to clean my house. The miracle of achieving a clean house without giving up my Saturday made me giddy. Figure out what you can hire out and what you want to or have to do yourself. You don't need to prove your worth at home and the office by perpetual perspiration. The only reward you get from working like a maniac is the workhorse award—and, of course, more work.

> **From the Pioneers: Don't feel you must do everything yourself.**
> **Maureen Kempston Darkes** (President and General Manager, General Motors of Canada): "It's okay to ask for help. Don't feel guilty about that. Get all the help you can get!"
>
> **Lulu Wang** (Partner and CEO, Tupelo Capital Management): "I think too often we hear about talented women just burning out, just dropping out altogether. I think with the women in our current generation, we still carry a very heavy load. We are still very much responsible for our families, often two-generational families, and often our husband's family as well as our own. If we don't set priorities, don't focus, then rather than distinguish ourselves, we'll extinguish ourselves. That's very important; if you don't have a sound personal life, it doesn't give you the foundation to go ahead and take the risk, and put in your best effort in your professional life."

---

*Ninety-three percent of the women with children in *Women in Corporate Leadership* reported using child care services. In *Closing the Gap*, we broke down the number: 81 percent used internal child care services and 38 percent external child care services at various times.

Life Strategy 2. Manage your time scrupulously. Obviously, you can't do all the things you want to do all of the time. Who can? Whether single or with a family, you're bound occasionally to have to put off until tomorrow what you can't do today, whether it's something at work or your workout at the gym. You must figure out what can't be done and decide not to do it. Set your priorities at home as you do at the office. Success in your life requires that you manage time strategically, no less than does your success as an executive.

Use time management tools. If it works for you (and personally I don't see how you could cope without one), buy an organizer—paper, or better yet, electronic—you can use for planning. Write out (or type in) what needs to be done and when, and check off what you've completed. I mark the priority items I have to complete each day. Although I don't plan every hour of every day, I do take down notes from nearly all my meetings and what I or others must do to follow up. I go through this list with my assistant daily, delegating whatever I can, and incorporating significant details into my organizer. That's proved to be a priceless record on many an occasion. I believe that if you have a prodigious amount to accomplish, the more carefully you plan, the more you'll get done. Judith Rodin agrees. She says, "Be absolutely compulsive about organizing your time. Keep notes. Figure out what you're going to do with all the minutes of your day to be productive. I'd been doing it for years, and I realized how compulsively organized I was one day when I took notes for my son's birthday party. I had every twenty minutes down." Was the party good? "They had a great time."

Life Strategy 3. Set priorities and make trade-offs. Executive women readily acknowledge making many trade-offs; what they trade differs as much as the individuals themselves. Some have circumscribed their social lives, some have postponed vacations, some have accepted dust on the furniture. I've also made many trade-offs throughout my own career. For one job I did a daily commute across a state, listening to many a book on tape. There were times when a traffic jam on the I-95 was heaven-sent. You—and only you—can decide what you can and can't do for your job, what's really important for you, and where and when you need to make compromises. Never forget that it's your life, even when it seems out of control. You can regain control. Take a deep breath. Then take fifteen minutes, half an hour, however long you need to set your priorities. The pioneers offer some philosophy on the topic.

From the Pioneers: There's no set formula.
Zoë Baird (President, The Markle Foundation): "Everyone has to make her own choices and decide what she can include in her life. The mistake is to think there's a right or wrong answer on whether you spend all your time at home or at work, or some combination."

Judy Sprieser (CEO, Transora): "You can't have career–life balance every day. It's a day-to-day decision. You do first things first."

Joan Leiman (Executive Deputy Vice President for the Health Sciences, Columbia University) says "there's no magic way" to balance work and personal life. She made her children her number one priority, but still felt "out of kilter" sometimes. She advises other working mothers to "accept the fact that it's difficult and that you'll always feel torn until they're adolescents. There's no easy answer, no right way. Only you can decide whether it's worth it. It takes organization and a tremendous amount of energy, but working women are able to give children what they need."

Lois Juliber (COO, Colgate-Palmolive): "The reality of dual-career, ambitious couples is that it's hard to spend much quality time together during the workweek. The focal point of my relationship is the weekend, so it's sacred. Partners have to work out a mechanism to spend real time with each other."

Lulu Wang (Partner and CEO, Tupelo Capital Management): "I think it's important to find interests to share with my husband because work will take me away from him. When I do have time for personal interests, I try to align them with his. It was his initial interest that brought us into vintage cars. Now we acquire them together and we race them together." She emphasizes, "Whatever free time we have, it's wonderful to find a shared interest with our husbands and families. It really is important to find enough time with the ones we love, to find that balance in life that centers us."

Carol Bartz (Chair, CEO, and President, Autodesk) commuted to California from Texas: "I hopped on a plane on Sunday night, and I came home on Thursday. I made it home three quarters of the time. Then I acted like a normal person for three days. I was 'Miss Mom.' When they'd call me with a conference call or fax, I'd ask, 'And what about this couldn't wait until Monday?' They're interested in proving to you that they're working."

Carolee Friedlander (Founder, President, and CEO, Carolee Designs): "I started my business in my home. Then I built an artist studio in the backyard and ran the business from there, with the kids in and out of the cabin. You're never really able to just do the business, but it's wonderful because you're right there. That's exceedingly important if you can't find adequate resources to help you raise your kids, and I had a hard time doing that. Then I opened a sales office in New York. I couldn't be there every day, so I hired someone to be there, and I went in once a week."

Life Strategy 4. Reassess your trade-offs frequently. A choice is only for now. When you make choices about what you've got time for, look at it as a decision for the time being. For today. For the week. Or, if you like, for the year. Continually revisit each choice. What works today might not work tomorrow. Certainly last month's priorities might have changed, especially when other people in the family are involved. Take time—whether early in the morning, before bedtime, or on Sunday night—to scrutinize what you're going to do and what must give way. Don't beat yourself up if you can't do everything you would do if you had a couple of clones of yourself.

Life Strategy 5. Hold the "right" job. Weighing into the equation of your trade-offs, of course, is the kind of job you hold. If you're just working at a job you feel is a good one but you're not thrilled, you're not likely to want to focus all your attention in that area and to work weekends and put off vacations. However, if you've planned your career and been fortunate enough to find a job tied to your values that excites your mind, the balance shifts. Find your passion at the "right" organization, and you'll have to make fewer concessions in order to make your life work.

> **From the Pioneers: Doing what matters affects your choices.**
> **Andrea Jung** (President and CEO, Avon): "You need a job you have passion for. Pressure of family versus work won't go away, but if you feel you can make a difference, then your job is an enhancement to your life."

Life Strategy 6. Do some things for yourself. If you're working yourself to the bone both at work and at home, you may feel as if you have little time for yourself. I advise you to take a second look at this. All work and no play makes Jill burn out (at the very least). Find time for some activity that gives you pleasure. The activity might be athletic, artistic, or family-oriented. Or it might relate to your career in some way: a conference, a class, an association. Fun doesn't have to be disconnected from everything else to be fun.

Despite the demands of their careers and families, the women interviewed for *Women in Corporate Leadership* reported being involved in a variety of activities outside work, including professional associations and board service at corporations and nonprofits.* For relaxation, the women participated in many differ-- ent activities, including travel, cooking, gardening, entertaining, exercise, and other hobbies. My idea of fun is cooking a really fancy dinner for my family and friends. The most common out- side activity noted by the women interviewed for the study was golf, but one of them said, "Golf is work."

Life Strategy 7. Have a support network. When you run into time crunches and frustrations with your schedule, you need to do two things: vent your stress and get advice. That's the time to call upon people who've been there, done that. If you have a woman mentor whose experience parallels yours, don't hesitate to ask her for advice on how to handle stressful times. In your networking with women in or outside your office, you've prob- ably met many women whose circumstances and histories offer solutions to the problems you're coping with. Ask them for ad- vice. Call upon your personal friends and your family for sup- port when the times get tough. Call on them in good times, too; sharing your successes will boost your morale. I never underesti- mate the need for appreciation and applause (at least of the fig- urative variety). Sometimes you need to hear kudos from someone who knows exactly how hard what you've accom- plished is; that's the time to chat with your mentor.

Life Strategy 8. Assume a positive frame of reference. I find that being careful about your choice of words will help you cope. How you speak about an issue influences, as well as reflects, how you feel about it. If you feel positive about a choice, you'll use positive language to describe it. That's why in this chapter

---

*By comparison, Canada's women are more likely to curtail their personal interests and much less likely to pursue personal interests than U.S. women. (*Closing the Gap: Women's Advancement in Corporate and Professional Canada* [New York: The Conference Board of Canada and Catalyst, 1998].)

I'm calling for a shift in the conversation about working women. The more we talk about how tough it is to "balance" work and family, the tougher it seems. For example, pioneer Linda Alvarado doesn't like to use the word "balance"; she prefers talking about what she calls "opportunity costs."

Working mothers need more strategies than anyone else. And to hear a lot of women talk, the first one is, before you do anything else, *marry right*! A key strategy mentioned over and over by the women pioneers in this book and participants in our surveys, interviews, and focus groups was having a supportive spouse. Of course, there's no guarantee when you're standing at the altar that a supportive bridegroom will mature into a helpful husband. But it's worth thinking about. The men coming out of college now certainly talk the talk, but only a time-tested marriage will reveal if they can walk the walk. I'd say the odds in favor of finding a supportive spouse are much better than they were in my day. I just lucked out in getting one of the best.

But, okay, if you're already married, I don't suggest you should divorce the guy if he's not Mr. Mom. Nobody's perfect. Nonetheless, negotiation often yields results. Talk openly with your spouse about what you need. Don't feel defensive about doing so; you're right to ask.*

STRATEGIES FOR MAKING
A WORKING MOM'S LIFE WORK

Working Mom Life Strategy 1. Weigh the family question carefully. Deciding whether and when to have children remains one of the most sensitive issues for working women today. Others may pressure you to do it or not, but only you (and a significant other) should decide whether to have a family. Not all women

---

*Learning how to negotiate personally is as important as it is professionally. The book *Getting to Yes*, by Roger Fisher et al., offers superb advice that you can apply at work and at home.

want to be mothers, and fortunately, the stigma attached to childlessness has lessened over the past decades. Some of the pioneers and women in our studies made a conscious choice not to have children, and some did so because they wanted to focus on their careers. It's not uncommon to hear from women that advancement in their organizations has depended on putting their careers before their personal lives.

It's not easy, though. Catalyst's surveys of women in corporate and professional Canada and executive women interviewed in *Women in Corporate Leadership* shed light on this issue. Among U.S. women, only 10 percent had chosen not to marry as a "balance" strategy, but 26 percent had postponed having children and 20 percent said that they had chosen not to have the children they would have liked to. In our Canadian survey, 41 percent of women had either postponed having children or had not had them at all. Nineteen percent had decided either to delay marriage or not to marry. I have a friend in academia who has two children. One she calls her "tenure child"; the other, her "professorship child." She planned them both, and it worked. She loves them; she loves her life; she loves the choices she's made.

The choice to focus on career and not have children is as valid as the choice to have a family and continue to work, or to have a family and stop working for a time or for all time. It's just personal. Many of the pioneers gave considerable thought and attention to the decision to have a family, and they graciously explained how they had made their choices. Let me also underscore their acceptance of their choices.

From the Pioneers: Weigh your choice.

Carolee Friedlander (Founder, President, and CEO, Carolee Designs) took short leaves as her children were born ("I feel it's important for women to take leaves because it's an irreplaceable time") and then returned to work. "If they want to, women should try to have it all. Life is a juggling act, and learning how to balance the different components isn't easy. Success comes from being able to prioritize what's important to you. It's a compromise, but both work and children can be a natural part of a woman's life."

Betty Beene (President and CEO, United Way of America) felt "called to do something in service to other people, and I couldn't do what I had to do and be a mother. I went to my pastor and asked about having children, asked how do you know what God wants you to do. He told me if I prayed about it, God would make good about whatever I chose. I feel he has."

Anne Mulcahy (President and COO, Xerox Corporation): "I'm a big believer in personal comes first. Kids come first. That doesn't mean that you don't work hard; I think it's about making choices. I gave up a lot of personal time and social time because I chose to be able to be very much a part of my kids' life and I really wanted a very rich, rewarding business life. . . . I always laugh when I have to write a résumé of any type, in terms of hobbies and special interests. How does none sound? There's just no room. Here's the part where you can't do everything. Your ability to make some choices and stick with them allows you to have some peacefulness and be happy."

Working Mom Life Strategy 2. Organize any maternity leaves. Your coming and going matter a great deal to your boss and your colleagues, as well as to yourself. How you arrange your leave and your return will affect how successfully you pull it off on both the professional and personal levels. Remember that with a male boss, you may be dealing with preconceptions about the difficulties that will ensue. But you can alarm any boss with the news that you're stepping away for a while. Who's going to pick up your work? You can make sure that your boss's fears are not realized by approaching your maternity leave as a project to organize. The guidelines below outline what you can do when you want a maternity leave.

Working Mom Life Strategy 3. Ask your employer for what you need. Not long ago, most women felt they couldn't ask for what

GUIDE TO A SUCCESSFUL MATERNITY LEAVE

Design your leave. Prepare a formal proposal spelling out how your leave will work. It should include the following:

- Do you want to work at home toward the end of your pregnancy?
- How much of your leave is covered by medical benefits? How much by leave policies?
- How much time do you plan to take off?
- Do you want to consider phasing back into work?

Make recommendations to your supervisor about how your work can be handled during your leave. (What is the status of your projects? What must be maintained, and what can wait until your return?)

Ascertain what child care resources are available through your employer (child care resource and referral programs, child care centers, etc.).

Stay connected and stay current when you're out on maternity leave. Stay in touch with mentors and colleagues; get active in trade associations or professional groups. Consider volunteer work. Keep up-to-date with the business press in your field, and especially don't let yourself get out-of-date on technology.

Determine when you will reconnect with your supervisor to discuss and plan your return.

they wanted and needed from their offices. When a child got sick, a mother might have ducked out the back door and returned the same way, to get in "face time." Or she might have called in sick herself. You might still feel you have to fudge a bit about going to your daughter's soccer game, while your male colleague gets accolades for being a good father when he brags about doing so. But at more and more offices today, you no longer have to resort to subterfuge. Many of the pioneers and women in our studies encourage being forthright about what you need. They say, "Go in and ask for it." That won't always work. I know some workplaces where this might be difficult, so use your judgment. But some of the pioneers did it and it worked for them, and this may be an area where you want to try to be a pioneer yourself. Once you're in senior management and you can take the time off you need, make your choices visible. You'll serve as a valuable role model.

From the Pioneers: Go for it . . . and compromise.
Roberta Gutman (Corporate Vice President and Director of Global Diversity, Motorola): "You must decide your own priorities and act on them. If you know what your priorities are, it's much easier to stand up. You'll have ferreted out the consequences of not following them." She gives a key example from her own experience, what she calls "an epiphany" that occurred when her son was six: "I was going on a trip, I had my bag ready to go, and he asked me not to leave. My heart was wrenched. I went to my boss and said I'd travel no more than fifteen percent of the time. I expected there would be career ramifications, but I took the chance. My boss was so flabbergasted by what I said that he said he admired me, and he kept me moving right along." She advises that you ask yourself, " 'How valuable do I believe I am, and what's important to me?' Decide that, and then stand up for what's real to you. You need to have the guts for it. Before I started each job after that, I went to my boss and said, 'My family is my highest priority, and I will go to their side if they need me. I need you to know that before I start here.' "

Barbara Paul Robinson (Partner, Debevoise & Plimpton) took the bull by the horns back in 1967, when flexible work arrangements were unheard-of: "I'd had my first child, and I needed control over my schedule. I wasn't a maverick, I just really liked working at the firm and didn't want to look for a new job. There had been three other women at the firm before me and they all left when they had kids, but I didn't want to do that. I went to the partners and asked to work part-time. They fussed around for a while," and she thought they were saying no. However, instead they said yes, if she'd change her specialty to trusts and estates. "So I worked a regular five days a week, then asked for four. After I had my second child, I asked for three and got it. But I knew it would be impossible to go back to litigation at that point." She worked part-time for four years, then asked to come back full-time, knowing she needed to do that to make partner. Still, the partners were surprised when she asked to be considered for partnership. "When it came time for my 'final exam,' a special crisis thing, I said good-bye to family and worked all the time with very little sleep. It was a crush for a few months."

You don't know what you can get until you ask. Your bosses or the partners at your firm cannot read your mind. They don't know what you need, and most need education on what can work. You can teach them by your example. Barbara Paul Robinson did, and she paved the way for other women. Today, her firm has institutionalized flextime partners.

Working Mom Life Strategy 4. Consider a flexible work arrangement. If you decide you need a flexible schedule of some sort, you need to plan it every bit as carefully as you would the maternity leave described above. You want a process that's as painless for your boss and for you as possible. You can consider flexible full-time options or reduced-time options, including the following:

- *Flextime.* This variation on the standard workday gives you the opportunity to start or finish the workday one to three hours earlier or later than usual. You and your manager determine mutually acceptable times. Obviously, if your office has core business hours, the manager will probably expect your presence at those times.
- *Flexible week.* Another full-time option; you work fewer but

longer days. Also called the compressed workweek, under such a plan you might work four longer days, or you might create a schedule of two or more weeks with some longer and some shorter days, with the average hours matching the standard for your workplace. Most common: the four-day week, the three-day week, and the nine-days-over-two-weeks schedule.

- *Flexplace.* Also known as telecommuting; you work at a location other than the work site: your home, a satellite office, or a branch office. You stay connected to the office by phone, fax, and modem.

- *Part-time work.* This schedule reduces your weekly hours so that you work a percentage of the weekly time expected of regular employees; or you reduce your annual number of hours. Transactional work also falls under this rubric; in it, you work full-time on a specific project and then take time off before starting a new project.

If your organization offers flexible work arrangements (FWAs), or if it does not and you're going to be the first to ask, you yourself must figure out how the arrangement will work. Plan it carefully, for not only does your superior's agreeing to it depend on your selling the concept, the success of the arrangement depends on your foreseeing the possible pitfalls and avoiding them.

GUIDE TO A SUCCESSFUL FWA

The following are some things you should think about in planning and organizing your own FWA.

What policies or programs does your employer offer in the area of flexible work arrangements?

What type of flexible arrangement will resolve the issues you face:

- Changing your work hours?
- Working from home on a regular basis?
- Working a reduced schedule?

Can you surmount the specific career challenges that accompany working part-time?

- How will you demonstrate your commitment to your career and job?
- How will you schedule regular conversations with your supervisor to discuss workload, assignments, and responsibilities?
- What are your personal goals for this period in your life, and how do they fit with your career goals? (Are you willing to "plateau" for a period of time, and how will you ensure you can return to the "fast track," if that's your goal?)

Are you suited to taking a flexible work arrangement? Certain skills are critical to negotiating and maintaining successful arrangements and to sustaining a career while working flexibly:

- Are you a self-starter who is comfortable with working independently? Can you be flexible with your schedule and adapt your arrangement as needed?
- Do you communicate effectively, both in writing and orally? Are you comfortable talking explicitly about schedules and logistics?
- Can you prioritize tasks and manage your time effectively?
- How will you maintain effective relationships with your supervisor and your colleagues?

What personal resources do you need for your flexible arrangement?

- If you want to work from home, what equipment do you need? What will your employer provide?
- Can your family survive on a reduced income if you work on a reduced schedule?
- Will you need child care or elder care services that fit with your arrangement, and can you find them?*

How will you evaluate the arrangement on an ongoing basis? FWAs need to evolve to fit your ever-changing personal situation and professional aspirations.

*If you have preschool children, most organizations require you to have a child care provider if you work from home.

Working Mom Life Strategy 5. Take charge of your kids' schedules. You can plan in advance for your children's scheduled activities and integrate them into your calendar so you don't miss the important ones. Call their schools and tell them that you need the year's calendar in advance, and don't take no for an answer.

From the Pioneers: Make the school cooperate.
Marie Knowles (Executive Vice President and CFO, Atlantic Richfield): "It's like guys who schedule golf dates. I schedule field trips with my kids' class. I put it on the calendar, and I do it. The school my boys go to puts out a calendar the first day of the year, so you know in September what activity will come in May. That's critical. The school has to do that for you."

Judith Rodin (President, University of Pennsylvania): "I used to demand of the school that they put out a schedule early enough so I could get the important things on my calendar before it got locked in. I pushed them to give me the swim meet dates. As a working mother, I had a right to demand that. You need to be assertive about your priorities."

Tosh Barron (Clinical Associate Professor, Stern School of Business, New York University): "Get mechanistic! Block off your calendar. I attended every school event. As I got higher up in the organization, I got big meetings changed. Xerox was open to that."

Working Mom Life Strategy 6. Integrate family and work. I'm noticing that as women find themselves more at home in the work environment, they're bringing who they are to how they do things. And as a critical mass of women builds, they're finding it easier to intermingle aspects of family and work—both at home and at work.

Once children reach a certain age, their curiosity about your work could increase. Start in early talking to them about what you do. Share anecdotes about your work, about the workplace, about your colleagues. Consider asking them for their viewpoints. I advise omitting gripes, at least until you're sure they're mature enough to see them in perspective.

The pioneers show a pragmatism about their families, especially as their children grow older. Most feel that their work makes them better mothers, as well as more interesting, better people. Several of them, such as Judy Sprieser, have involved their children in some way with their work.

From the Pioneers: Talk to your kids about your work.
Geraldine Laybourne (Chair, CEO, and Founder, Oxygen Media) used her work at Nickelodeon children's television "to involve the kids (now twenty-four and twenty-seven) in everything I did. Our dinners were brainstorming sessions. The kids tested my stuff; they were completely integrated. It was sort of a family business, like a farm," she says.

From the Pioneers: Bring down the wall between work and family.
Judy Sprieser (CEO, Transora): "For fifteen years, I thought I had to draw a firm black line between work and the person I

was outside work and not let one overcome the other. Now they're firmly overlapping all the time: I set up a laptop in the kitchen or in the room where the kids are practicing. We can perform multitasks as women: I can make something on the stove, give my son his spelling words, and talk on the phone at the same time. My husband can do one thing at a time, but I can blend it all together. I chat on the phone while styling my daughter's hair. I have conference calls with teachers at my desk. My daughter and I trade e-mails at work. When I speak at events during an evening or weekend, I bring my daughter so I can spend time with her and she can see me in this capacity. She critiques my speeches." Sprieser explains that she doesn't do anything else but work and family: "Every bit of leisure time is with the family. I love to play piano, so I play nothing but duets with the kids. I horseback ride with my daughter. I've adopted her sports as my sports, so we're together all the time."

Zoë Baird (President, The Markle Foundation): "I'm there until the kids leave in the morning, but they're in school a lot of the day, and they have play dates, and they have music lessons. Sometimes it's frustrating how little time you get with your child, even if you're home. They wouldn't have time to hang with me until I get home from work anyway." She considers the effect of work on her children: "If I felt it wasn't good for them, I'd not work. I try to have them benefit from the work I do. Work contributes to the person I am. My nine-year-old loves that I'm working in something involved with new media and is interested in the things the foundation is doing."

Working Mom Life Strategy 7. Take the larger perspective. Let me throw in some common sense here. If you do decide to have a family and continue working, don't let it slip your mind that you're pregnant only a short time or that your kids aren't young forever. And don't worry that you're not perfect. You do what you can on a day-to-day basis.

From the Pioneers: Swear off perfection.
Barbara Paul Robinson (Partner, Debevoise & Plimpton): "There's no one right way to do it, but it's worth trying to have both. In a long lifetime, the period of raising kids is relatively small, and it's worth the struggle to balance it with work."

Andrea Jung (President and CEO, Avon): "[What changed me was] changing my own expectations. I'm not too hard on myself. That's made the difference in how I manage. The day I decided I wasn't going to be perfect, I began to manage better. For me it comes down to what's important on any given day. You have to be able to admit the ten things you can't do out of twenty-five. Winners pick the right fifteen."

Rebecca McDonald (Chair and CEO, Enron Asia-Pacific, Africa, and China): "I made a choice to be a whole person by my definition. You have to decide what makes you whole, and you should do that. From moment to moment, the trade-offs might not seem right to me, but on balance, they've been worth it. I'm not convinced anyone can evaluate their life without looking at it on balance."

KNOW YOU CAN DO IT

As president of Catalyst, I firmly believe that it's right for women to work if it's right for the individual women who choose that option. So I repeat what I said earlier: Make the choices that work for you, and continually revisit your choices. Try not to let others influence you to the extent that you're not doing what you want and need to do. You have more control than you think. Make your decisions in a conscious, well-thought-out fashion. So much hinges on your attitude. If you're prepared—well organized, savvy, confident—to handle anything that comes along, you won't be thrown off balance and you won't be influenced by people who would throw you off.

In my experience, the women who have found a viable compromise between their work schedules and their personal schedules have been the happiest. How you do so depends on you. The precise compromise—if that's what it is—will be your own invention. And how you feel about your choices will make all the difference.

CHAPTER 8

Find a Mentor/Be a Mentor

From the Pioneers:
Andrea Jung (President and CEO, Avon): "The first woman CEO at Federated Stores had been my mentor at Blooming-dale's. She's the person to whom I attribute a lot of my success. She believed in me."

Nancy Karch (Retired Director, McKinsey & Company): "[I had] three important mentors in New York almost sequentially. With each of the mentors, I'd write notes on note cards and say, 'I don't understand these three things people said in the meeting.' "

Marie Knowles (Executive Vice President and CFO, Atlantic Richfield) says the most important thing she's gotten from mentors was "honest feedback about what I needed to change or develop. That's the thing women don't get. We don't get told to stop doing that, or 'Gee, you're really good at this, but you need to be thinking about developing that skill, too.' Or 'Do you know how much you ticked off that person in that meeting?' "

Janet Hanson (Founder, President, and CEO, Milestone Capital Management): "I've had a number of male mentors—before, during, and after my career at Goldman Sachs, and now as the head of my own firm. These people made a difference in my life by helping me to unlock my own potential. . . . They showed me how to identify and fully leverage opportunities as they arose. And they instilled in me a strong sense of self-confidence."

I'm happy about serving as your mentor-in-a-book, offering advice on meeting the gender-related challenges of today's workplace. I've told you many things that real live mentors might have told you and much that they wouldn't have, calling as I am not just on my own experience, as mentors do, but also upon that of the women pioneers interviewed for this book, the thousands of women Catalyst has talked with, and all the experts on the Catalyst staff.

Nevertheless, you still need a flesh-and-blood mentor, one who knows you and your career. If you haven't found one yet, I advise you not to give up. For optimal career success, you really do need people who are actually (not virtually) in your life. You need someone who knows the people and the politics of your office, who can give you insight on individuals' motivations, and who can boost your career with senior management. And if possible, you ought to have someone whom you can observe in action, someone to model yourself upon.

A mentor in your office is ideal. But if you can't find one there, I have suggestions on how to find mentors elsewhere. Yes, mentors, in the plural. You'll be surprised at how many people out there really will help you. And it's my firm belief that the more perspectives you can get on your career from those in the know, the better.

WHAT DIFFERENCE DO MENTORS MAKE?

"Everyone Who Makes It Has a Mentor" proclaimed the *Harvard Business Review* two decades ago.[1] Further research and studies confirmed that in men's experience at work, mentoring made the difference in their advancement opportunities. One survey reported senior male executives as saying that "influential mentors were second in importance only to education as a factor in their career success."[2] Catalyst's research with women confirms that this is not gender-specific; mentors make the difference for everyone. Four out of five of the senior women executives who participated in *Women in Corporate Leadership* emphasized the importance of a mentor to their success. Similarly, in Canada, women in corporations and firms considered mentoring critical. And in Catalyst's study *Women of Color in Corporate Management,* these women listed "not having an influential mentor or sponsor" as the major barrier to their career advancement.

Mentors play many different kinds of roles—all important in their varying ways—throughout the entire careers of those they coach. Virtually all of the women pioneers interviewed for this book had mentors of one or more of these types and often more than one. And virtually all of the pioneers attributed an element of their professional success to having been mentored.

When do you need a mentor? A mentor can help you throughout your career, at all stages from entry level to senior management. As you're starting out, you can use help in learning the lay of the land, and your relationships with your mentors can be quite informal. It's good to have people pulling you into a corner and saying, "Here's what you need to do." When you've made it to senior management, feedback and information from others in senior positions will prove invaluable when you're making business decisions, as well as career choices.

There are times when having a mentor will be critical to your mobility. For example, if you're working in a securities firm and you move from the trading floor to management, it's hard to learn the new skills you need to coordinate a staff without a mentor's guidance and support. If you're experiencing a seismic shift, such as moving from field sales management to a headquarters job or moving from bench scientist to management, a mentor's help and moral support can be crucial to your success. Once you make such a move, there's often no turning back, so your mentor's information and protection may mean the difference between your making it and not making it.

During the first few years of your career, you're likely to advance relatively smoothly. This movement often loses its rhythm in middle management, when you're ready to move upward, roughly at the director level or its equivalent, the time most women hit the glass ceiling. You'll probably need a mentor most to help you at this point, to tell you about opportunities, to talk about you to the higher-ups, and to "sponsor" you.* Plan ahead so you have mentors for this time in your career. And keep in mind that you'll need different kinds of mentors at different stages of your career. One woman put it well, saying that early in her career, a mentor had "turned the lights on for me" by describing the political landscape for her; later, she had needed someone to "turn the light onto me," and she had found others to act as sponsors and give her visibility.

HOW CAN YOU FIND A MENTOR?

The best mentor relationships evolve from a natural affinity between two individuals. They begin informally, generally after the two have worked together for a while and developed a mutual respect. Talent usually draws the mentor to the protégée, and accomplishment and power draw the protégée to the mentor. You like each other; you ask questions; the mentor shows interest and offers advice. It's all quite casual. No proposal, no engagement ring.

If this has not happened for you, don't sit around and wait for the magic to happen. In the real world, mentors don't go out mentee hunting. Mentors want to associate with winners, with

---

*I'm putting together under the mentor umbrella those who offer support as well as those who sponsor you. For women, these are often different people.

rising stars, so that some of the stardust will brush off on them. Generally your mentor will not be an altruist. Rather, he or she mentors to fill a departmental or broader organizational need.

What do you want in a mentor? Take out your career plan and decide what you specifically need. Make a list, and put things into their order of importance. Do you need advice on how to move to the next level? How to manage your support staff? How to write a report, press release, or presentation? Do you need the scoop on politics at the organization or on what it really takes to rise to the top? Do you need assistance in grasping the nuances at meetings?

Next, match what you need with people who might be able to give it to you. You don't want to hitch yourself to someone who will only praise you, nor do you want someone who will bury you under criticism. You do want someone you can get along with. The ideal mentor will be astute enough to observe others' reactions to you and forthcoming enough to offer honest tips about your style. You want someone who can assess your performance, someone in the loop who can alert you to information, rumors, and gossip. In addition, it would be great to have a person who will go to bat for you and praise you to influential people, someone who believes in you and will proffer you for opportunities, including moving on. Indeed, you want someone who will push your limits and help you develop your potential.

Only the luckiest of people will ever get all that focused on one individual. Athena comes to mind once again. But since you're not Telemachus, don't count on her materializing. Instead of searching only for the perfect mentor and becoming her protégée, strive also to become the mentee of several talented people. You need to think about who at your organization can give you some of what you've put on your list. Who's had the experience you're seeking and so knows the path and the prerequisites? Who has the skills you want to acquire? Who's the best manager? Who's the most effective at meetings? Who has his or her ear to the ground? Make a list of those people.

Then give some thought to whether anyone on this list has shown an interest in you, has helped you in any way. If no one on the list has, but others in your office have cottoned to you, should they be on the list? Also, consider someone senior with whom you have an easy relationship. And, of course, think about who has the influence to be able to help you move ahead.

Should your mentor be a man? In many organizations, male mentors are all we have. Not many of the senior women Catalyst talks to have had female mentors; the continuing scarcity of women in senior ranks limits their supply. For the women pioneers in this book, finding a male mentor was the only option, and most said they had had at least one important male mentor. I know I did. Some women find that men are especially good at giving objective advice. And, of course, these male mentors, with their preestablished networks and credibility, can be very effective at sponsoring their mentees in senior management circles, bringing key assignments and visibility their way. So don't underestimate the power of a male mentor.

Be alert to the pitfalls of male-female mentoring. The most common problems reported to Catalyst include the following:

- Stereotypical gender assumptions
- Paternalism
- Sexual tension
- Innuendo from others about the true nature of the relationship
- Jealousy of respective spouses
- The inability of male mentors to meet specific needs, such as how to deal with bias
- Differing preferences in social activities

I don't think these problems should deter you; most can be surmounted with tact when needed and straightforwardness the rest of the time. A formal mentoring relationship reduces the risk that they will arise.

Should your mentor be a woman? In most organizations few women have the clout of men at the senior level, but a woman mentor offers certain things you can't get with a man. You certainly can't get better advice on how to advance as a woman than from a woman who's made it. Women mentors can help you avoid the kinds of mistakes they've made. They may offer specific style advice, something you are unlikely to get from a male mentor, who might justifiably feel inhibited discussing, for example, what you're wearing or whether there's something wrong with your makeup.

A woman mentor might also help you with strategies for time management essential to work/family balance. She is more likely to have experience with maternity leaves and with flexible work arrangements, for example. You may not need this advice at the moment, but it's not a bad idea to have someone who's savvy about these matters on your side.

Keep in mind that women executives generally have less time to mentor than do men, especially if they have small children. But as you seek out senior women who've seen your work, don't rule out the busy ones, even if they already have mentees. Often the busiest people are most willing to help. Don't give up. Later in the chapter I'll tell you how to go about finding a mentor.

From the Pioneers: Men and women mentors fill different needs.

Geraldine Laybourne (Founder, Chair, and CEO, Oxygen Media): "Women get caught in a nasty bind with the notion they need some guy to be their mentor. Finding wise people whose judgment you trust, as opposed to looking for hierarchical mentoring, should be your focus."

Women say:

Senior vice president, health care: "There are advantages to both sides. The women can empathize with you more, and the men can give you probably more of an objective response. Whether we like it or not, it's still a man's world . . . and to understand that world, I found it very helpful to get a perspective from a man."

Woman of color vice president, chemicals: "When I became pregnant and had children, my mentors and role models changed to women who had done it and came back to work and were still fully functional. By God, they still had their brains left."

If you're a woman of color, should you have a mentor of color? For women of color, the race and gender of a mentor play an important role in whether a mentor relationship leads to success. Virtually all the women of color pioneers in this book had white male mentors who offered measurable assistance. In Catalyst focus groups, some women of color said they had chosen white male mentors specifically for their clout at the organization.[3] Following are the benefits reaped from mentors by women of color pioneers:

From the Pioneers: Cross-race mentoring offers insights and help.
Roberta Gutman (Corporate Vice President and Director of Global Diversity, Motorola): "All my mentors have been white men. They were just friends of mine; they just told me things. In hindsight, I can tell you that cross-gender and cross-race mentoring teaches us nuances about upward mobility in organizations. There's not enough women to go around. And white men are not afraid." She advises African-American women to "use your sororities. Black sororities have systems set up, and this can work for finding mentors."

Rita Wilson (President, Allstate Indemnity Company): "All of my mentors have been white men, and throughout my career, I never actually selected a mentor, they 'selected' me. My first mentor was a regional vice president in Florida when I was pretty low in the hierarchy. He saw something in my abilities that I, quite frankly, had not recognized in myself at that time.

There were few women in positions of influence, with the kind of corporate experiences that could be of real value. Fortunately, that's changed an awful lot over the years."

There are important things that a woman of color can get only from having a mentor of color, including advice based on shared experiences as a minority. If you need race-related job advice and gender-issue advice, there's no one better than someone who has learned the ropes firsthand to teach you how to deflect or move beyond difficult issues.

Must your mentor be older? Not necessarily. You can learn from anyone and everyone. But I cannot overemphasize the importance of having an experienced mentor whose advice comes with seasoning. Think about choosing someone two to three levels above you. Their experiences might have more in common with your own, than, say, those of a person in the very top tier of your organization would. Not that a top person wouldn't have a great deal to offer you, but you'd expect a different kind of sharing.

Can your mentor be your boss? Yes. A good boss wants you to make him or her aware of any problems you're having. There's no vulnerability here, just appropriate teamwork. Your boss, after all, is charged with developing you and may indeed see himself or herself as your coach/counselor. You can and should have certain expectations of your boss as your coach, even if your relationship doesn't develop into a personal mentoring one. Many people have developed powerful and effective mentor relationships with their bosses. But you might need to save the personal issues for conversations with your other mentors, your network, your personal friends, and your family.

From the Pioneers:
Anne Mulcahy (President and COO, Xerox Corporation) affirms, "Good bosses make great mentors. Where it works, that's the best mentorship you can have."

Make compromises. Compromise on what you expect from one person, knowing that the relationship may expand and that the potential exists to develop other mentoring relationships in the future. But never compromise when it comes to the other person having respect for you as an individual and for your work.

STARTING A MENTORING RELATIONSHIP

Although it's nice to be straightforward in your approach to matters at work, this may not be the best way to go about landing a mentor. Sometimes a mentor wants to believe that he or she has discovered *you*. So, with your list of possible mentors in front of you, proceed with caution. I recommend starting with someone who has seen the best of your work—better yet, a person who has responded positively to it. Supposing no one fits that category, what then? Make yourself visible to a potential mentor and do some investigating. Find out what you can about that person's career trajectory. Know where he or she has worked and what he or she has accomplished, so you know the right questions to ask. Talk to others who have worked with the person, and read back issues of company newsletters to find out more. Volunteer for projects that your first or second choice works on so you can strut your stuff. If members of your network know the person, ask them to consider praising you. Learn what that person does outside of work, for example, nonprofit work, boards, etc., and join up if you can. Do good work there that he or she can see.

Then you can test the water. At an office event or social occasion, approach your target. If such a moment doesn't occur, you might arrange a meeting. One of your network friends might help set one up. Even a cold call at the person's office door at the right moment can work in your favor. I don't recommend lurking around the coffeemaker, but keep your eye open for that person's comings and goings, and you might find an opening.

When face-to-face with the person, ask a question. Women who've had great mentors suggest asking for advice about something related to your career or something about your career linked to something in his or hers or something about your work. Most people are flattered to be asked for advice.

Start small. Don't scare off a potential mentor by asking for too much. The idea of mentoring can seem like another major responsibility; the person might turn you down if the job seems too big. So don't lay it all on your potential mentor at first. Let the relationship evolve. Be realistic about what someone can give you. Build your rapport over time. When seeking an informal mentor, it's not a bad idea to try a little subtlety. Leave the word "mentor" out of the conversation.

Base your approach to a potential mentor on what you know about him or her and on the kind of relationship you have. Use your judgment. If you're working with the person, you know his or her schedule and know how much time he or she has available. If you don't, you might want to develop a phone or e-mail mentoring relationship or one that includes this aspect. Face-to-face contact creates the closest relationships, but compromise where necessary in order to get the mentor you want.

Give back to your mentor. Your mentor generally has a goal in taking you on. There's nothing wrong with that. When starting out, don't give your mentor the impression that you're out only to implement your own career plans. Let him or her know of your respect and support and show that you're going to be helpful right back. Be loyal. Return favors. Be his or her press agent, offer information you pick up in circles the senior folk don't run in. Don't underestimate the value that you, as a protégée, can bring to the relationship.

A good mentor takes pride in the growth and accomplishments of a protégée and often garners respect from others as a result of working with you. Your mentor will bask in your accomplishments along with you. Celebrate both your successes together.

OTHER OPTIONS FOR FINDING MENTORS

Formal mentoring. Does your organization offer a formal mentoring program? If so, you have much to gain from participating. As mentioned earlier, the more diverse the advice you receive, the better, so don't stop at one mentor in a formal program. Over the past few years, I've seen more organizations creating formal programs to fill the mentor gap for women and people of color.

Formal mentoring programs generally choose a mentor for you, in a kind of matchmaking service. In Catalyst's experience, a good formalized relationship sometimes does achieve the depth, scope, and level of commitment experienced in relationships that have developed informally. More often, though, formal relationships are more task-oriented than informal ones, with a focus on specific goals. I advise you to go into such a program not expecting the personal and emotional intensity that an informal relationship may provide, and then you can be pleasantly surprised if it develops. What matters is furthering your career. Don't let your expectations or hopes for closeness overshadow the professional advantages of formal programs.

How do formal mentoring programs work? Some bring people together through social events, so that they can meet and pair naturally. Other programs rely on supervisors to match mentor and mentee based on mutual interests, compatible personalities, and other criteria. Your mentor need not work in your field, and formal programs sometimes emphasize this point: some of the best pairs arise when mentor and protégée work in different functional areas, thus expanding the protégée's network and opportunities for exposure and allowing him or her to communicate openly about sensitive issues, such as problems with a supervisor. Some formal programs use mentors from outside the company.

Some companies have created fairly imaginative mentoring options. Catalyst has worked with "mentoring quads" and mentoring groups or circles, where one or two mentors take on four to nine mentees. In such programs, more men and women are mentored and there are better options for finding good chemistry with a mentor. Catalyst has also worked with companies that create peer mentoring programs, as well as programs in which senior women or men are "mentored" by junior women or men.

Good formal programs have procedures for changing partners and for either of you ending the relationship without retribution. "Divorce is okay," says one program coordinator. And even if the match is not made in heaven, you can benefit from whatever learning your assigned mentor has to offer. As with any mentoring, you and the mentor must commit enough time to give it a good try. Don't give up if the chemistry doesn't seem right in the beginning. Beginnings can be awkward. Set up a minimum of one meeting per month, and if getting together is tough, use e-mail. Work out together how to make the relationship work. You can go to the opera together, go to games together, have breakfast or drinks together.

If your workplace doesn't offer formal mentoring, you might bring that fact to the attention of management. If you decide to play a leadership role in establishing such a structure, you'll achieve the visibility that might attract potential mentors. If you have a women's network at your organization, that's another way to approach the matter.

External mentors. After all is said and done, if it's still impossible to find a mentor in your office, look outside. Mentoring organizations have popped up in recent years across the country; they will pair you with mentors and fill the mentor role with training or tips.* They teach everything from negotiation skills to presentation. The mentor they pair you with will not be able to help you with your office politics, of course, but he or she will

---

*Menttium Corporation, operating out of Bloomington, Minnesota, markets mentoring programs to corporations, creating and monitoring mentoring partnerships; Women Unlimited, New York–based, offers programs in Boston, San Francisco, Orlando, and Chicago. It provides coaching as well as pairing.

be able to give support, advice, and perspective based on his or her own workplace experiences. This external mentor's objective views may prove invaluable, and you may be able to reveal yourself more freely than you'd dare with an inside mentor.

Women's mentoring has evolved into relationships that may be "more about commitment than about chemistry," according to Jean Otte of Women Unlimited, one such mentoring organization. Otte finds that formally forged external mentoring relationships, as well as internal formal programs, focus on "personal growth and development, not on promotions and plums. They are more about learning than power. Mentoring, then, is not about who you know; it's about who knows what you need to know."

When you're seeking an external mentor, control the process in the way I described for seeking informal mentors. Figure out what skills you need to get where you want to go. Learn in advance about any proposed mentor. You can do this by going on the Internet, perhaps, or by calling his or her assistant, looking in *Who's Who*, doing other research at the library. Outline in advance how you'd like the relationship to work and what will be the frequency and type of contact, and then amend it together with the potential mentor. It's important to have a structure in the beginning of such a relationship, as in any formal mentoring relationship, even if that structure changes. And as with any mentoring relationship, stick to it until you're sure it's not working, but don't stick it out forever. If you find it's not working, terminate it as amicably as possible.

CALLING ALL TECHIES: MENTORS FOR THE CLICKING

If you are pursuing or even considering a degree in engineering, science, technology, or mathematics, you may be able to sign up with a Web-based organization called MentorNet (www.mentornet.net) for a year of regular e-mail mentoring from established professionals. The low number of experienced women in technical fields makes mentors hard to find, and MentorNet, which is supported by several large corporations that want to recruit more women in those fields, makes the search more productive and the mentoring process easier and more readily available. Testimonials on the site confirm its success.

Multiple mentors: More can be better. With few people out there to perform the be-all mentor role for women, and with the increasing complexity of career decisions, the word "mentor" has acquired a broader connotation than a traditional adviser on whom you rely.

From the Pioneers: Find mentors in different places.

Lulu Wang (Partner and CEO, Tupelo Capital Management): "Sometimes when young women say there are no role models in their business, I tell them that I think they should look wherever they can, because you can learn excellence even from a distance."

One excellent way to go is to create a panel of mentors at many levels of experience, in a wide range of areas, inside and outside your company. That way, you can get the inside dope from one person, style tips from another, feedback from the third, and so on. It's a win-win situation: you'll get advice on a wide range of career path options, more opinions, and a broader perspective. And you won't exhaust anyone in the process. Consider soliciting advice on a given topic from someone you respect as a "one-shot" mentor, without moving it into a more formal relationship. Instead of focusing on mentoring as a relationship, think of it as learning wherever you can. Mentoring expert Jean

Otte emphasizes that "you don't need a single mentor helping you throughout a career; you need a mind-set that allows you to learn from those around you."

Bad things happen to mentors, too, and you may find your guardian angel disappearing before your eyes, transferred or promoted or downsized or gone by choice. Having other mentors will lessen the blow.

> **From the Pioneers: Get different mentors for different areas.**
> **Carol Bartz** (Chair, CEO, and President, Autodesk) says that when someone asks her to be a mentor, "I don't know what that means: Be their mom? Be responsible for their career success? Share my life secrets with them? I advise women to build a personal mosaic of experts and guides that will cover each of the areas where you need specific information and advice. Someone who's good at office politics, someone who's a good time manager, and so on."

> *Women say:*
> **Vice president for human resources, manufacturing firm:** "Whenever I had an impasse or a conflict, I would call one or more of my mentors and chat with them and get some additional ideas. It's important to have a wide-ranging network of people you can talk to on a variety of issues."

> **Woman of color Catalyst focus group participant:** "You have to talk to different people, almost put your career on your own path and think about it, 'Okay, I want to make this move. I talked with this person and they said this, and this person said this. What do I feel is the best?' You really stand alone and just find people to give you advice in different areas when you don't just flat-out have one person as your mentor."

ENDING A MENTORING RELATIONSHIP AND OTHER STICKY ISSUES

Moving on. You need to know when it's time to move on from a mentor. When the lessons have been learned, the bird must fly.

Let go when you start to need new skills that your current mentor cannot provide or if your mentor can no longer boost you forward. Let go if your mentor shows signs that you're ready.

Some mentors might not want to let you go, especially if you've made a mentor of your boss. In that case, it's important to execute the maneuver with delicacy. You might not even have to say you're ending the relationship; you can just let it wither naturally.

In any case, letting go doesn't mean forgetting your mentor. When you move on, whether for reasons of your own or your mentor's, try to arrange a way to keep in touch. Many women find that being able to call upon mentors as friends later in their careers creates important support, information, and other connections. And as you move on, whenever you get the chance, offer support, information, and connections to your former mentor. I count some of my former protégées among my best friends.

What about backlash? At Catalyst we hear that supervisors sometimes feel threatened or undermined by a subordinate's strong mentor relationship or resent the fact that a mentee now has opportunities he or she never had. Good formal programs take this into account, because a supervisor's cooperation is critical to the success of the program. They include educating supervisors about the program's intent and objectives. If you're in an informal mentoring relationship that incurs animosity, your mentor may be able to find ways to continue your rapport, as well as to minimize your supervisor's fears.

Similarly, you might feel resented by peers and others who do not have mentors. If so, you might pass along some of the pointers in this chapter to them, or give them a copy of this book.

What about bad advice? No mentor is infallible. Some mentors may provide poor advice or outdated views from time to time. Mentoring is a one-on-one relationship, so no one but the mentor controls the information passed on to the mentee. You must use your own judgment, as you would in taking anyone's advice anywhere. Never feel obligated to do what your mentor recommends if it doesn't feel right to you. You can also always get a second opinion.

BE A MENTOR

If you've been fortunate enough to have an effective mentor, you have probably turned the tables and are now mentoring other women. If not, I strongly advise that you do so. Many women want to give back to other women once they've advanced to a certain level. You have a lot of knowledge now, not only about what you do but also about how to deal with issues related to advancement, how to deal with bias, how to crack some glass. I wager you'll enjoy passing that knowledge along.

According to the *Harvard Business Review*'s seminal article on the subject, mentoring is a basic duty of an executive. *HBR* sums it up: "Executive responsibility involves assisting the people down the line to be successful . . . after it helps them, it helps the business."[4] In other words, your mentoring ensures the development of future leaders at your organization, and thinking of the future must be part of an executive's job.

From the Pioneers: Help others.
Roberta Gutman (Corporate Vice President and Director of Global Diversity, Motorola): "We have to reach back and find sisters and say, 'I know something that can help you.' "

Women say:
Vice president, chemicals/manufacturing: "As my career has progressed, I have very consciously taken on the mantle of mentoring. I work at it because I think it's part of the obligation . . . to make sure to get people, especially women who are coming up in the field, out of a 'there's only so many slots for women' mentality."

Woman of color vice president, manufacturing: "It's important to give something back. As you help others, you continue to help yourself. As black women, it's especially valuable that we help each other. If in the wake of being what I am I can leave a space for somebody who looks like me to also succeed, then I will have done something good."

How can you find a mentee? Many young women are out there looking for women to advise them. Make a conscious search throughout your organization. Don't wait for the perfect protégée, and not only because some talent may not be obvious but also because there's much good to be done. Create a shortlist covering a wide range of potential candidates. Begin by showing your admiration and respect for a potential mentee's work and offering words of encouragement. The relationship can evolve from there, with your offering tips and humor as you observe her in action. And although I say "her," I have found that women who mentor young men gain new insights into organizational workings that they might have missed on the way up. And your network will expand. Think diversity. Mentoring people different from you will offer you new insights. I believe women have a responsibility to break the pattern of mentoring only those who resemble ourselves.

How soon can you mentor? I think you'll be ready to help other women quite early in your career. I've found that many women feel they're too junior to mentor, but they're operating under the false idea that you have to know everything in order to give advice to others. When I started out as a teacher, I quickly learned that I needed to know only the subject at hand to pull off a great class. Sometimes I was only one lesson ahead of my students. It is never too early to mentor. Indeed, make mentoring a habit you practice early and often.

Can anyone mentor? Not all people make good mentors. I once worked with an individual I'll call Jack, who was one heck of a role model. When I tagged along with him, I learned a lot about how to handle colleagues and clients. But if I asked him a question about how to do something, impatience would spread over his face. If I didn't do something as well as he would have liked (or would have done it himself), he couldn't turn his annoyance to productive pointers. When I needed him, he stood up for me like the best of champions, and when I wanted inside advice, he was there. He was simply not a teacher.

Don't feel you must be a mother or a be-all-and-end-all adviser, or the job could turn out to be overwhelming. Do what you can. Start small, and if the relationship seems right, then do more.

Finding the time to mentor. Your responsibilities at work and at home may preclude much after-hours mentoring during the week, but a lot of mentoring has always taken place after hours, over dinner or drinks, or during business travel. If you can do that, fine. If not, think of creative alternatives. You might propose mentoring play dates where one or both of you bring your kids to the park and you talk organizational strategy while the kids play.

Don't think of mentoring as requiring face-to-face meetings. Phone mentoring relationships work well, once the one-on-one relationship has been established. More and more women now carry on e-mail mentoring.*

Mentoring benefits the mentor. The benefit for you as mentor is far less subtle than you may think. You will feel more accomplished in your own career when you realize how much you have to impart to someone else.

My mentees often give me the straight scoop when no one else will. A mentee can often offer information or feedback I'd not otherwise have access to. In the same vein, mentoring extends your own network into that of your mentee. If your mentee succeeds, mentoring will continue to work in your favor. In other

---

*In fact, some new mentoring services work completely by e-mail.

words, the relationship will increase your influence base. You need to know what middle management thinks and how the rank and file feel about issues. Have your protégée tell you, but never exploit your relationship by prying into confidences or personal gossip. And have him or her give you the feedback you need at critical junctures in your own career, such as informal performance assessments when you're looking to move up.

Sometimes it's appropriate to get help from your protégée with your workload or to use him or her as a sounding board for your ideas. You've probably picked a smart mentee, and his or her ideas could complement yours. Especially as the relationship matures, you can work together, with you accepting the challenges and insights that come from the younger mind because you have the self-confidence to make argument productive.

But the payoffs of mentoring amount to more than these. I find that little in life satisfies me as much as watching someone "get it," seeing someone learn and gain in confidence and then grow beyond you. Seeing through your protégée's eyes, you'll always be learning as you teach. And mentoring keeps you young—not to mention tuned in to the latest vernacular.

CHAPTER 9

Conduits to Top Leadership

There's a big secret out there that lots of women in the work world aren't told: certain jobs, no matter how good they are, won't take you to the very top of most organizations. If you have your sights set on the pinnacle—(and why shouldn't *you* be the woman CEO who finally brings our membership in that exclusive club to, say, a double-digit percentage?)*—you must have some experience with the bottom line. That means a line job— one with profit-and-loss responsibility. It's important for you to understand just what that means.

This chapter is addressed specifically to those who aspire to (or already practice) management, a discipline that requires specific skills and responsibilities. Some people are promoted to manager because they are good at their jobs, and then they find

---

*As of August 2000, women held fewer than 1 percent of Fortune 500 CEO positions.

that managing doesn't appeal to them or that they're just not suited to the task. For example, one Catalyst study showed that nearly a third of both men and women in business-to-business sales positions were not interested in moving up the career ladder; they wanted to stay in field sales.[1] Their reasons: sales may offer greater compensation than beginning management positions as well as a certain security in the face of layoffs; it offers greater independence and control over schedules; and they may just plain derive job satisfaction from it—they love doing it.

Scientists and engineers, too, often don't want to move up to management. They know that in technical fields, a few years away from the bench can preclude ever returning to the discipline. Getting into senior management probably means, for them, the end of their careers as bench scientists or working engineers. If you fall into one of these categories, the line/staff concept may not be as important to you. But, if you don't, line and staff realities are vital.

Knowledge is power. Many of you probably enjoy management (or will when you get the chance) and are good at it. As to climbing the organizational Everest, some of you will be happy with a success far short of the summit, while some will be determined to reach the top. But one way or another, as you plan your career you need to know all about the business of staff and line.

Most organizations have two paths. One path includes the jobs that involve running the business; these are line, or operational, jobs. The other path is the staff side—human resources, legal, communications, finance—the functions that support those in line jobs. Both play an essential role in the work of any organization.

The line/staff distinction holds sway not only in corporations but also in firms, nonprofits, foundations, and other large organizations, although you'll find differences in various fields regarding what is and isn't a line job. If you're selling consulting

LINE JOBS	STAFF JOBS
• You generate revenue or manage people who do.	• You advise and support the work of people with line (or bottom-line) jobs.
• You have "P-and-L" (profit-and-loss) responsibility.	• You may engage more often in interdepartmental, team-based work.
• You have direct involvement with products, services, or customers.	• You have a broad view of your organization's work.
• You wield direct power.	• Your power lies in influencing others.

services, for example, your consultants are line. If you're producing widgets, line divisions include sales, production, division, and group operating executives. (If you're in human services, the line jobs have client or patient contact.) Line positions always include the chair, CEO, president, chief operating officer, and general manager of an organization. Whether executive vice president, senior vice president, and vice president are considered line jobs depends on their functional area; for instance, executive vice president for human resources (staff), senior vice president for finance (staff), vice president for sales (line).

Line, not staff, positions are the conduits to senior management. There are exceptions, but basically, to reach a top management position, one must spend time working with the nuts and bolts of the business—and prove that one can build revenues as well as manage the business.

A manager who has worked only in a staff support area, such as communications, human resources, finance, or, for the most part, legal, will not have had the opportunity to learn the skills of revenue generation. If you've always worked in staff posi-

JUST THE FACTS

Which jobs are line and which are staff?

Line jobs: Sales, operations, marketing (in some organizations), some finance positions (mergers and acquisitions, for example), manufacturing, product design, consulting, service provision.

Staff jobs: Organizational (or corporate) affairs (assistant to chair, chairman's office, communications, external affairs, investor relations, public relations, government affairs), human resources, CFO and finance, general counsel and other legal, advertising, some marketing, information services, customer relations, customer service, strategy and planning, R-and-D merchandising, product development.

tions, you may indeed have those skills, but you will have had scant opportunity to show them off or to hone them. This means you are likely to lack the kind of experience required for the very highest management positions.

That said, let me add a few important considerations:

1. You may genuinely prefer staff positions. In general, more people work in staff positions than in line positions. More than 60 percent of the senior executives in our *Women in Corporate Leadership* survey held staff positions. One reason many women elect to work in staff positions is that they're considered more women-friendly than line positions. The hours may be more predictable; you might find, for example, it's easier to regulate your work to allow for personal life. Then again, you might not. Staff jobs have inched closer to line jobs in America lately, with people on both tracks working overtime—to prove themselves and get ahead. Another big reason to prefer a career in staff may be that the last thing in the world you want to do is run an operation and be responsible for the P and L.

2. Senior management positions of great responsibility exist in both staff and line; it's simply that the staff-job ladder usually stops short of the very top.

3. The times are changing, and talent is in short supply. These days, there are companies trying to work out ways for that much-needed talent to get to the top by a much greater variety of paths. I know of at least one CEO who came up through a corporation's legal department. (However, since being a woman executive is already rather unorthodox, my advice is to stick to a more traditional path if you're determined to reach the top.)

And, of course, there is what might be number 4: Very few people ever reach the pinnacle of their organizations, no matter what career path they've selected or fallen into, yet many people can have extremely successful careers in senior positions, line *or* staff.

Functional rotation between line and staff may be the best way to get into top management. Not only do you need line experience to get to the top of your organization; as a general proposition, you need staff experience, as well. You'll need at least one rotation into a staff job, and probably more. Why? A line job focuses on a particular operation of the company. If you're a buyer, it might be for menswear. If you're in pharmaceutical sales, you take your pharmaceuticals out to doctors and hospitals. If you're running a muffler factory, you concentrate on getting mufflers out. You have a specific focus; you don't have the big picture.

You simply can't learn everything you need to know to run an organization from a single line job or even a series of different line jobs. With a series, you'll know more, but you still won't have the overview of the whole operation. By taking the right staff job, you can get that big picture, plus broader experience. Staff positions work a different set of muscles than line jobs do. In them, you exercise the skills of negotiation and wielding influence; you learn tolerance for ambiguity and lack of closure;

you are more likely to perform team-based work. You might more often find interdepartmental work part of your responsibilities.

Although line work can provide you with visibility that carries back to headquarters, the right staff job, actually located at headquarters, offers great exposure and will show you off, up close, to senior management so they know who you are and how you work. Staff positions offer a window on corporate politics that most line positions lack. In addition, the right staff job at headquarters will give you an overview of the overall business. You'll learn how information moves from the field to headquarters, how headquarters deals with it, and how decisions are made. One woman pioneer explained that before she held such a job, she didn't understand how difficult it can be to get the correct information from the field, the information one needs before decisions can be made. The jobs that offer such experience include strategic planning, high-level financial work, certain types of positions in the legal department, assistant to the chair, and certain high-level human resources jobs.

How long should you remain in one of these positions? For about the same length of time you'd stay in a line position: two to three years, until you've learned what you need to know. Note how the men in your organization do it: they rotate through jobs and move on to senior management roles.

From the Pioneers: Switching functions is the key to success.
Rebecca McDonald (Chair and CEO, Enron Asia-Pacific, Africa, and China): "I thought it would be a great opportunity to sit at the right hand of a talented person, to see how decisions got made in the head office. I had just enough business maturity to know I wanted to understand how strategic and tactical decisions get made."

Carol Bartz (Chair, CEO, and President, Autodesk): "I knew that people who got rewarded had pretty broad knowledge, and I always liked corporate, not believing as some did that it's just a bunch of politics. Staff jobs are part of a journey. It's an invaluable thing to get a stint with the head of the company. I liked looking through corporate eyes. If I'd stayed in the field in sales and sales management, I wouldn't have had the broad experience."

Maureen Kempston Darkes (President and General Manager, General Motors of Canada): "Use staff jobs to gain as much knowledge of the business as you can. Then get as much operational experience as you can—go after the operational jobs, let it be known you want the opportunity to get them."

Anne Mulcahy (President and COO, Xerox Corporation) supports the strategy of switching functions: "I went and took the human resources job for Xerox as chief of staff. I departed from my previously mentioned approach," where she went straight for the line jobs, avoiding the staff positions. She explains, "I really decided I needed to look at the company from a different perspective. This was about eight years ago. I worked on both the organizational designs and culture change. That was a breakthrough in terms of coming out of the functional ladder approach to a much broader state of experience in terms of my career."

The perception of "women as staff" can hinder your mobility. The majority of women who participated in Catalyst's *Women in Corporate Leadership* survey* were on career paths that would not take them to the highest management levels, where they could run their organizations. The majority of these women

---

*Catalyst surveyed more than 1,200 senior executive women in Fortune 1000 companies at the vice president level and above, as well as Fortune 1000 CEOs. The vast majority were within two reporting levels of the CEO. Average annual income was $248,000. Seventy-two percent were married, 64 percent had children, and two thirds of the latter had children under eighteen. A third had MBAs, and most had twenty-five or more years of experience. (*Women in Corporate Leadership: Progress and Prospects* [New York: Catalyst, 1996].)

held staff jobs—some by choice, some because they'd advanced too far in staff before realizing they were stuck, some because they'd taken well-intended advice that had steered them into a situation where "glass walls" had blocked their mobility and stifled their ambition. "Glass walls" is a term coined by Catalyst to represent invisible barriers that prevent women from moving between functions and getting the experience of the variety of responsibilities that organizations require for upward movement. When they'd started out, these senior staff executives in our survey simply hadn't known enough about the workings of the work world to be aware of the necessary components of an upward career path. They learned by trial and error, and many have passed along what they learned in the verbatim remarks quoted in this book.

Organizations and the individuals in them have positioned few women to make it to senior management. (See "Just the Facts" box on page 186.) A decisive 82 percent of CEOs interviewed for *Women in Corporate Leadership* said that a lack of significant general management or line experience is the most crucial factor holding women back. Forty-seven percent of the women agreed, indicating that they, too, believed that women still need to grasp the importance of line experience to their climb.

CEOs say:
CEO, Fortune 500 company: "The reason there are not many women in the senior ranks is not that women haven't been in the pipeline long enough to advance; it's what they've done while they are in the pipeline."

I've found that many women starting out today still do not know the right questions to ask of their bosses about the career paths leading to senior management. What if it happens that you're more talented than your boss and he or she refuses to see

JUST THE FACTS

Women Occupy Few of the Top Positions in Corporate Leadership*

There are two women CEOs in the Fortune 500.

Among corporate officers of the Fortune 500, women hold 6.2% of the top titles (CEO, chairman, vice chairman, president, chief operating officer, senior executive vice president, and executive vice president).

Women hold 139 of 1,376 executive vice president and senior executive vice president positions.

Line Positions Remain Male-Dominated

Men hold 93% of all line positions among corporate officers.

*2000 Catalyst Census of Women Corporate Officers and Top Earners of the Fortune 500 (New York: Catalyst, 2000).

---

your potential? What if your boss tells you that what you want isn't for you? Whom should you go to? You need to exercise caution in going over your boss's head; it's a dangerous game. Some ways to go: learn about company advancement programs; talk to women who have succeeded; go outside your department; or connect with senior line women and get their advice. Speak to your outside mentor or your network. If you still can't get yourself moved into the functional role you think you need, go outside the company. Take your marketability seriously, get in touch with headhunters, explore options. This is why people jump from one company to another.

A cautionary word about changing functions: when a woman is offered an opportunity to move from line to staff, a different scenario may result from that which occurs when a man makes such a move. It's not unheard-of for a man to move through a stint in human resources or strategic planning, then in a year or two move out into another line job. Historically, women have not fared so well at this. The pioneers who have succeeded at it are the exception rather than the rule. Try to get your plan in writing if you know you're going to want to rotate out—or you might find yourself stuck.

> **From the Pioneers: Changing from staff to line is a challenge.**
> **Anne Mulcahy** (President and COO, Xerox Corporation) explains that when she moved to a staff position, "I had fifteen years of experience managing P and L at Xerox. My experience and timing were important. If you have a track record, it can ensure that you don't get caught in a staff ghetto. I went into a staff position in a position of strength. I did it to stretch my capabilities and experience. It was clear I had demonstrated the line performance. Now it was time to expand my core performance."
>
> **Ellen Hancock** (Chair and CEO, Exodus Communications) took a job managing a staff function at IBM that subsequently paved the way for greater P-and-L responsibility. "If I'd said no when the corporation said they wanted me to get certain experience, I might not have gotten my later assignments," she asserts. However, she lays out strong caveats and some terrific advice about deciding whether to take a staff job. "Some staff roles don't lead to a line position. When looking at any job—line or staff—look two jobs out. Look at the current one you're addressing and the most probable assignment after that one. Think about where the job will go and if it's going where you want to be. Ask if you like the trajectory. Don't box yourself." Her second caveat: "Be sure you have the right mentors, properly placed, that can vouch for you and assure you will move on." Third, she says, "Always talk about the next step. No one will sign a paper on it, but at least be sure that you and your boss are going into it the same way, that both of you see it as a broadening assignment to give you greater strength going forward." She adds a fourth piece of advice: "Then trust your instincts. It's a combination of conversations and trust that will assure your continued upward progress."

Cross-functional rotation. Some organizations offer formal rotation programs for career paths that include both line and staff positions. Most career paths that take people to senior management involve rotations, but they're not necessarily well planned, balanced, or strategic. You want them to be so, if possible. If you can work with your organization in a formal rotation program, you're likely to get the breadth of experience you need to run the place. Or you can do so informally, making a career path for yourself that allows you to gather varied experience. For example, you can go first into sales and sales management, where you're in the field, then move to a job in corporate headquarters, where you can see the general lay of the land as Anne Mulcahy described. At headquarters, you're closer to the line of sight of senior managers, who can see you work and learn to rely on you and take risks with you. More than one of the women pioneers included in this book moved into corporate from the field or from business units and found it gained them experience and exposure. Their bosses saw their promise, and that led to their taking chances on them by offering them line assignments. Their success in the new positions led to their moving up.

Beware of the wrong advice about functional areas. It can and does happen that someone you respect and trust and who cares about you and your future gives you bad advice. Be on the alert for "negative mentoring," such as when a well-meaning individual praises you as a "people person" who would surely excel in human resources or public relations. This may well be true, and

---

IF YOU'RE LOOKING FOR A LINE JOB

Ask the right questions of your potential employer. When you're interested in landing a job in line management, you need to know specific things about the organization you're considering before you can make a decision about whether you can succeed there. Does it care about developing employees? Does it have a system for identifying and advancing people who demonstrate leadership talent? Have women made it to the top? Ask questions such as the following (although not all at once) when you're considering a position:

- What are the opportunities for lateral movement and cross-functional rotation?
- Have many women made the shift from staff to line lately?
- Do you offer management training?
- How can I learn about opportunities? Are jobs posted?
- How are high potentials identified?*
- What is the career path for the track I'm getting onto?
- Is there a succession-planning process? How does it work?
- Who are the success stories? Are they in line positions, in top positions? Can I meet them?

---

* "High potentials" is a term used in business to represent employees who should be channeled into the fast track to senior management. There's always a way of identifying them, but it may be secretive and biased.

---

if it's what you want, go for it. But what if it isn't? Well-intentioned but incorrect advice has stymied many a talented woman's upward progress. Don't let it limit you.

You should also know that you may not get help—even if you get the right advice—from the human resources department. Although many human resources professionals know that one key way to develop high-potential employees is to provide line opportunities, many organizations have not yet managed to practice what they preach. On paper and in theory, they affirm that promising women in staff should gain this experience. But in actuality, many organizations continue to assume that women in staff roles lack interest in line positions or the qualifications for them. Even human resources departments still have stereotypes to shed. And, of course, most have many other concerns besides your career.

Beware the possible pay cut. Another glitch in your moving from staff to line may result from pay issues. Your organization may even hesitate to offer you a job for this reason. If accepting a line job requires taking a pay cut, should you consider it? A few of the pioneers in this book accepted a pay cut as the price of a lateral move. But you may not have to today. Many organizations have implemented broadbanding, which groups jobs together in a way that offers a wider range of salaries; you might move to the top range of the new band you're in, so that you can keep your current salary during your transition phase. Women have more leverage now than they did five years ago, so remember to negotiate.

Seek line assignments early if you want to aim for the top. Remember, it's harder for a woman to reach top management than it is for a man. The particular challenges women face mean that you should consider taking a line position during your earliest job planning if you want to work toward a senior executive position. You have the best chance to succeed if you plan your career early on.

I can't stress this enough: working in a line position as early as you can will start to give you the experience in management and revenue responsibility that is critical to advancement. If you're already working, look around and decide where you might like to land a line job; then make it known that as soon as possible that's what you want. In the earliest stages of your career, when you're most likely to be flexible, you might be amenable to

BEFORE YOU TAKE ANY JOB

Ask yourself first, "How far do I want to go?" Some of you may know right off that you want to head toward the corner office and vie for the position of chief executive officer. But not everyone in management wants to advance all the way to the top. You may prefer a job in middle management that pays the salary you want. Or you may want a balance between your life and your work that precludes putting in the time required to reach the highest levels of management or even to work full-time. Or you may delight in the type of work you can do in communications, public affairs, or human resources.

Still, just to keep your options open, consider starting out on the fast track. You can always jump off, but—right or wrong—you can't always jump on.

working the unpredictable and often long hours that line jobs entail. Things get harder when you need to relocate, say, to a plant situated in a place where a spouse will have difficulty finding work. Some jobs may require traveling or taking international assignments, which you should go for while you're the most mobile. Try to get the jobs with the most travel or relocation requirements under your belt while you're young.

If you're currently in midcareer, do not despair. Many of our pioneers have demonstrated considerable cleverness in making the switch; take their tips to heart. But there are problems. For example, from the company's point of view, a division might resist taking on an expensive person, which you're more likely to be once you've been working at the company for a while. Sometimes a CEO's budget includes a fund to encourage such rotations without your having to cut your salary and without taking a chunk of the division's budget, so if you're considering a switch and you're relatively high in the organization, ascertain if your organization has such an opportunity for you.

From the Pioneers: Go for the line jobs.
Dorrit Bern (Chair, CEO, and President, Charming Shoppes): "The first couple of years are critically important. If you start early enough and demonstrate you have an ability to make

money for the company, men won't have trouble giving you bigger jobs. The beauty of being able to make a profit is that your talent can't be ignored. But if you get maneuvered out of P-and-L responsibility into a staff position, even if they promise you'll be brought back, nine of ten times you're not. Once you're shoved off into support functions, you'll never make it to the top. If women want to be successful and move up, they have to have ahold of the P and L."

Anne Mulcahy (President and COO, Xerox Corporation) understood the importance of line: "I started in sales. The reason I did it was because it was line, it was core to the company, and it was a totally tangible way to measure my success. It was a performance-oriented assignment. I wanted something that could be judged on absolute performance. It was a tactical decision."

What constitutes a line job? An entry-level line job at a manufacturing company might be at one of the company's plant facilities where you would supervise a phase of production in the manufacture of a product.* These jobs may be called "operations" positions. On the other hand, starting in a sales job offers immediate experience in revenue generation. A sales position may lead to sales supervision and on up the ladder. In the retail field, you might land a job as a buyer. Another example: brand management is at the heart of the business in a consumer products company and makes a good place to start.

What your organization sees as a line job might not be what another organization does. Marketing jobs are a case in point. Most organizations consider marketing a staff job. However, if you have a marketing job with a brand for which you hold responsibility for the P and L—and consider yourself unusual if you do—and for making numerical goals based on brand

---

*Some organizations would never put a nonengineer in a product-manufacturing slot; others have begun to experiment.

performance, your job is closer to line than staff jobs. Again, P and L is the key. Our pioneer Andrea Jung moved up the ladder at Avon via this route.

Is a line position right for you? Line positions serve as key steps to senior management jobs, but they do have their drawbacks. Women make up a mere 7.3 percent of corporate officers in line positions in the Fortune 500. As indicated earlier, you'll be in the minority wherever you go, and you could easily be the only woman in a factory or plant—you could be the woman pioneer, breaking ground as the first woman whom men have reported to. You may face stereotypes harbored by male managers about women's potential, women's commitment to their jobs, women's mobility, and women's family responsibilities—but you'll probably face these anyway. You may find your sense of humor working overtime to deal with the kidding and comments. The time commitment necessary to succeed may make a flexible schedule well nigh impossible, and work schedules may be unpredictable, or they may involve shift work. In order to get the right experience, a change of location will almost always be involved as well.

If it is impossible to get into a line area, take a staff position close to where line activities occur; for example, in a human resources position at a manufacturing facility. While there, take on tasks that expose you to senior management. Or working at corporate headquarters, performing brilliantly at a job in planning, might show off your strategizing skills and give you an overview of the organization; it's also a visible position where senior management might pick up on you. Or grab a beginning job in distribution at headquarters. That may lead to other line positions, especially if you take on the tough tasks. Wherever you are, make it clear to your boss right off that you are interested in learning the business.

Staff positions offer power and influence. If you are a person who likes to have influence, a career in staff may be right for you. In staff, you work behind the scenes, and you might not get a lot of recognition for your accomplishments. You won't have the same kind of direct power that an individual who wields a P and L has, but you have power nonetheless; and if you have the ear of the CEO, you will have more power than line executives out in the field. Indeed, if you work your way up to senior vice president or executive vice president in human resources or legal, you'll have the power to make things happen or stop them from happening. You'll have the power to change organizational culture. In certain areas, such as human resources, legal, and strategic planning, you can have a direct influence on molding the organization and its policies, both internal and external. You may even play a role in influencing the direction of the organization. In communications, you have responsibility for how the organization is presented to the world and can work on the organization's image.

Understand your options and know your organization. Make an informed decision when determining the job track you want. If you're interested in gaining experience in both line and staff jobs, there are ways you can help ensure your success. First, know the history of the company with others in your kind of position: Have promises been kept? Have people been moved through staff positions and back into line positions? Do your research. Do you trust the person making the promise? Can you get it in writing, in case that person moves on during your sojourn?

Control your advancement. You can avoid waking up when it's too late to do anything about your career direction if you understand career paths, know the difference between line and staff, keep yourself on track, and clearly communicate what you want. Since you can't be sure that one organization is like another, if you're interviewing for a new position or trying to change functions, ask about the path for each job you're considering. And once you land the job, continue discussing this with your boss and others in the know; it should be part of an ongoing career dialogue so that you get the opportunities that have been promised to you. It would be great if a fairy godmother–boss would monitor your ongoing career and assure you that you're moving in the right direction, but that probably won't happen. The primary responsibility for your getting onto and staying on a career track lies with you.

≈

CHAPTER 10

What to Expect at a Firm

Professional women tell Catalyst they love their careers and the rewards they reap. However, they also tell us that life at a firm poses specific challenges for women. In this chapter, I will help you prepare for those challenges. If you're in the process of deciding where you want to work, you'll find here the pros and cons of professional firms' culture and how to parry the cons and catalyze the pros to realize a satisfying career. If you're already established at a firm and are familiar with the issues, you'll find insights here about what you can do to enhance your success.

THE BASIC DIFFERENCES BETWEEN
A FIRM AND A CORPORATION

At a firm, you'll find ways of working, conducting business, and achieving power and influence that make your career totally different from one you'd have as a professional at a corporation or nonprofit, a foundation, and so on. These differences result not only from the kind of work being done but from the very structure of a firm. In essence, firms consist of partners who share in the profits and associates who are working their way up to partnership. By contrast, corporations and other organizations have many more layers of hierarchy, and advancement comes by working one's way up a ladder of salaried positions.

Since you'll find upsides and downsides to each option, you need to assess them according to your own needs and ambition. If the advantages and opportunities uniquely available at a firm are right for you, if they fit your personality and ambition, you should go with a firm and stick with it. On the other hand, many people start in firms and move to other organizations once they've gained experience. Others start in the public sector and then move to a firm or other private-sector setting. Your options may be determined by the time demands of your personal life weighed against your professional goals. Go in with your eyes wide open, and you'll be in a position to reap the considerable rewards of a firm career.

What Do Firms Uniquely Offer?

1. *Partnership.* Partners own their firm, run it, and perform client service. It may take up to twelve years working as an associate before you achieve partnership, the locus of power in a firm. As owners, partners have considerable autonomy and freedom in the kind of work they do (normally within their specialty) and work both collaboratively and independently. Costs and profitability loom large as concerns for partners, as their own earnings come from the firm's profits. Partners are evaluated by their peers. Such positions rarely exist at corporations.

2. *Criteria for partnership.* The first eight to twelve years of your career will be devoted to doing whatever is required to

make partner.* The criteria for partnership vary from firm to firm but usually entail bringing in money, billing a certain number of hours, doing notable client work, having technical ability, building strong (often social) rapport with clients and with partners inside the firm, having an executive presence, showing fealty to the firm, working in firm-related projects, and sometimes doing pro bono work. You need expertise in a particular area, as well as broad skills that facilitate integration of the firm's resources for your client. Proving yourself to be of partner quality may require several years of a nose-to-the-grindstone approach to the work you're assigned. Some associates join a firm for the experience and leave when they've had enough for their purposes.

3. *The role of an expert.* At a firm, you're an expert adviser in your area. By contrast, most professionals in legal, financial, human resources, or PR departments at corporations perform a generalist role.

4. *Client service.* You focus primarily on clients and their needs. You need to be accessible to them and may work on their site for days or weeks at a time. It's sometimes said that when working at a firm, you "advise"; in corporations and other organizations, you "do." An adviser lacks the ability to implement what he or she knows needs to be done, so for some, advising may be frustrating.

5. *Deal making.* Depending on your specialty, you're more likely to find opportunities for deal making (e.g., buying and selling businesses) at a firm than at a corporation, where you'll get the chance to buy and sell assets only if you're in mergers and acquisitions or are a senior manager. Investment banking firms are the prime area for deal makers.

*Time to partnership varies by individual firm and by type of firm: some accounting firms have switched to twelve years to partnership; at some New York law firms, associates wait eight to twelve years; while some management consulting firms consider associates for partner six to seven years after they start.

6. *New-business generation.* Part of making it to partnership and partnership itself includes bringing in new clients, which is known as rainmaking. You're selling your professional expertise and that of the firm to new clients. At corporations, those in marketing and sales have the responsibility of new-business generation, but in other corporate areas, you're not likely to have to focus on this activity.

7. *A multiplicity of roles.* While you're working your way to partnership, you may have the opportunity to work for different industries. When working on teams, you're exposed to the expertise of many different individuals at the firm, giving you a breadth of contacts and potential supporters.

8. *Growth spurts.* At a firm, you may have the opportunity to do exciting, even heady, things that would normally be ahead of your years. Young partners at some firms have the chance to work directly with the CEOs of prestigious companies and have their counsel valued. You can see your own growth. At a corporation, your learning curve is likely to be slower unless you're unusual in garnering high-risk assignments at an early stage.

9. *Compensation.* Firms usually pay better starting salaries than you'll find elsewhere, and after you make partner and share in the firm's earnings, you'll earn more than you would in middle management at a corporation. This difference may narrow or disappear as you progress at a corporation, as senior-level corporate counsel positions often pay salaries equivalent to what you'd earn at a firm.*

10. *Heavy time and travel demands.* For the most part, the time demands at a firm are more acute than at a corporation.

---

*A 1998 PricewaterhouseCoopers survey found that the highest-level in-house corporate counsel positions pay as much as the average partner earns at a top-fifty law firm (1998 U.S. Law Department Spending Survey). Corporations often offer stock options to senior-level people, while in a firm, profit sharing boosts income. You should research salaries and add that information to the pot before you decide which option is better for you.

Certain types of firms require intensive time commitments, some at specific times of the year (e.g., tax time) or at specific stages of your career (especially the two years before partnership), others whenever you're working closely with clients. You're responsible for billing a certain number of hours at most firms, and those numbers have climbed over the past decade, increasing the time commitment you must make to client work. At firms with project-oriented work, each project generally has a well-defined time of completion, so things can let up if you organize your work to take breathers between projects—for example, to take a vacation. Since some firm jobs necessitate work at a nonlocal client's site, travel may take considerable time as you commute back and forth each week. In addition, long and sometimes unpredictable hours on the job, as well as travel and having to put in extra hours without notice and beyond your control, will have ramifications for your lifestyle. For those who love the work, this adds to the sense of a job well done. For others, it can be a significant drawback.

CHALLENGES FOR WOMEN IN FIRMS

A professional firm may offer you a career that's challenging and exciting. But the playing field for women and men is no more level at firms than at other kinds of organizations, and at times the terrain may be even more uneven. Firms in general have responded more slowly to the demographic changes in the American workforce related to women and people of color. I don't present the challenges that follow, with insights from women who've been there, to discourage you but to inform you: forewarned is forearmed.

Challenge 1. Firms change at a snail's pace. This slowness to change results in part from the partnership structure. Partnerships require a great deal of consensus management, making it difficult to hold partners accountable for women's advancement and retention, whereas a strong leader at another type of organization may choose at any time to hold subordinate managers accountable. Where client service takes precedence, firms find little incentive to invest in internal structures or initiatives that would catalyze such change. Partners become partners for their expertise and their client service, not because they excel at managing people. Those in support functions at firms—for example, those doing internal work—are not on the partnership track, which clearly communicates the lack of importance placed on such work.

You can find firms that focus on people management skills and systems, but they're unusual, and obviously that has negative implications for the women who work there—and often for the men as well. A lack of such systems leaves a management void that unfortunately is filled by relationship-based decision making. As one might expect in such a situation, the all-too-human tendency to hire, develop, and promote those one is most comfortable with (read: *those most like oneself*) comes to the fore. Too often, that doesn't include women.

Challenge 2. Myths and stereotypes still flourish.

Women say:
Partner, law firm: "The atmosphere is fairly alienating to women. Even though I've been successful and . . . am respected as a lawyer, I think I'm also found to be threatening. I'm just not one of them."

Catalyst focus group participant: "Ninety-five percent of the [securities] industry is men. I don't know if it's just that they don't want to let women in, they don't want to train them and work with them. They see them more as sales assistants than colleagues."

Senior manager, professional services: "Frequently you're asked to relocate if you want to be partner. I don't know if the question even gets asked of women. Sometimes it's assumed that because their husband works and has a good job, they probably don't want to move."

The culture at many firms has served to perpetuate the "old boys' network," wherein biases and myths regarding women loom large. Just like managers at other types of organizations, many male partners fall prey to false preconceptions about women's abilities and commitment. That continues to thwart women's progress at firms.

Although the stereotypes damage women's chances and opportunities, the most pernicious is "the client trump card," which can be played by partners at whim. It means that partners can fail to assign women to the teams serving the most highly visible, most important clients, and so women miss out on the experiences, contacts, and exposure that grease the fast track to partnership. It makes women reluctant to ask for flexible work arrangements: "Clients don't want women who won't be accessible all the time." This assumption and others have been disproved by Catalyst research, but they are so instilled in many firms' cultures that it may be years after women reach a critical mass before the myths disappear.

Challenge 3. Women need to learn business development. Business development is integral to partnership. But a common preconception about women in firms is that we're not good at business development, we're not rainmakers. Rainmaking serves as one of the key criteria for partnership in most firms. You don't want to be someone others must bring work to, or you'll end up a principal, not a partner, and not by choice. In some cases, the importance of new-business development has not been made clear. In others, women have found it intimidating. Either way, women at firms too often don't focus on developing this essential skill. (See "Ten Ways to Make Rain" on pp. 215–17.)

From the Pioneers: Firms seek rainmakers.
Barbara Paul Robinson (Partner, Debevoise & Plimpton): "You can't just be good at servicing clients, you can't just do a perfect job, you have to bring in business. For women, developing business—in financial services, as well as in legal services—is really hard. You've got to woo clients, and big high-paying clients are what matter. It's hard for all young people to develop business, and harder for women to get the large corporate business controlled by men as clients. These men went to the same all-male schools, they know each other, they socialize, play golf. That stuff is alive and well and continues in grown-up life. I'm now working in a rainmaking network of women lawyers. We're working out other strategies for bringing in new business, like going to the ballet or the theater."

Women say:
Partner, management consulting firm: "Too many women believe they can't sell. They hide until late in their career, then panic. They don't understand the mechanics of selling: that you need ten pitches to close one. There is a fear of not being liked, of not being accepted."

Partner, tax firm: "The firm is frustrating and challenging. Each partner is expected to generate $3.5 million in fees each year. I can never do a good job at everything."

Partner, tax firm: "You are promoted based on how much money you are making the firm. You have to grow the practice."

Partner, management consulting firm: "Rainmaking is the key yardstick. We tolerate a lot of people who bring in business who chew people up."

Some say that rainmakers are born, not made, and there's some truth to this. Like a born salesman, a person who is adept at bringing in new business often does seem to have a natural affinity for that work. It's also true that if you're lucky enough to land a born rainmaker as a mentor, useful pointers and leads will come your way, and you can become a rainmaker by nurture, if not nature. Yes, male mentors teach protégés how to develop business, and, yes, since women often lack such mentors, you might miss out on this opportunity. In fact, this lack is key to men's making it to partner more quickly than women. Catalyst finds that many women can get caught off guard by the criticism "You're not a rainmaker" when they're up for partner.

Challenge 4: The up-or-out model. The career path and the pace of advancement at most firms have traditionally been to move to partner on a preset schedule or you're chopped liver. This up-or-out model,* with its emphasis on achieving partnership in an inflexible, immutable time frame, creates difficulties for both women and men. If you're heading for partner, you're always aware of having to make the grade. You need to know the right people and make the right connections both inside and outside the firm. Since the eight- to twelve-year partner track often falls during your mid to late thirties, you can get caught between your professional and family goals. The toughest time comes during the hard push for partnership, as at sixth year for law associates, or eighth to tenth year for senior managers in professional services firms. Many women tell Catalyst that the partner track and the biological clock are on a collision course. The partner track rarely provides suitable flexibility for those whose talent a firm would do well to retain but who want both career and family. Once you're a partner, though, things may calm down; I've heard from many women that it's easier to have a family after you've made partner.

---

*"Up or out" usually entails moving along on the partnership track: for example, holding the classifications of staff, senior, manager, senior manager, or partner. Employees spend three years at each level, working full-time and being measured against other same-year hires. Anyone who doesn't make partner or is not perceived as partner material must leave.

Some firms offer an alternative to partnership (sometimes called principal), but it's often considered a consolation prize. The only career track to power at a firm is full partnership, and principals don't have the same clout as partners, either outside or inside the firm. Second, a firm may not have laid out how the position of principal differs from that of partner and may have made the former an attractive option. Indeed, "principal" means different things at different firms; some use the term interchangeably with "partner." In some instances, a principal is a niche expert, a specialist without the broader experience of partners; in this case, he or she serves as a resource to client teams. In others, a principal might be accomplished in all areas, but less so than partners. Or he or she might be outstanding in every area except business development. One also finds principals in professional support positions: for example, in human resources, finance, or compliance, with as many as 80 percent of the latter being women. Individuals functioning in capacities other than partner or on the partner track at most firms don't get the same financial rewards or respect as partners or those on the partner track. Principals lack voting rights in the partnership.

Because of the lack of power, prestige, and financial rewards, many professionals, both men and women, find the alternatives to becoming a partner unattractive. In the past few years, registering their objections with voice or feet, they've forced some firms, including high-profile firms, to recognize the limitations of the up-or-out model, especially for women whose talent they want to retain. These firms have felt the cost of attrition. They are working to create a viable, long-term career model that is attractive to those who want to have options about how they work at different career (and life) stages.

Challenge 5. *Client service calls for immediate responsiveness.*
The client service focus of a firm may create an environment with erratic and tight time constraints. Your success depends on

delivering service to your clients, and clients want what they want when they want it. There may be times when you have to be ready at any hour of the day or night or weekend to handle unanticipated requests. "Face time," the amount of time you're seen in the office, matters a great deal in some firms—so that it's evident that you're available for clients. The best survive through skilled time management, but thriving requires learning to manage clients' expectations and demands.

Men and women alike express distress at the demands of today's firms, as is evident from the verbatim statements in this book from those who've been through it. Some give up on their firm aspirations and move to organizations where they have greater control over their schedules. This is not to say that other organizations won't call on you to work late hours or weekends, to travel at the last minute, or to choose between attending your son's school play and closing a deal, but you won't have to cancel such important personal events as frequently. Attrition for such reasons has increased, and some firms have taken note and responded, though the syndrome is tough to break in competitive and fast-paced environments.

Women say:

Former senior associate, management consulting firm: "It goes beyond my imagination to think about having a baby and working at the firm. I really enjoyed being a consultant, and I probably wouldn't have left if I could have seen myself balance a family with a job."

Partner, law firm: "You could talk about a lot of different issues such as turnover, but the main one is, can you be a partner here and have a family? And there is no partner, no woman partner, who has any children."

Woman of color associate, management consulting firm: "The partners have a short-term outlook on people. They really don't care whether you are there until two or three in the morning.

They know people come and go, and there is always an associate who is willing to work really hard. The attitude is that associates, and to a certain extent, senior associates, are fungible."

Challenge 6. The billing system is a tyrant. In many law, accounting, and consulting firms, you record your "billable hours," time that gets billed to your clients.* Some law firms require 1,800 to 2,000 or more billable hours per year. To accomplish 1,800 hours of billability, you have to charge clients thirty-five hours each week for fifty-two weeks. Some big-city law firms reward associates with bonuses if they bill more than 2,500 hours. If you're billing at such high rates, forget about vacation time, sick time, and internal business—you're working more than ten hours a day. Many firms of all types require that you be at least "70 percent billable" or more. In big cities, associates and partners alike may work at least one day every weekend. Add onto this the time you need for new-business generation—a top priority that does not get billed—and you're spending maybe another ten hours at work each week.

Firms consider billability a gender-neutral partnership criterion, but it clearly poses a disadvantage for women. Billing 2,000 hours a year leaves little time for child rearing or anything else. A study by the Center for Research on Women at Wellesley College states that firm culture "[mandates] a lifestyle standard that assumes 'successful' lawyers have no family obligations and/or have an invisible life support system supplied by a spouse, and [enacts] organizational dynamics that favor men."[1]

Challenge 7. The flexible work arrangements paradox. Such a situation would make anyone loath to ask for a work schedule that would reduce the number of hours they bill or their time in the office, even at the growing number of firms with such poli-

---

*Other types of firms, such as public relations firms, also require you to bill your hours.

cies on the books. Women in firms are not alone in this, as corporate women report a similar situation. Indeed, most women—and men, as well—fear the career repercussions of using flexible work arrangements. Catalyst has found that some professionals who officially work part-time, two to three days per week, for example, actually often work more.[2] Even in the best-case scenarios, women lawyers who go part-time and remain on the partner track (or already are partners) frequently find they must switch their specialties to areas considered more family-friendly.

You're much more likely to find flexible work arrangements at a corporation than at a firm, although at a corporation, too, the "face time" required may get in the way. In firms, if a woman partner goes part-time, she may find her commitment questioned by the full-time partners. Part-time partners who return to full-time work often find the cultural barriers higher than ever, maybe even impossible to surmount.

Challenge 8. Exclusion. Client service includes not only performing outstandingly on projects but also socializing with clients and with key players at the firm. Women often undervalue the importance of the social aspects of client service or may even be oblivious to them. Similarly, women may not focus on developing the personal relationships with colleagues and partners that are requisite to success. Even when they do focus on them, they must work hard to be included. Women at some firms tell Catalyst they feel ostracized from an "all-boys club," that they aren't "part of the clique."

The choice of venue for socializing remains an issue in some firms, and, believe it or not, men still take clients to topless bars and wonder why women lack a sense of humor about it. This may astonish many of you, especially Generation X women and younger, who were treated as peers by the men you went to school with. In many jurisdictions, all-male clubs only recently lost their tax-exempt status and thus there are powerful pressures to change their gender policies, but some golf clubs continue to limit the times when women can play, and so women miss opportunities where partners may woo potential clients.

Women say:

Senior associate, management consulting firm: "At a seminar, some of the partners confessed that they didn't ask women to lunch because they didn't want to be in an awkward situation if they were seen alone with a woman associate."

Catalyst focus group participant, securities firm: "I would walk into the office, and they have naked women up on the Internet. I would say, 'This is really inappropriate.' But you get treated as, 'Oh, she doesn't know how to have fun.' "

Catalyst focus group participant, securities firm: "One of my colleagues said to me, 'I think you're being overly sensitive. Why can't we go to topless bars?' He took a poll and two days later said, 'They all think you're being pretty sensitive.' I said, 'Do me a big favor. The next time we have a function and we're all out to dinner, why don't you propose we go to a topless bar? Then I will sue you and become wealthy and retire.' "

Challenge 9. Finding a mentor is critical. Chapter 8 covers the importance of mentors to your career, but I want to underscore here that for people in firms, mentors often make a career. Since most firms have a scarcity of women at the top to act as mentors, and since men generally mentor men, women face hurdles in finding a mentor. This lack of mentors for professional women is a major disadvantage. As a newcomer, you need people to teach you what's what, pass on valuable pointers, position you for advancement, and invite you along to meet their contacts and connect you to their networks. Mentors help you land the assignments that offer the experience you need to make partner in the specialty you want.

ISSUES FOR WOMEN OF COLOR

Women of color stress that exclusion hits them hard, as inhibitive of both mentoring and networking. Catalyst's landmark study *Women of Color in Corporate Management: Opportunities and Barriers* found that women of color have even less access to mentors, particularly those influential enough to promote their career development. Such exclusion becomes a major obstacle to achieving partnership.

Women say:

Woman of color senior associate, management consulting firm: "Who you know affects assignments. Women and minorities are hurt because they have a harder time getting to know the partners to get the right assignments."

Woman of color senior associate, management consulting firm: "The main barrier for women and minorities is that there are not enough of them. They do not have social and informal networks to work with."

Woman of color associate, management consulting firm: "To move up, you need a partner who is really pulling for you. Partners often did not reach out to women to be project leaders. This made women feel on the outside."

Woman of color senior associate, management consulting firm: "I saw it happen to people who had been chosen. He may have skipped a stage in his development, he may be a lousy manager, but he is smart and well connected. His mentor is very influential. So this guy will be successful."

HOW TO SUCCEED AT A FIRM

Some aspects of firm life have clearly improved for women, more quickly at some types of firms than others. One is tempted to say to the firms, "It's the demographics, stupid." Women make up nearly half of graduating law students, more than half of accounting graduates, and about one third of MBAs. Some of them join firms and learn the ropes, then seek more amenable environments. Even when women tell their firms they're leaving for other reasons (for example, to have a family), they tend to turn up shortly thereafter in corporate, nonprofit, foundation, or entrepreneurial settings. They tell Catalyst that they need better opportunities and the chance to control their schedules and time.

Some firms have found that losing human capital means lowered productivity, interrupted client service, and lower morale. Some firms are being pressured by women clients who want to work with women. Others have found that the women they've recruited, trained, and come to value leave after a few years, meaning a lost investment. Turnover can be expensive, often costing 150 percent of a year's salary or more. More and more firms, accounting firms in particular, have seen the potential handwriting in red ink on their wood-paneled walls. Accountability for retaining and advancing women is key. But if a firm doesn't care about turnover, or indeed, if it profits from turning over hot new talent in factory-like conditions, it's not likely to respond to changing workplace demographics.

Therefore, you need some advice on how to succeed when you've chosen a career in a firm. I've broken down the best strategies into eight basic categories, with tactics that will improve your chances to achieve partnership and succeed once you've become partner. And for those of you who don't go firmward, read on anyway. These tips are helpful in many work situations.

EIGHT STRATEGIES FOR SUCCESS AT FIRMS

Strategy 1. Head off whatever biases you can. Many misperceptions about you can be avoided or altered once you know they exist. Expect to encounter the biases detailed in this chapter and Chapter 1. Keeping them in mind, choose your moment to initiate dialogue with the partners. Once you've built something of a reputation as a solid, committed worker, you have leverage. Tell them what you want. If you want to be on the fast track for partnership, let the partners know. Ask for the high-visibility clients. Put yourself forward for important work, and don't expect it to be assigned to you otherwise. Let them know you're available to travel, if you are. Use humor to educate others about misconceptions.

Strategy 2. Do what you can to improve your chances. You know the criteria for partnership, but if you're hazy about them, ferret them out and focus on those. First, the firm has to make a business case for your partnership, which includes your specialty, your revenues, and how that fits into your particular office. Second is outstanding personal performance, as in billings, technical ability, managing people, and client service. The third category presents greater problems for women, as it's the subjective area: Do you fit their perception of partner? The perception that a partner is male has not died out at firms across the country. So they may wonder, Is she committed and will she stay, does she have executive presence, and can she be polished in dealing with senior executives? You need to demonstrate that clients will treat you as a peer.

Take becoming partner into your own hands. Sit down with the firm's partners—especially your mentor(s)—and make sure they see your commitment. You may think they already do, since you're performing well and concentrating on bringing in revenues and new business. But they might not. Don't underestimate the power of the myths about women's commitment, or they could affect your future. Be preemptive about the issue.

Tactics for improving your chances for partnership:

- Make time to socialize with the partners and your peers. Developing these relationships leads to opportunities.

- Early in your career, identify the knowledge areas where you want to develop expertise. Then ask for clients that afford the experience you need to gain that expertise. Beware of "negative mentoring," the well-intentioned advice that might steer you in a direction you don't want to go, simply because the partners feel more comfortable about it. Retain control over your career path.
- Cultivate relationships with the senior people who can pull you onto assignments, and do so early on.
- Work with as many different senior partners as possible. Ask for guidance in areas you want to develop, such as interviewing, negotiating, dealing with difficult clients, and so on. You'll garner a variety of skills. Equally important, you will show a diverse group of partners what you can do, and you want partners to perceive you as a potential peer.
- Develop a style that works. Flexibility of style matters; those who move up fastest emulate traits and techniques they see working in successful seniors and partners.
- Be aware of the importance of client networking activities. Initiate informal contact with clients in social venues that work for you.
- Develop credibility. Primary to your success in any field, credibility can come fast in firms, where the hierarchy has but two tiers. At a consulting firm, where there is what Nancy Karch of McKinsey & Company calls "immediate cause and effect," one great client success may mean you're home free. This is part of the appeal of working at a firm, where your destiny lies in your own hands perhaps more clearly than in other organizations. Firms being self-starter businesses, success with a big client leads to more clients, which brings in more money, which leads to partnership.
- Focus on your reputation early on. A strong reputation means that senior management will seek you out for their assignments and teams. During your first year, you can establish your reputation as a hard worker who delivers results, has or

is developing expertise, and demonstrates confidence with clients. A solid reputation established early will guarantee your landing the kinds of projects you want and the mentors you need to advance.

- Contribute to the knowledge management process by writing up what you've learned from a project. Look for new insights, write them down, take what you've written to experts in the area for editing, and then publish it. You not only show you're smart, you demonstrate your entrepreneurial side and become known.

- Demonstrate your team leadership skills. Don't wait for the formal designation of "project manager"; be entrepreneurial. Take the leadership within the team you're on so you can prove you have these skills. Show that you can mobilize other people to solve clients' problems and that you're able to delegate.

- Speak up at team meetings. You have the obligation to contribute, even if you're an analyst just out of business school and you're sitting next to a thirty-year partner. When you lead meetings, create an environment where everyone can speak and everyone can dissent, so that you get all the ideas you can out on the table.

- Volunteer to participate on prestigious committees. Keep volunteering. Take other committee assignments and prove your worth, then volunteer again.

- Volunteer to help with organizational training or events. This gives you increased visibility and a chance to work with others in a more informal setting. Building connections like this can lead to mentoring relationships.

- Take on pro bono clients. All firms do pro bono work, and such projects will offer you the visibility both inside and outside the firm that will expand your network into the community. You also might enjoy the diversity and the breath of fresh air such atypical clients can bring to your workday.

Strategy 3. Learn to develop new business. This, of course, will improve your chances for advancement, but if you haven't done any selling, you may think it's more difficult than it really is (see box "Ten Ways to Make Rain," below, for some tips on how to meet the new-business challenge). Let me start by assuring you that rainmaking is not rocket science. Nor is it a gift; you don't need to have a "sales personality." See sales as a skill you can learn, just as your male peers learn it, albeit with help from their mentors. There's no mystery, no magic. Rainmakers focus on selling their competence and that of the firm. So take a look at "Ten Ways to Make Rain" for some tips on how to meet the new business challenge.

TEN WAYS TO MAKE RAIN
(AND CAUSE THE SUN TO SHINE ON YOU)

1. **Develop a marketing plan.** Pick your field, decide what companies you're going to approach, and go out and talk with them.
2. **Learn how to sell.** Selling is no big deal, and it really is part of your job. Get into the mind-set of knowing you can do it.
3. **Find mentors.** You need to pick out a person you can watch in action. Get that person to take you along during new-business efforts. Listen in on conversations as he or she is pitching. This gives the best training possible. Today, successful rainmakers "take along" mostly their favorite young men. Not even all men get this benefit, as it's hard for partners in their daily rush of work to spread this kind of teaching around. I recommend that you spot a senior partner who's good at it and come right out and ask to be taken along. A mentor—the same person or another—can also give you pointers as you're going for new business and help improve your approach. If you can't

find a mentor on your own, perhaps your organization has a formal mentoring program. If so, by all means get involved with that.

Get feedback from your mentor. When you're nearing partnership, you need honest, in-depth feedback. Get that feedback and fix what's not working. Real or perceived problems can keep you from partnership.

4. **Be a good protégée.** Once you've cultivated the partners you admire, offer to help them with proposal development. When they let you go on calls with them and sit in on phone conversations with clients, offer to do follow-up work. At the end of client projects, write up what you've gleaned for the firm's knowledge management system and ask the appropriate partner to review your work or even to coauthor it with you.

5. **Establish connections.** Rainmaking requires connections. See if one of your mentors will share access to his or her connections to help you bring in new business. In the parlance of the securities business, this mentor might just "share his or her book" with you. You have nothing to lose by approaching such a person diplomatically, and much to win.

6. **Develop your network.** Your own connections will also bring in new business. Get all the help you can. Develop relationships with your peers. Join networking organizations. Join professional associations. Who you know will make all the difference in your success at a firm.

7. **Generate "follow-on" business.** That means additional business with your current clients. Most business comes in through repeat clients. As you're working on a project with them, identify the needs within their organizations and suggest ways your firm could help. If you're an associate in your first year, it will give you a real leg up when you bring these needs to the attention of the partners on the project.

8. **Entertain potential clients.** But don't presume that the only way to bring in new business is through established

methods, such as golf and other common social venues. Come up with your own approach. Take clients to places you enjoy, whether it's the theater, ball games, or a spa.

9. **Tell partners you want to be included** when they make proposals to "walk-ins," a major source of new business at many firms.

10. **Once you make partner,** although the rainmaking pressure will increase, you can target clients with high potential and will thus need fewer new clients to make any quota.

Strategy 4. Determine if an alternative career track will work. If you don't want to become partner but you do want to stay and work at a firm, you might be able to do that. Although at many firms, the role of principal does not command the same respect as that of partner, some firms are now seeking to create other viable alternatives in order to retain highly valued individuals who are not interested in partnership. Some have targeted the rigidity of the "up-or-out model." The firms that have dismantled this system may offer a choice between the traditional partner track and a slower one that permits greater balance between work and life.* You just have to be aware that once you are a principal, you step away permanently from the partner track.

Strategy 5. Plan your leaves carefully. It may be possible at certain types of firms—for example, management consulting—to

---

*One firm has established a new career model that permits creating paths that allow you to progress at your own pace. You can choose to move up in the traditional manner, or you can slow down your advancement in order to balance your work and personal responsibilities. Involving coaching, career development, and the developing of expertise, this career model also helps smooth the path for women who want or need flexible work arrangements and has changed the perception that you can't advance if you work a reduced schedule. Women report that the new career model allows them comfort in working such a schedule. Since the firm implemented the career model, its turnover of women has been reduced and the number of partners has increased.

take maternity leave when you complete an assignment. (See Chapter 7 for effective strategies for organizing maternity leaves.) And no matter what the type of firm, be smart about your return. Talk to the partners you've worked with prior to your leave. One management consultant tells of how she visited the office two weeks before her return. First, she chatted with the staff coordinator about what partners were working on what assignments. Then she popped her head into the offices of the partners she wanted to work with and said, "Say, I'm coming back; what's up?" She got her plum assignments before her first day back.

Strategy 6. Choose the right firm. You may be able to find a firm where retaining women does matter, where you will have a degree of control over your time and the shape of your career, and where you will find the work fulfilling. When choosing a firm, whether it's your first job or a change of positions, learn which ones have begun to rectify the female attrition problem. Find out how many women partners a firm now has and how the numbers have changed over the last few years. Learn not just whether flexibility is offered, but whether associates and partners actually use it and if they remain on the partner track. As discussed in Chapter 2 on career planning, there are specific questions you can ask at a firm to learn about the environment so you can figure out where you will get a fair shot at the top and where you will be able to find your work/life balance needs more nearly met. Learn about whether a firm's glass walls might keep you from developing the particular expertise that interests you. You might want to select a firm where you can move back and forth between types of clients; for example, in management consulting, working on a project with a tight deadline, followed by a long-term study. That way, you won't be pigeonholed and you'll have the chance to have some breathing space when you need it.

Don't fantasize that things will change overnight or that your fabulous talent, though it really is fabulous, is going to take you swiftly to the fore. Firms, by nature, change more slowly than corporations, and some of the former change over the dead bodies of their senior partners. Do your homework, and you will discover which firms have the best track records.

As some firms have demonstrated, it is possible to find creative, effective ways of attracting and retaining talented women. At Catalyst, we have been working with several firms—in accounting, management consulting, securities, law, and public relations—in the search for new and creative models. By working with these firms to create change, we hope that in the future, you will have the even playing field you need to succeed.

WHAT TO LOOK FOR IN A FIRM

- *Look into the facts.* How many women partners are there? Are these women senior partners in the management ranks? Is there a viable alternative career track? Are there "glass walls," with women clustering in certain areas, unable to move into the higher-powered ones? How are assignments handled: Is the process monitored or is it informal? Do men and women take parental leave? Are there part-time partners? If so, do they participate in the life of the firm—for example, business development and pro bono work—or do they spend all their time at billings? Do women head up important committees and practice areas? What are the requirements for billable hours, and are they different at different levels? Has anyone used a flexible work arrangement?
- *Look into the policies on travel, site work, career progression.* Ask for examples of how they are used. (Some firms now permit you to travel to a client on Monday morning instead of Sunday night as in the past. Other firms have you return from the client on Friday and be at the office that day.)

- *Look into the culture.* Check out the firm's reputation regarding women. Check the Catalyst Award winners. Find out if there is a women's network; some firms have networks that even host clients at events in order to help women begin to sell. Find out if the firm offers formal mentoring.

Strategy 7. Break some ground for other women. If you meet the obstacles I've discussed in this chapter and you still want to stay at your firm, take a chance. Your firm may be ready for change. As mentioned above, some firms are working to make formal flexibility (part-time, job sharing, and so on) a viable option. If you love firm work, you might consider being a change maker, rather than leaving when you face critical issues.

For instance, if you need a different type of work schedule and the firm doesn't offer alternative work arrangements yet, you might be the trailblazer. Consider asking for what you want. Be imaginative if you do this. One option: suggest you reduce the size of your client portfolio for a certain amount of time. You might approach the partners, as Barbara Paul Robinson of Debevoise & Plimpton did many years ago. She did it, and so might you. The more women who stay and try, the more real flexibility will become.

Find support among colleagues and peers inside and outside the firm. If the climate is right, you might join with other women at the firm to form an informal or formal network that can at some point advise the firm on what works to retain women.[3] Or join a professional association, where you will find support as well as networking and mentoring. Seeking out support when you don't need it will mean it's there when you do.

If you're a change maker, you might take it upon yourself to make your firm's partners aware of whom they're including and excluding. Attack the myths. Consider whether getting together a group of women and letting the partners know is a good approach. Or you can do this through a women's network at your office.

Strategy 8. Persist if you like the work. It's a reality that the playing field for women in firms remains uneven. You can help slant it your way by taking the tips in this chapter to heart. Working at a firm offers many women careers that are fulfilling, exciting, remunerative, and challenging. The benefits of working at a firm—as laid out at the beginning of this chapter—can be found nowhere else. If these match your talents and your needs, don't let the challenges discourage you. Should the firm you work for not meet the standards you seek, you can always change firms. And no matter how tough it may get, don't let the turkeys get you down.

≈

CHAPTER 11

Wisdom from the Pioneers

Now that you know how to be your own mentor, I can exit gracefully. But not before these parting words. Each of the pioneers was asked, "If you could tell your favorite protégée only one thing to help her to succeed, what would that be?" They winnowed their advice down to one gem as they each articulated what they consider most critical to your career success. Coming as it does from the female stars of the workplace—women with strength, tenacity, power, influence, intelligence, many skills, and a deep fount of experience—their hindsight is worth a million bucks.

Their advice covers a broad spectrum, from the skills and attitudes that breed success to networking to the kind of work to choose, when to move on, work style, and lifestyle. I hope you'll find them an inspiration.

WHAT YOU NEED TO DO TO SUCCEED

Do your job better than anyone else. Every item of advice in this book is predicated on a categorical imperative: Perform! Do what you do so well that people cannot help noticing. Deliver the goods and then some, over and over again. That will lead to a reputation that expands outward and then pulls new opportunities toward you. People will count on you, call on you, recommend you. Your achievements will give you the credibility that's particularly precious to women. I've stressed another common refrain throughout the book: most successful women must work harder than most of their male peers. But the simple fact is that you must outperform everyone else if you want to achieve a senior leadership position.

Rebecca McDonald (Chair and CEO, Enron Asia-Pacific, Africa, and China): "Performance counts. Talent notwithstanding, education notwithstanding, on a day-in and day-out basis, that's what gets people's respect."

Jill Barad (former President and CEO, Mattel): "Love what you do, do it from your heart of hearts, and do it better than anyone else. Then put yourself in situations where other people can see your passion and see its results."

Build your self-confidence. Some people are born with self-confidence, and some people achieve it. Most of us, I think, develop our self-confidence from our successes and from how well we learn from our failures. Superior performance and the concomitant recognition will augment your self-assurance. Self-confidence means you know you can trust yourself in the varied circumstances that will test you throughout your career, and it will lead others to trust you as well. In the soil of self-confidence blooms leadership, credibility, power, prowess, and courage, all of which you need to move to the top of whatever field you have chosen.

Zoë Baird (President, The Markle Foundation): "Be confident in who you are; that comes through and creates confidence in you by others. Understand how you're perceived by other people, but if you're going to be a leader, understand who you are yourself."

Joan Leiman (Executive Deputy Vice President for the Health Sciences, Columbia University) counsels women to "believe in yourself." She cautions that you not disregard external factors: "We'd be fools if we didn't make judgments about what the environment demands of us to succeed. But if that's all we do, we won't matter. Trust yourself and others will trust you. Liking you helps, but if they don't think you can do the job, you won't get far."

Judy Sprieser (CEO, Transora): "Trust your gut and take chances. You may have marvelous intuition and if you have the confidence to trust it, it's a powerful asset."

Nancy Karch (Retired Director, McKinsey & Company): "Worry less about avoiding risk. Risk is what gives you competence, helps build your confidence, and lets you break out of the pack."

Nothing will boost you like succeeding at a risky endeavor. When I took over running a psychiatric institution, I faced serious staffing and morale problems that threatened the entire venture. I knew this when I took the job, and although I also knew my own strengths and had confidence in my ability, the risk factor ran high. My success at reorganization proved that I could steer a large institution through rough waters, and this track record reinforced my penchant for risk taking.

Get what you want by insisting. In a work world governed by men, the men in charge expect that if you want something, you'll ask for it. Make your goals and aspirations clear to your boss. Don't sit on your ambition. When I and the women pioneers entered the workplace and began our ascent, we tried to blend in, not make waves. It took a while to figure out that no one would offer us what we didn't expect or ask for. We had to learn to ask for what we wanted. Women who have made it to senior management have not displayed timidity. They have set their sights on their goals, have determined what they need, and have made their cases in the most effective way in the right places. When necessary, they have wrested success from the hands of those who would have overlooked them. Several of the pioneers stressed taking the initiative as the most important advice they could give their protégées:

> **Barbara Paul Robinson** (Partner, Debevoise & Plimpton): "Figure out what you want, figure out if you're developing the skills you need, and figure out how to get them. Don't sit back and wait for the luck of the draw. How you develop is happenstance of the work assignments you get, and women don't always get fair treatment in assignments. Reach out and grab what you need."

When it comes to getting through the glass walls to hold jobs with profit-and-loss responsibility, you must not only call upon your initiative but also summon up chutzpah and determination. You don't have history on your side—to this day, few women hold revenue-generating positions. If you want a line job, tell your boss. If he or she says you don't have the experience, convince him or her to take the risk. Let your boss know you're risk-worthy. Job rotation through both line and staff areas will build your experience, but if you go back to the staff side, the glass walls can quickly close back in on you.

Learn to read your organization. Women too often work at their tasks and tend not to get involved in the nuances of what's going on around them. Watch the nuances of interactions. Use your radar to get the lay of the land. Intuition, perception, and intelligence applied to the way things work in your office will reveal a lot about what you need to do to make progress. One of the pioneers emphasized that you need to focus your sights on the chain of command.

> **From the Pioneers: Choose the right company.**
> **Ellen Hancock** (Chair and CEO, Exodus Communications): "Be in a company that wants you to advance. . . . Understand the climate. You know how your peers talk; you know how managers feel. You should not be the first female corporate officer. Let this be the litmus test: check the numbers, and if after 2000 they don't have women on the board or women corporate officers, it's a boys' club, they're in the stone age, and it's not worth it to work there." Hancock categorically recommends leaving if you're meeting bias. "If it's from one particular manager, you can get yourself a new manager. But if your company has a reputation or a culture limiting to women, if you're on hold, go to a different company. Don't try to fight it. Life is too short to think you're going to change a company's culture."

Part of learning the lay of the land and how to operate in the workplace includes developing effective communication skills. One of our pioneers stressed the critical importance of learning the lingo of your workplace. Make a practice of comparing notes with your male peers. Emulate their skills. Work on how you speak, so that others receive the messages you intend, and on how you listen, so that you understand the nuances, both spoken and unspoken. You can't do it alone.

WHO CAN HELP

Seek and accept assistance in your career. Another of the pioneers stressed the importance of getting help from others. Recognize your need for a helping hand and find ways to get it—from bosses, sponsors, mentors, family, or friends of all sorts with whom you've connected and who can link you with others. You will hear of opportunities for yourself and others. You will become privy to information that will prove useful both professionally and personally. You will benefit from other people's connections. Moreover, you need the support and insight they can give when you're succeeding and when you're stuck, when you've had a triumph or a failure, when you're happy and when you're down. Entrepreneur Carolee Friedlander considers that her network has been critical to her continuing success in her own business and that connections, no matter what your field, make a difference in how far anyone will progress.

From the Pioneers: Build bridges.
Lulu Wang (Partner and CEO, Tupelo Capital Management): "I think you need to learn to build bridges in front of you. No matter how junior or senior you are, you should always be willing to reach out and help others. The abundant help and goodwill I received when I started Tupelo came from all the bridges I'd been building since I started working. They opened up so many new avenues for me. I think that's something women always have to remember. It's wonderful to be mentored, but we should also reach out and offer our help to others. We should think generously, act generously, and that generosity will come back to bless us."

You will need the insights and wisdom of others all the way to the top of the ladder. Since I've been at the helm of Catalyst, I've repeatedly called on friends and associates from previous positions as well as on those I've met since taking the job. I can't afford to be out of the public policy loop if I intend to keep the organization current and viable. From my network I get data, new information, ideas, and other connections. I can't imagine staffing without it; for instance, when we needed a vice president for our Canada office, I called on academic friends in the United States and Canada, who cast a wide net for us.

WHEN TO MOVE ON

Keep the faith. No matter what path you choose, sometimes the going gets tough. The pioneers who've "been there, done that" talked at length about many a difficult moment they had hit as they made their way upward. All of them faced challenges that might have daunted them. All of them, in chorus with me, say, *"Don't give up."* Keep your eye on the larger picture. Whatever's giving you trouble—obstacles to your advancement, troubles with your boss, problems with managing—don't abandon ship. Focus on navigating around them, over them, or through them. And if something goes sour, patch it up as best you can, turn the page, and move on.

In a career of risk taking, many things you try won't pan out. Others will. Don't expect everything you attempt to succeed. Success is built on learning from failure. Three pioneers focused their most critical advice on your stick-to-itiveness:

Linda Alvarado (President and CEO, Alvarado Construction): "Don't give up too quickly or too easily on your hopes and dreams. If two out of ten of your projects succeed, you're doing well. Sometimes you win and sometimes you lose, but remember, as in baseball, you will have another season."

Carol Bartz (President, CEO, and Chair, Autodesk): "I want a woman to know she's packing her bags for a long experience. She'll do many things, have many jobs, relationships. If she believes there are many steps on the journey, she won't get discouraged when a couple of them get tough. Her whole career isn't doomed when something goes bad. Stay calm. There are a lot of things in that bag. We can all get emotional; we all have a tendency to believe we screwed up: 'Why didn't I do that?' Just recognize there's still time, there's room."

Lynn Forester (Founder and Co-chair, FirstMark Communications International): "Men are used to playing the game hard and losing sometimes. They just go out and have a beer afterward. Women take no personally; they shy away from asking. Failure is temporary. Accept it, have more confidence, and start over again."

Know when it's time to go. Now that I've counseled persistence, let me also say that you must move on when it's time.

Sometimes you can figure out how to make a situation work where you are; sometimes you can't. Sometimes you can start afresh in the same workplace after a difficult transition, and sometimes you can't or perhaps you shouldn't. Sometimes you can find a way around glass walls or to shatter a glass ceiling, and sometimes you hit adamant opposition. How can you know the difference? Four of the pioneers homed in on this as their most important offering to a protégée:

Judith Rodin (President, University of Pennsylvania): "Don't say, 'What's wrong with me,' but, 'What's wrong with the system, and are there ways I can change it?' Most problems are systemic, and you need to analyze them dispassionately. If you can't fix them, be ready and willing to move on."

Yvonne M. Curl (Vice President and Chief Marketing Officer, Avaya Communication): "Have the courage to change, to pursue what you want to do. The longer you stay in the same role, the tougher it is to make a change."

Rita Wilson (President, Allstate Indemnity Company): "Don't allow yourself to be a token. Don't sit on the sidelines. Once women and minorities allow that to happen, there's no coming back. We don't have that luxury and we have far too much to offer to be 'humored.' Two things are important for me: I must have the opportunity to do my job according to my own criteria for success—the opportunity to make a difference—and I must have opportunities to succeed."

Carole St. Mark (Founder and President, Growth Management): "Go where you know you can get a fair shot. If your antennae are up, you can sense an environment that won't be good for a woman. If in your business or your division you feel a hostility, it doesn't pay to stay and fight the system because you're likely to lose. Find a place where it's not like that. Leave. Unless you're Joan of Arc."

When you face a career crisis, ask yourself certain questions and examine your symptoms. Is it personal? Is it a repeating pattern? Then it may be you, and perhaps you can work through it. But maybe it's not you. Can you see yourself growing and moving? If not, there's no reason to assume that growth will happen someday. Do you find yourself at a dead end at your organization? Are you exceeding expectations, yet nothing is happening? Then you should think of leaving. Don't disregard the signs and the omens. "Nobody has you stapled there," says Bobbi Gutman, corporate vice president and director of Motorola's Global Diversity Department. She recommends that when things get rough, you should consider looking around. "Even if you simply start to look for a new job but never leave," she says, "you gain a sense of power and control. Sometimes a bad situation becomes quite tolerable when we have a sense of our own control."

As you look around, assess the situation. If you're not sure that you can change things, the passage of time may reveal that all you need to do is make an adjustment or negotiate for what you want. Career coach Sheryl Spanier recommends that you give a problem job six months. She believes that "people can stand anything for six months, as long as it's not abusive. Instead of leaving in a state of chaos when you're vulnerable, if you can find a way to live with the tension for six months and work through it, you might come out farther ahead." Time will increase your awareness of cause and effect and give you the chance to rebuild your self-esteem and self-awareness.

When you've tried everything you can think of, used every trick in this book, called upon your mentors and your networks, yet still nothing gets you where you want to go . . . then it's time to move on.

Stay alert for opportunities. Consider complacency an enemy. No matter who you are, no matter what you're doing, don't allow yourself to get too comfortable. Even if you're lucky enough to work at your dream job, you don't want to stagnate. Look for the signs: Are you learning, are you challenged, are you moving toward the goals you've set? To advance, you need to expose yourself to new ideas and to learn new skills. One of the pioneers focused on this area, urging you to remain open to new directions, to possibilities, to serendipity:

Barbara Aronstein Black (Professor, Columbia School of Law): "Be flexible, because trite as it sounds, one never knows what's coming around the corner. We all know something dreadful may happen, but we're not so open to the opportunities. My experience shows you really never know, so it's necessary not to have so rigid a life plan that something that comes along unexpectedly can't be fit into it."

When you least expect it, an unusual, even fabulous new avenue might open to you. As I explained in Chapter 2, that's what happened to me. When I became president of Catalyst, the business arena was a real stretch for me. But it has paid off handsomely in new experiences, new opportunities, and the chance to make a difference for women in the workplace.

WHERE YOU WORK

Choose where you work (and what you work on) carefully. Several of the pioneers emphasized the importance of where you work. In sum, they say to pay attention to where you put your energy and your time. Just about all the pioneers stress that you should spend your time doing things that interest you. Coalesce your work and your interests. Know yourself. Determine what you love and what you're good at, then match them with your field and your job as closely as possible. Make midcareer shifts to correct your course, if necessary. Great things can emerge from your passions at any time in your career. Best yet, link together doing what you love with a job at an organization that shares your values or even inspires them.

From the Pioneers:
Carly Fiorina (Chair and CEO, Hewlett-Packard) wants you to "believe you can do anything you want to do. Really believe it." Then, she advises, "Do what you really want to do. It's important to throw yourself into it, to be who you really are, and not let anybody take that away from you. There may be people who will get in your way, and there will always be people who will help you. You can accomplish great things only by working with other people." As an afterthought, she adds, "Never sell your soul, because no one will ever pay you back. When all is said and done, you've got to be happy with who you are."

The best and happiest careers occur when you work at what moves you, what excites you, what matters to you, what you love. When I received my initial paycheck at my first job, I stared at it as if someone had handed me a gift. I was young and idealistic, sure, but the moment was an epiphany. The company had paid me for something I loved doing! It didn't take me long to grow fond of the interface between my paycheck and my career and to know that that was how I wanted to live my life. And I have.

HOW: STYLE AND LIFESTYLE

Accommodate, but be yourself. As a woman, you are still in the minority in most workplaces, especially in the highest ranks. Women of color must deal with double minority issues. The most successful women learn what works and then adapt their work habits and self-presentation so as to make the people they work with comfortable. Finding a way to do this while retaining who you truly are presents a challenge to all women. Our pioneers have made accommodations. They advise you to do so, too, but with certain caveats. Two pioneers, both women of color, singled out this area for where they wanted to offer cardinal advice to protégées:

Roberta Gutman (Corporate Vice President and Director of Global Diversity, Motorola): "Women have wasted time being chameleons, who we think we should be in a given situation. We should be *melding* who we are, not *changing* who we are. Don't try to blend into norms that make you behave less than the way you really are. Or you'll lose who you really are, both in behaviors and in priorities."

Rita Wilson (President, Allstate Indemnity Company): "Stay true to what makes you unique as a woman, whether with family, friends, or business associates. You'll have to make adjustments, some concessions. Everybody does. But don't leave pieces of yourself along the way, because you can't go back and recoup them."

Know what matters. If you're going for a career in a leadership capacity, neither you nor I can pretend it won't preoccupy you at certain times of your life. If you throw yourself totally into your job, make it your conscious choice and your satisfaction will shine through. I haven't a doubt in my mind that a fabulous job may provide extraordinary fulfillment. For others, a strong home life plus a career loom large among their fulfillment criteria. And for others—the work world may simply never fulfill them. That's okay, as long as it's a choice, not a fallback. One of the pioneers weighted this topic as the most important area to cover with her protégées:

Marie Knowles (Executive Vice President and CFO, Atlantic Richfield): "Make sure you have more than a briefcase to go home to. Career or positions can go away in a snap. Every day, jobs are being eliminated in my industry, and men who had only their careers—never mattered if they had wives—are devastated and don't know what to do. What matters is what you are as a person."

THE FUTURE FOR WOMEN IN THE WORKPLACE

Here in the Information Age, women and men come equally well equipped for what Peter Drucker calls "knowledge-based jobs."

In 1997, women earned 56 percent of bachelor's degrees, 40 percent of MBA degrees, 44 percent of law degrees, 41 percent of Ph.D.s, and 41 percent of M.D.s.[1] Options for working now exist that allow for greater flexibility of time and place; you can work from an office or from home, or indeed from a park bench. The good news is that companies and firms in ever-increasing numbers know this and are acting on it. They know that their businesses cannot succeed, that they cannot build a robust, prosperous future for their companies, if they don't use *all* of the talent available to them.

That's a far cry from the conventional wisdom of earlier decades. When Catalyst was founded in 1962, opportunities for women were few. Most married women who worked had "jobs"; it was their husbands who had "careers." Let's look at one woman who was collecting her first paycheck in the early 1960s. She got married young, and started a family shortly thereafter. Her first job waited until her kids were spending all day at school. Once she got to the workplace, what did this woman of the 1960s face?

I began my career in 1968, and I can tell you that whenever my boss wanted to praise me, he'd smile and call me his "right-hand girl," and I knew he meant it as a compliment. I was unlike most faculty wives at that time. I was hardly the only professor's wife who worked, but I was one of the very few whose jobs didn't revolve around their husbands' work—proofreading galleys, typing correspondence. I had my *own* job—and both my husband and I knew I was building a career.

Like most women of my time, I couldn't imagine myself in the executive suite. Things have certainly changed. And there's no turning back for women now—or for men, either. We used to think the issues that Catalyst has been working on all these years were "women's issues." It turns out they are *everybody's* issues. Today it's not just working mothers who need attention. Fathers feel the same tug between work and family.

You have likely seen signs that we are in the midst of an extraordinary transformative period. It's an inflection point, a confluence of events that has the potential to change the competitive landscape so fundamentally that nothing can ever be the same again. There have been few moments like this in human history.

Stephen Ambrose writes that when Lewis and Clark set out to chart the Pacific Northwest, their journey was not much different from those of the ancient Romans. In all the years since Caesar, not much had changed: explorers, isolated, still relied on hardy pack animals and sturdy footwear. Then came the steam engine, the telegraph, the railroad. And travel and communication were never the same again.

Today we're in the midst of another fundamental shift. Time and space constraints are being obliterated. Companies do business around the clock and measure their markets globally. Information gathered in one city can reach people on every continent in an instant. These new realities require new kinds of companies that value the contribution of the entire talent pool, and that take advantage of women's unique contributions to the workforce. Today we see companies where teamwork matters more than hierarchy, and where intellect is valued above brawn, where the content of one's character really is more important than the color of one's skin, as Dr. King dreamed it would be one day.

Because of these changes, women—and men—are different today. That woman I mentioned from the 1960s—she's not the same person. She and her husband have a whole new set of aspirations for their daughter—*and* for their son. They have different expectations about how a family should be structured. They expect that if their daughter stays home to raise children, it will be because she chooses to do that, not because society tells her she must.

More and more women are leaving large, old-style organizations when they meet obstacles to advancement and are starting their own businesses that soon may scoop the crème de la crème from the talent pool. And much of that is female. Women will not continue to work where their endeavors go unrecognized and unrewarded. Women will find a workplace—or they will found one—in which there is no intrinsic exclusion. Women will find or found a workplace in which opportunities are color-blind and gender-blind. We will find or found a workplace in which there is an environment that expects achievement for women and men alike. The competitive pressure on more conservative companies will, I believe, hasten change there as well, so in the next decade we may see old wrongs righted and slanted playing fields leveled.

As your mentor, I have filled this book with the actions, approaches, and attributes that my experience, Catalyst's knowledge, and other successful women's achievements demonstrate will bring success at work. No matter whether you're working for a hot new dot com, a professional firm, a nonprofit, a Fortune 500 company, or your own business, I hope you will turn the advice here to your own ends. I hope and believe that this book will help you go out into the workplace better equipped to be your own mentor.

〜

Pioneer Profiles

LINDA ALVARADO, PRESIDENT AND CEO, ALVARADO CONSTRUCTION

Running her own successful multimillion-dollar construction firm in Denver as a Hispanic woman has been a challenge for Linda Alvarado, but she has never flagged in her optimism and her determination to succeed. Of her first job on a construction site, she says, "My boss liked to go off and play golf, so he taught me how to do things," and she thus found her calling. To succeed in an all-male industry, however, Alvarado had to find a niche "with an expertise that most men didn't have. I took courses in surveying, estimating, and other classes from both industry associations and universities, but most important early on I learned computerized scheduling programs. I could do critical path method scheduling, which revolutionized the industry. Without that technological background that set me apart, I wouldn't have made it."

She lists four basic success strategies: (1) Understand and embrace risks, "particularly where [you see] no role models ahead to say what you should and shouldn't do." (2) Don't personalize. "Know that if it doesn't work the first time, it's not you. Women personalize their lack of initial success, while men, because of their involvement in sports, don't. Men miss the goal and blame the wind factor, while women say, 'I blew it.' " (Alvarado, who has five brothers, played softball and knows that "you may strike out once, but you get another turn at bat.") (3) Persist: "Go back and have a debriefing. Find out what you did wrong so you can do it right the next time." And (4) Network: "No matter your business, it's people that make decisions."

As a part owner of the Colorado Rockies—and the only woman entrepreneur to own a baseball team—Alvarado now has a high profile and has been approached to run for mayor of Denver. She is married with children and serves on the boards of Pitney Bowes, Qwest Communications, Pepsi Bottling Group, Minnesota Mining and Manufacturing Company (3M), and Lennox.

Career path:

Gemini II: Contact administration on construction site
Alvarado Construction: President and CEO

ZOË BAIRD, PRESIDENT, THE MARKLE FOUNDATION

Zoë Baird served as the first woman general counsel at a major American company. Her career has spanned the White House, a law firm, two corporations, and a foundation. She was President Clinton's initial nominee for attorney general.

Baird's career shifted from the public to the private sector when she had to leave the office of White House counsel upon President Carter's defeat. She rejected an offer from one firm when told by a partner she should do corporate law because women were "unsuitable on client visits where you met them in the field wearing a hard hat." Instead, she went with the firm of O'Melveny & Myers, which she found had a good track record with women. She appreciates the irony that one of her first visits to a client entailed donning a hard hat to see the client's liquefied natural gas plant. "I kept that symbolic hat," she says.

Marriage to a Yale law professor took her from Washington and into corporate legal work at General Electric in Connecticut. Then Aetna successfully wooed her away "because any company that would offer a general counsel position while you're on maternity leave is a company to talk to." Baird sits on the President's Foreign Intelligence Advisory Board and is writing a book on global crime. She is married with two children.

Career path:
U.S. Department of Justice: Office of Legal Counsel
U.S. White House: Attorney
O'Melveny & Myers: Associate
    Partner
General Electric: Manager, Legal Department
Aetna Life and Casualty: Senior Vice President, General Counsel
The Markle Foundation: President

JILL E. BARAD, FORMER PRESIDENT AND CEO, MATTEL

Jill Barad, until recently one of the few female CEOs in the Fortune 500, got there as a result of her fabled marketing talent. She started at Mattel as a product manager. A few years later, she gave Barbie her now-famous makeover to a professional woman and increased the company's revenues from $200 million to $1.9 billion. Barad explains her basic success strategies: (1) "bold risk taking backed by sound analysis and logic, so you break out of the model as it's always been"; (2) strong communication skills, "especially in marketing, where you take a product through your vision, getting those internally behind it and convincing the customers they need it"; (3) being visible "so your good work gets seen"; (4) "doing things that make you uncomfortable," such as when her career sidestepped out of marketing into product development, rewarding her with vital new experience; and (5) "volunteering if you're not chosen for the job you want."

Barad stopped working when she first married, but her high energy soon sent her back to the job market, where she landed a post at Mattel, which made her highly visible both internally and externally. For years near or at the top of her game, she has "most often been the only woman in any corporate situation." She deals with that by "not thinking of myself as a woman in a man's world, but as another person on the team defending what I believe to be true. You've got to believe that."

As CEO, she strove to ensure that her greatest strength—her aggressiveness—was not a liability: "I tend to believe people can make miracles happen if they believe they can. The hurdles can be high if the people climbing them know they will get the recognition for delivering results. Give them the credit. So much is about the way people feel about their work: the better they feel, the more they put out." At Mattel, Barad implemented flexibility policies and gave employees time off to volunteer at local schools. She serves on the board of Pixar and is married with two sons.

Career path:
Wells, Rich, Greene/West: Advertising Account Executive
Coty Cosmetics: Brand Manager
Mattel: Product Manager
   Marketing Director for Barbie
   Vice President
   Executive Vice President, Marketing and Worldwide
      Development
   President, Girls and Activity Toys Division

President, Mattel USA
President, Mattel Inc., and COO
President and CEO
CEO and Chair

PATRICIA "TOSH" BARRON, CLINICAL ASSOCIATE PROFESSOR, STERN SCHOOL OF BUSINESS, NEW YORK UNIVERSITY

Patricia Barron, known as Tosh, pioneered a career at Xerox that included a mélange of staff and line positions. Barron notes the challenges women continue to face in the upward climb: "Women have to overcome gender bias and functional bias. They have to communicate that they can do the line job." Her successful movement between functions resulted from doing her job right: being successful directly under the eye of the CEO. After finishing foreign assignments in China, "I came back to the U.S. operation because I knew that was where top brass mined the talent. It was a step backward, but it meant I went forward." It led to her job as president of the company's largest unit.

She advises dealing with gender bias head-on. When she didn't get one of five regional manager positions, she questioned the decision: "I asked to understand the criteria so I would know what I had to do to get the job next time. He told me that previous line experience was really important, and I pointed out that three of the five men didn't have the kind of line experience I had. He was a 'good old boy,' but I didn't beat him to a pulp. I got the job the next time." She advises asking questions, rather than taking an aggressive approach. "Don't go in and say, 'I want, I want.' Say, 'I'd really appreciate your career advice.' People are flattered when you ask for career advice. Ask, 'What kinds of experience do I need for you to feel comfortable putting me in a job, and can you help me get there?' Always put it in questions, so they do the thinking; otherwise they can be lazy in answering."

Now retired from Xerox, Barron is keeping her hand in as a professor at New York University's business school, and as a member of the boards of Aramark, Quaker Chemical, Teleflex, and USAA. She is married with two grown sons and one teenage boy.

Career path:
McKinsey & Company: Consultant
Xerox: Director, China project
   Manager, Future Products Integration
   Mid-Atlantic Region Sales Manager
   Vice President and Regional Manager, U.S. Marketing Group
   Director, Corporation Information Management (Information Systems), then Vice President
   President, Office Document Products Division
   President, Xerox Engineering Division
   Vice President, Business Operations Support
New York University: Senior Fellow in Research, Executive-in-Residence, Stern School of Business
   Clinical Associate Professor

CAROL BARTZ, PRESIDENT, CEO, AND CHAIR, AUTODESK

Carol Bartz says that she never imagined being a CEO, yet she now runs Autodesk, an $820 million company that is the world leader in desktop and Internet design and multimedia software. Her key success strategy, she says, has been taking risks, especially "turnaround assignments that no one but Mikey [of the cereal commercial] would try, not glamour jobs." That built her own confidence and the confidence of others in her. No actual plan guided her, yet she stresses that "you should build a career like a pyramid. It's important to have a strong foundation. Mine was in sales and marketing, with a technical background, then experience in management and customer relations. Too often people want a promotion and get 'verticalized.' You can't have an unstable base if you want to succeed."

Bartz's career demonstrates that it can be advantageous to move between line and staff positions, although she counsels doing research on how your organization has dealt with women in the past: "If your company doesn't have a history of pulling people from staff positions, avoid them like the plague." Moving from a revenue-generating field position in sales (line) to corporate headquarters (staff) gave her a visible stint near the CEO and an overview of the business. "Broad experience gets rewarded," she says. If you're not clear what that is at your organization, she recommends, "find out what the guys do to get ahead, and do that."

Bartz assumed her current job while fighting breast cancer. Since she arrived, Autodesk has consistently been listed as one of *Fortune*'s best companies to work for. She serves on the board of Cisco Systems. She is married with a daughter.

Career path:
First National Bank: Sales Representative
3M Corporation: Sales Representative, Systems Analyst
Digital Equipment Corporation: Sales Representative
    Sales Manager
    Program Manager
    Product Line Manager
Sun Microsystems: Customer Marketing Manager
    Vice President, Marketing
    Vice President, Corporate Marketing Workstation Division
    President, Sun Microsystems Federal
    Vice President, Customer Service
    Vice President, Worldwide Field Operations, Executive
        Officer
Autodesk: President, CEO, and Chair

BETTY BEENE, PRESIDENT AND CEO, UNITED WAY OF AMERICA

Now running the nation's largest charity organization, Betty Beene did not plan on having a career at all. She took a job at a Girl Scout council because she'd once attended camp, an experience that led to her working for the Houston Girl Scouts, where she reached the top post in six years. "It was a terrific place to be a young woman at that time," Beene says. "You were never limited because of age or sex." Here she honed her fund-raising skills and mastered "the fundamentals of mobilizing volunteers to accomplish what a staff never could achieve." She applied "as a lark" for the top position at Houston's United Way and landed the job, much to her surprise. "It's easy for me to ask major leaders in the private and public sector to give money and time," she says of her current post. "I present them with an opportunity to take their gifts—their financial or their intellectual firepower—and affect people they don't know and never will see. Giving answers the question 'Does it matter if I was here?' "

She recommends that women volunteer at organizations with outcomes they care about: "I meet people in those venues that I wouldn't normally meet in my line of work and learn from them things I wouldn't normally learn." She advises getting feedback and never makes a fund-raising call with a key volunteer (often a leader of a major corporation or a ranking government official) without asking what she could have done better. "Sometimes you have to press them, and they might just say, 'Great.' You have to initiate the questioning to be sure you're getting the coaching you need. I work best when someone challenges my judgment." She looks on these people as mentors, saying, "I know a lot about the subject matter we're dealing with, and they know a lot about processes. The nature of the nonprofit sector puts you in a position to get remarkable advice from all sorts of people."

Beene believes that "what gets counted gets done" and has focused on creating a board and staff that "reflect the composition of the country we serve in age, race, and sex." Pleased that the United Way has just been named one of the 110 best nonprofits to work for, she points to a growing feminization of nonprofits and the opportunities they present for women. But she says, "We hire a lot of people from the private sector who expect non-profits to be slow-paced. What they find is that it's as intense if not more intense than the private sector because we're so mission-driven." She holds an MBA in finance, is earning a doctorate in human resource development, and is married.

Career path:

Girl Scout Council: Field Executive
   Manager, Cookie Sales
   Director, Administrative Services
   Director, Human Resources
   Director, Field Services
   Assistant Executive Director
   Executive Director
United Way, Houston: President and CEO
United Way of Tri-State (New York, Connecticut, New Jersey):
   President and CEO
United Way of America: President and CEO

DORRIT BERN, CHAIR, CEO, AND PRESIDENT, CHARMING SHOPPES

On her first job interview, Dorrit Bern told the interviewer she wanted to be president of the company. Because she was a professional golfer, she says, "I'm terribly competitive and my single focus is to win. It doesn't hurt to be an athlete if you're working in corporate America." Bern's mother was a buyer, and Bern herself has been in the retail business all her life. She had early profit-and-loss responsibility as a buyer and made divisional merchandise manager at age twenty-seven. "That was unheard-of. Most buyers were men—even of dresses and bras."

Bern became known as a fixer of broken businesses and advises this as a success strategy: "Women should take tough jobs men don't want, right from the beginning. Women sit back and think, 'One more year, then the boss will call me in.' They must bust into his office and say, 'I want the job; give it to me.' That's what guys do." At Sears, she started junior apparel and revamped the women's department and, having the largest responsibility for the "softer side of Sears" businesses, she played a major role in the company's turnaround. "Turnaround opportunities come up every day, and women need to look for them. That's how you get noticed and become valuable."

Bern knew instinctively when it was time to move on. She left Bon Marché, a division of Allied Stores, when it traded up from its strong position as a moderately priced department store. "I didn't want to work for a company that wasn't going to win," she says. She left Sears "when I knew I wouldn't be president. Charming came after me for years, but I wouldn't leave for less than a CEO position." She currently commutes between her office in Philadelphia and her home in Illinois, where her husband and three sons live.

In 1996, Bern began the Keeping Kids WARM Coat Donation Program. Today over 6,500 new winter coats have been given to inner-city elementary school children in Philadelphia, Newark, and Baltimore, and in Canada. Bern also initiated donations to Working Wardrobe, an organization that helps women who have completed job training and are entering the workforce. Bern serves on the boards of Southern Company in Atlanta and Brunswick Company.

Career path:
Allied Stores: Merchandising
    Department Manager

Buyer
Divisional Sales Manager
Sears, Roebuck and Company: Category Vice President for
    Women's Apparel
Group Vice President and officer of the corporation and for
    Women's Apparel and Home Fashions
Charming Shoppes: President, CEO, and Chair

BARBARA ARONSTEIN BLACK, GEORGE WELWOOD MURRAY PROFESSOR OF LEGAL HISTORY, COLUMBIA UNIVERSITY SCHOOL OF LAW

The first woman dean of an Ivy League law school, Barbara Black came late to an academic appointment. Achieving tenure at age fifty-one, then catapulted into the deanship at Columbia's law school, she "learned on the job. I lacked experience in administration, in governance, in chairing academic committees, but I felt a responsibility not to turn it down. I thought I would be encouraging to women and that I could help out my colleagues. I had made snail's progress in my career because I had given so much time to family, so it was exciting. But I knew how risky it was." She advises women to take risks "in a direction that one is reasonably well prepared for."

With a father, uncles, and brothers who were lawyers, Black earned her law degree at Columbia in 1955, "a matter of less moment than it seems when looking back." She then married a law professor, raised three children, and cared for her ailing mother. In her spare time, she completed a Yale Ph.D. in Anglo-American legal history. While a grad student, she taught part-time, and comments that since at age thirty-eight she was a " 'quarter-time acting instructor,' I could presumably make full-time instructor by age 152." The pace obviously quickened when she assumed the post of assistant professor of history, then associate professor at Yale Law, before moving to Columbia

Law. A year and a half later she was dean and in that position brought in women as key appointments in such fields as feminist studies, race theory, and modern jurisprudence. She is a member of the bar in New York and Connecticut.

Career path:
Columbia University: Associate in law
Yale University: Lecturer
   Assistant Professor of History
Yale University School of Law: Associate Professor
Columbia University School of Law: Visiting Professor
   George Welwood Murray Professor of Legal History
   Dean

CATHLEEN BLACK, PRESIDENT, HEARST MAGAZINES

As the highest-ranking woman in magazines, Cathleen Black has moved around in order to move up, taking major risks in the process. She used her experience as advertising manager at *Ms.* magazine to boost herself into the role of publisher at *New York.* She tried a brief stint in San Francisco with Francis Ford Coppola on a start-up magazine that didn't work out, and didn't hesitate to return to New York and *Ms.* "If you find a situation that is not reverberating well, pick yourself up by your bootstraps and move on," she recommends. Soon after, another start-up challenged her. It was *USA Today,* which she calls "my biggest risk. It was a killer, hemorrhaging red ink, ridiculed by the eastern establishment press. Now it's the number one newspaper in the country." She left when the learning curve flattened and so moved on to run the Newspaper Association of America, an industry organization representing 1,500 newspapers in the United States and Canada, a job she says "taught me how to look at the big picture, as opposed to hands-on operation of a newspaper." Hearst Magazines came calling and now she's its president.

Black began in magazines in advertising sales and marketing, building a tangible track record. "A lot of women began to break through by taking the sales route," she says, "because you could prove you were successful. You could demonstrate you delivered." Based on her own experience, she believes that "women work harder than men, by and large to prove—either subliminally or not—that they would be able to do the job. That's starting to change now." Her hard work has paid off in her satisfaction. Of her career, she says, "You don't start out wanting to reach for the brass ring. It's an evolving thing. Now there's not a day that goes by that I'm not excited when I wake up." Black sits on the boards of the Hearst Corporation, Coca-Cola, and IBM. Married with two children, she professes that "having an important personal life as well as business life is the best solution of all."

Career path:

New York magazine: Advertising Sales

Ms. magazine: Advertising Manager

New York magazine: Publisher

City of San Francisco Magazine: Advertising Director

Ms. magazine: Associate Publisher

Gannett Company: President, *USA Today*
   Executive Vice President, Marketing
   Publisher, *USA Today*

Newspaper Association of America: President and CEO

Hearst Magazines: President

YVONNE M. CURL, VICE PRESIDENT AND CHIEF MARKETING OFFICER, AVAYA COMMUNICATION

Yvonne Montgomery Curl worked her way up the ladder during her twenty-three years at Xerox, starting in sales and then gaining a variety of experiences in staff positions. She considers her staff-side stint as executive assistant to the chairman as central to her success: "I had the chance to see the company in the broadest perspective you can and to learn what the CEO does." In a case of being in the right place at the right time, Xerox "had just gone through a reorganization. I was on a task force that mapped out how to run the company, which gave me a role in deciding how the company would operate. I had many links with the field," and as a result, she built a wide network she could later call on. In November 2000, Curl joined Avaya Communication Inc. as a vice president and chief marketing officer.

Curl offers an overview of a successful career. She says that "early on, you're primarily judged on performance. But moving out of your comfort zone is an important decision you have to make. You'll succeed if you're identified as someone who can play a bigger job. Relationships with the right people help, but they're not enough. If you have a mentor who cares about you, that's important. I've used mentors as mirrors to get feedback. I ask, 'This is how I'm seeing it; am I missing something?' "

She advises women to network. "Information is power," she says. "The old-boys' network is a forum to share information. It's hard to be on the outside and be totally effective. You need to know what's going on when you're in a meeting. So make up for it as much as you can. Network internally so you know some specific things that are going on. But don't just network internally, or you'll be too narrow. It's good to talk to people outside who have similar experiences so you don't think you're just crazy. That's helpful in putting biases into perspective. And you learn new ways of approaching things and new things about the business."

She is married.

Career path:
Xerox: Sales Representative
    Sales Planning Manager
    District Sales Manager
    District Manager
    Manager, Quality and Business Process, U.S. Marketing
        Group (staff job in line organization)

Vice President, Field Operations, New York area
Executive Assistant to Chairman and CEO
Vice President, Marketing and Strategy Integration, Americas
   Customer Operations (ACO) Latin America (in line
   organization, but a staff job)
Senior Vice President and General Manager, Southern
   Customer Operations for United States Customer
   Operations (USCO)
Senior Vice President and General Manager, Public Sector
   Worldwide, Document Solutions Group
Avaya Communications: Vice President and Chief Marketing
   Officer

MAUREEN KEMPSTON DARKES, PRESIDENT AND GENERAL MANAGER, GENERAL MOTORS OF CANADA

Maureen Kempston Darkes held staff jobs prior to running the Canada operation. "You can take a number of different paths to the top," she says. She started as a labor lawyer, then moved to GM's legal department, "where I quickly got an overview of the business, and that base of information served me well." She ran several departments, including tax, corporate affairs, and legal. She restructured the tax department, then took the challenge of a move to New York. "My strategy in every job I've had is to grow it, to add value, and then grow out of it so I can go on and do something different." She finds that women may lose opportunities for being "too task-oriented. The task is important, but an overview is equally important. Men have a broader perspective. We tend to believe that if we do something well, we'll naturally get ahead. Not true. You need to stretch yourself, have a higher scheme of things to accomplish, and then you'll be rewarded."

GM of Canada shows her influence. A leader in women's advancement, she says, "If you're going to have diversity, you've got to identify people early, get their career paths in place, and stick with them. It entails risk for the individuals involved, and we need systems to support them. Young people coming into business want new opportunities; they want broad-based careers. If we're going to hold on to them, get the best value from them, we need to develop them." She has implemented flexibility, which is "important to the organization and important to the individual if we want to attract and retain good people. Some companies may fear losing control, but I get a better product from people. They get the job done well once they know the standards and you allow them the means to accomplish them. If not, I step in quickly. My experience is that people respond well to that level of trust." Kempston Darkes serves on the boards of CAMI Automotive, CN Rail, General Motors of Canada Ltd., Noranda, and Thomson Corporation. She is married.

Career path:

Osler, Hoskin & Harcourt: Associate
GM Canada: Legal Adviser
   Head of Tax Department
   General Director, Corporate Affairs
   Vice President, Corporate Affairs
   General Counsel and Corporate Secretary
   President and General Manager

CARLY FIORINA, CHAIR AND CEO, HEWLETT-PACKARD

Carly Fiorina, who assumed the top role at Hewlett-Packard in 1999, finds that "women spend a lot of time asking for power, or demanding it." But power, she says, "comes not by waiting for others to give it to you," but by using it. She counsels women to "do the most straightforward thing and exercise power!" She has experienced the frustration women at all levels have had to deal with, that of not being heeded by men at the table, "but it's been a long time since I've felt I wasn't heard when I needed to be." The way she has dealt with this situation is worth emulating: "If it was important to be heard or it was important not to let another claim my idea, then I made a practice of going at it until I was heard."

Fiorina worked her way up the ranks at AT&T, and she admits she had some lessons to learn about how to succeed. "One assignment had me scared for two years," she says, "when I was managing a government contract and we were suing a customer. I was terrified of failing in that one. It was the formative experience of my career because I conquered my fear." The high-profile venture of spearheading the launch of Lucent Technologies not only catapulted her to success, but also taught her valuable lessons. Such visible risk taking, she says, "lets people know what you're doing and what you're capable of. I found out—and others did, too—that I could learn a whole bunch of new things in a hurry. I also learned that you don't have to be an expert to be effective; you just need to learn and to get help from the right folks."

Fiorina professes that "nobody accomplishes any great thing alone. I've been helped every step of the way by many people," including immediate bosses and her boss's boss, "who believed in me and believed I could pull it." She applies this in her current position as HP's CEO. "Leadership," she says, "is accomplishing results through others. That's the difference between leading and being an individual contributor. It's a great thrill leading teams to accomplish more than they thought possible."

Fiorina is married with two stepdaughters and a granddaughter, and holds an MBA. She serves on the boards of Kellogg and Merck, was elected to the U.S./China Board of Trade, and has topped *Fortune*'s list as the most powerful woman in American business.

Career path:
AT&T: Sales Representative
   Account Executive
   National Account Manager

Vice President, Strategy and Market Development
President, Atlantic and Canada
President, North America
Senior Vice President, Global Marketing
Lucent Technologies: Executive Vice President, Corporate
    Operations
President, Consumer Products
Hewlett-Packard: CEO

LYNN FORESTER, FOUNDER AND CO-CHAIR, FIRSTMARK COMMUNICATIONS INTERNATIONAL

While Lynn Forester was at Columbia Law School, a professor, Ruth Bader Ginsburg, warned her that she'd "run into situations as a woman that you won't like, but, trust me, it will be easier than anything I ever ran into." Forester considers that any sexism she's met was "not malice, just stupidity," including a time in 1980, while on an interview lunch for a firm, when she was "sent into another room with the wives." She took a position at a New York law firm in corporate and banking law "as a classic associate, working more hours than I thought existed in a day," and during that time cut her telecommunications teeth with a male mentor who "bet the bank on cellular and gave me opportunities to do important deals." A client wooed her away.

She recommends that women find work environments where their style fits in: "Look at men who are successful in different industries; which ones do you most identify with? Once you figure that out, go into that area." Knowing herself to be an entrepreneur, "results-oriented, independent," she bought TPI Communications in partnership with Motorola, tripled its size, and moved into Latin American markets. She sold it and focused on her own wireless business company, FirstMark Communications International, which later merged with a public company, and she now works with a partner, Michael Price, a former partner at Lazard Frères, as founder, co-CEO, and chairman of First-

Mark Holdings and FirstMark Communications International. A subsidiary of her company, FirstMark Communications Europe, raised $1 billion of private financing in June 2000, making it the largest private financing of a telecommunications company in European history.

A definition of success for Forester came from a mentor "who told me not to focus on the money I'd make but only on the vision of what I wanted my company to be. If you are excited about that, other things take care of themselves." She developed credibility at FirstMark Communications International "according to standards men understand. I've made a lot of money, so men think I know something." Forester is a member of the Council on Foreign Relations, the U.S. National Information Infrastructure Council, and the Secretary of Energy advisory board. Until April 2000, she served on the board of General Instrument Corporation, and until 1999 served on the board of Gulfstream Aerospace. She has two children.

Career path:
Simpson, Thatcher & Barlett: Associate
Metromedia Telecommunications: Executive Vice President, Development
TPI Communications International: CEO and Chairman
FirstMark Communications: President and CEO
FirstMark Communications International: Founder and Co-chair

CAROLEE FRIEDLANDER, FOUNDER, PRESIDENT, AND CEO, CAROLEE DESIGNS

Carolee Friedlander started her multimillion-dollar jewelry business at her home in Greenwich, Connecticut, in 1972, having worked in store design and jewelry design since college. Told by a bank that her husband would have to cosign her $6,000 loan, she borrowed money elsewhere. Soon she opened a New York sales office, going there once a week but working primarily from her Greenwich office, despite advice to the contrary. Calling herself fiercely independent, she says, "Everyone tells you, 'You can't do this' and 'You can't do that.' Don't believe in the world of 'can't.' Eternal optimism is part of the 'head-set' of being an entrepreneur."

She advises women to go to business school "to get a broad framework in areas where you don't have strength. . . . I wish I'd gotten an MBA," she says, "because though I was strong in marketing and design, I had to run a business." She stresses the role of other people in career success: "Seek out people smarter than you in areas where you're lacking. Women today are lucky to have the networking opportunities they do; they need to take advantage of them. I wish I'd had my contacts a lot earlier."

"We live in a man's world still today," says Friedlander. "We've come a long way and haven't come anywhere. Progress is very slow. It goes back to having the right 'head-set.' It's easier for me as an entrepreneur, because I don't have a boss. If I'm meeting with a man and don't agree, I say it. If there's an issue of some kind, I raise it. I'm blunt about it." Friedlander has served as president of the Committee of 200 and on the President's Export Council. She is married with six children: three her own, three joining the family with her second husband.

Career path:
Freelance jewelry design
Store design
Carolee Designs: Founder, President, and CEO

ROBERTA GUTMAN, CORPORATE VICE PRESIDENT AND DIRECTOR OF GLOBAL DIVERSITY, MOTOROLA

Bobbi Gutman's early ambition was to "help bright people understand the folly of keeping black people down," and, she says, "my history professor at Cornell said the way to do that was neither through Congress nor the Supreme Court, which 'follow public opinion.' He said, 'It's multinationals that make change in this country; you must excel by their standards, change them from inside, and they in turn will change the country.' " She built a career in multinationals, and in her current position at Motorola, she has become one of the world's most sought-after diversity experts.

"Women must ask what they want from a career, not from a company," says Gutman. "Few people ask, 'How valuable do I believe I am, and what's important to me?' " Her career path shows that she practices what she preaches: she left behind good jobs with great bosses because "I just had to leave." To one wonderful boss she said, "You keep telling me how good I am, but I don't know that because I don't have a comparison. I have to get out and see how good I really am. If you love me, let me go." She urges women to move beyond "comfort, a powerful human feeling, so that when we don't like what's going on where we are, we have the courage to move on."

Known for an outspoken style and humor that have served her well, she tells how "every place I've been, middle managers have told me that women don't curse, that sometimes I'm too direct, or there's too much levity. But one top manager said to me, 'The hardest part of my job is getting accurate data. You're refreshing in that you are direct and tell the truth.' " Assessing her candor, she says, "I never talk to a title, which is what people usually do in corporations. I talk to individuals."

Gutman is married with one son.

Career path:

Scott Paper Company: Assistant Personnel Manager

SmithKline Beecham Corporation: Manager, Personnel Services and Policy Coordination

Motorola: Director of Personnel for technical professional staff

Digital Equipment Corporation: Manager, headquarters employment

Motorola: Director, Executive and Management Development
   Director, Human Resources Diversity
   Vice President and Director of Human Resources Diversity
   Corporate Vice President, Motorola's Director of Global Di-
      versity, and Executive Director, Motorola Foundation

ELLEN M. HANCOCK, CHAIR AND CEO, EXODUS COMMUNICATIONS

In a recent speech, Ellen Hancock led off by quoting an Apple ad:
"People who are crazy enough to think that they can change the
world are the ones who do." This is an apt description of Hancock herself, who today heads one of the fastest-growing companies engaged in Internet-related services, and who could rightly
be considered one of the pioneers of the Information Age. When
her company acquired Global Crossing Ltd.'s Global Center Inc.
in October 2000, Hancock became one of the wealthiest women
to head a public technology company. Her experience in high
tech spans several decades. She spent twenty-nine years at IBM
(where she was the first female vice president in company history), followed by a COO appointment at National Semiconductor and a top post at Apple in charge of research and
development before becoming CEO at Exodus. Hancock emphasizes that she made each transition only when she felt she no
longer had the support to help lead and grow the company. "I
always promised myself that if I was not moving ahead, if I was
leveling off, or the day came when I was no longer contributing
to the leadership of the company, I'd leave," she says.

Hancock believes that the responsibility for women managing
profit-and-loss jobs falls on women themselves. "Too many
times we've been offered what is a convenient job for people.
When I left IBM, search firms called to ask if I'd go on boards. I
said, 'Yes, but I'm looking for a line-management job.' Women
have to insist on that, to take it on themselves, to say, 'Is this job

I'm about to take going to lead me to the next one, and do I really want that one?' If you can't see it leading in a straight trajectory to where you want to be, don't get sidetracked by what in fact might not be a very good promotion."

An advocate of mentoring, Hancock endorses the formal mentoring program she participated in at IBM: "I had the names of individuals I was responsible to mentor, both women and minorities. And I would agree to mentor in the informal sense. I think women still need to push on their own, but it doesn't hurt to have a little of that pull, to have an organization that wants to see women and minorities get ahead."

Her journey in the Internet world has generated several lessons, which she describes as follows: (1) Women have to work harder to get ahead. "Is it fair? Absolutely not, but I believe it to be true. When you are in the minority, you stand out." (2) Stereotypes exist, and we have to overcome them. "One stereotype is that women lack the right instincts, and lack the ambition for the top-level jobs." (3) Women have to develop a style that makes male managers comfortable with us. "I did it by being one of the guys. I tried to be part of their system rather than forcing them to be part of mine. I believe you first have to be invited into the club before you can change any of the rules."

Hancock is married and is a member of the board of directors of Colgate-Palmolive, Aetna, and Marist College. She is also a member of the Council on Foreign Relations and the Committee of 200.

Career path:

IBM (29 years): Last position: Senior Vice President and Group Executive

National Semiconductor: Executive Vice President and COO

Apple Computer: Executive Vice President of R and D and Chief Technology Officer

Exodus Communications: Chairman and CEO

JANET TIEBOUT HANSON, FOUNDER, PRESIDENT, AND CEO, MILESTONE CAPITAL MANAGEMENT

Following a successful fourteen-year career with Goldman Sachs—which included being the first woman in the firm's history to be promoted into sales management—Janet Tiebout Hanson left to launch her own asset-management firm, Milestone Capital Management. "To excel as a manager in a larger corporate or professional setting, you need to maintain a complex network of formal and informal relationships. In my experience, this is generally a lot harder for women to do than for men. Because these networks are typically male-centric, it takes longer for women to make the right connections, pick up on the correct signals, and speak the 'language' of management."

Hanson also believes that it is more difficult for women to build or sustain their professional networks during periods of career transition. "Promotions, leaves of absence, flextime positions—all of these events create 'disruptions' in your network. Making the management ranks is a great accomplishment, but you soon figure out that there aren't many other women around to serve as coaches, mentors, or role models as you begin to build a whole new set of relationships. And after I returned to work following a leave of absence I found it really challenging to reenter a business and a network that certainly hadn't stood still since I left."

Reflecting on her decision to leave Goldman Sachs and start her own company, Hanson views entrepreneurship as a "tailor made" opportunity for many women. "Running your own firm allows you to focus on the business in your own way and on your own terms. My experience and training at Goldman actually gave me the skills and confidence I needed to succeed as an entrepreneur. I was fortunate to have had a number of male mentors who not only helped me to establish myself as a manager and develop the right set of relationships, but who also showed me what it means to build a business rather than just manage an organization. Now I focus on both in a way that makes sense for me and my lifestyle."

Hanson advises other women, particularly those at Wall Street and other professional service firms, to think of their careers "in terms of a business that needs to be actively managed. Too many women don't make career decisions the way they would make business decisions. You would never attempt to run a business without a clear vision, achievable goals, a well-thought-out strategy, a definition of upside potential and downside risks, and concrete measures of success—why think about your career any differently?"

Hanson is married with two children.

Career path:

McGraw-Hill: Assistant to the Senior Economist
Goldman, Sachs & Company: Vice President and Co-manager, Money Market Sales
   Vice President, Internal Marketing, Asset Management Division
Citibank: Independent Consultant
Milestone Capital Management: Founder, President, and CEO
The Milestone Funds: Chairman of the Board of Trustees

LOIS JULIBER, COO, COLGATE-PALMOLIVE

When Lois Juliber went on her first job interviews, she said, " 'I want to run the company.' But I didn't believe it. My real goal was to be product manager on Kool-Aid." This combination of moxie and actual targets has formed her career as she subsequently achieved this first goal, and she says, "I continue to amaze myself." Instrumental in Colgate's North America turnaround, she focused on morale, "getting the company to grow again by getting people to believe they were good at what they did, that they could make decisions, and that they would win."

Her fifteen years at General Foods followed a clear career path for general marketing. As success strategies, she points to hard work, high energy, tenacity, listening, and strategic thinking: "I could step back and see the bigger picture, stick with things, build on other people's experience." She describes "standards I had to achieve because I was a woman" but had the good fortune to be identified early as a high potential and "was stretched and put into opportunities before I was ready." She tells how she left General Foods to enter the global marketplace, "leaving a secure job to work outside the U.S., based on the other side of the world. Yes, there was risk involved. You have to take smart business risks as a professional."

Juliber has broken ground as a woman, but she didn't do it "by being 'one of the boys.' However, to succeed in the kind of business I'm in, you must be respected by them. You don't need to drink with them for them to know who you are. My approach, whether it's a business decision or social activities in the company, is to be true to myself consistently." Like many successful women in business, she plays sports, including competitive tennis, and is learning to play golf with her husband. Juliber serves on the board of Du Pont and is married.

Career path:
General Foods: Assistant Product Manager, Kool-Aid
   Product Manager, Kool-Aid
   Category Manager, Post Cereals
   Marketing Manager, Post Children's Cereals, Dry Grocery
      Business Unit
   Strategic Business Unit Manager, Dry Grocery Products
   Corporate Vice President, Meals Division
Colgate-Palmolive: Vice President and President, Far East and
      Canada
   President, Colgate North America

Chief Technology Officer
COO, North America and Europe

ANDREA JUNG, PRESIDENT AND CEO, AVON

Andrea Jung began her career as a buyer at Bloomingdale's and was named to her current position as president and CEO of Avon Products, Inc., in November 1999. As she advanced in the retail world, she built a reputation in merchandising—creating and marketing brands—a track that, it turned out, prepared her for her current corporate work. She attributes her success at Avon to spearheading a global marketing push. Says Jung, "Avon is the example in the beauty business of a turnaround. It involved real risks. We had to discard some products and upgrade others, raising prices and raising the bar on performance." She has superb advice on how to manage risk: "Believe in what you want to do and communicate the risk up and down. You can't be alone in it. Share the risk, pro and con, with a boss, and peers, and with people you manage."

Her job as a Bloomingdale's buyer gave her early P-and-L responsibility; at Avon, she began with a staff position in marketing. "It's great to have both line and staff experiences. In staff jobs, I learned negotiating and communication skills and I gained a breadth of understanding. I had a wide lens on the opportunities and barriers of organization and governance." She urges women "to check to see if you're in a company that's willing in their developmental process to give women line opportunities. I truly love the beauty industry and everything Avon stands for. This passion for my work is fueled by the pride in what Avon represents as a global company and as the company for women."

Jung sits on the boards of Avon and GE, and is a member of Princeton University's Board of Trustees. She was named as one of *Fortune*'s "50 Most Powerful Women in American Business" in 1998 and 1999. She has two children.

Career path:

Bloomingdale's: Assistant Buyer
  Buyer
  Group Buyer
  Vice President and Merchandise Manager
Robinson's: Senior Vice President and General Merchandise
      Manager
I. Magnin: Senior Vice President and General Merchandising
      Manager
Neiman-Marcus: Executive Vice President, Merchandising
Avon: President, Product Marketing Group for United States
  President, Global Marketing
  Executive Vice President and President, Global Marketing
      and New Business
  President and COO
  President and CEO

NANCY KARCH, RETIRED DIRECTOR, MCKINSEY & COMPANY, MEMBER, MCKINSEY ADVISORY COUNCIL

Formerly one of four women directors (senior partners) at the time at her firm and the first woman to hold regional management responsibility at McKinsey, Nancy Karch served as managing partner of McKinsey Southeast United States. Her success stems from having carved out a new field for the firm and establishing a global retail practice. Now a leading adviser to the retail industry, she sums up her success strategy as risk taking and innovation. "I broke out of the pack because of that experience," she says. "The beauty of risky things is that if they pay off, they're very noticeable. I became an expert in an industry and built a reputation with its leaders early."

Karch studied to be a mathematician but soon rejected the isolation of the theoretical and enrolled in Harvard's MBA program. She chose to enter consulting over investment banking because "neither numbers nor deal making interested me. In consulting, you do things ahead of your years, and they're exciting. As a young partner, I worked directly with the CEOs of prestigious companies, who clearly valued my counsel. The first time that happens, the light goes on and you say, 'Holy cow, these are the big guys running companies, and they want to talk to me!' It's pretty heady. You have days when you see your own growth."

Karch credits mentors for abetting her success: "Having mentors was important during the years I was starting to build our retail practice. The firm didn't have retail as a priority. When you're building something new, you must take risks, and you must find time for it. I was working on it when the evaluative committees wanted me to work for client X. If I got flak, my mentors were there. It was extremely important having important people stand up for me."

Career path:
Northeastern University: Lecturer in mathematics
McKinsey & Company: Associate
   Manager
   Principal
   Director and Senior Partner
   Office Manager, Southeast United States
   Member, McKinsey Advisory Council

MARIE KNOWLES, EXECUTIVE VICE PRESIDENT AND CFO, ATLANTIC RICHFIELD

Now one of the top women in the oil business, in 1970 Marie Knowles faced closed doors at every major oil or chemical research company, despite her M.S. in chemical engineering. "They told me they just weren't hiring women," she says. A friend got her a job in a small research firm, and she soon diversified by earning an MBA, which got her through the door at ARCO. There her twenty-six-year career has spanned sixteen jobs ranging from staff experience in finance and planning to a stint abroad to a line job at ARCO Transportation, where she headed the operations of the $900 million division. "It was a people management job; I don't have to actually operate the fleet of oceangoing tankers, although I did steer one once," she admits.

She says that "going back and forth between line and staff is important. You get different perspectives and insights, and you need all those experiences on the way to senior-level executive jobs. If you get a broad base of activities, they can't cubbyhole you." She took a pay cut to make a lateral move, one of her success strategies. She advises, "If you know where you're going and a pay cut is going to move you toward your goal—whether money or a more satisfying career—do the lateral move. If you always hold out for a promotion, especially as a woman in a corporation, it will limit your ability to get broader experiences. You'll have to compete head-to-head with men in that experience line, and you may wait for a long time." She was "thrilled" to take the position of CFO, although it meant returning to a staff job. "There's a big difference being one of the top five," she says. For a short time she sat on the board, until the company abolished inside directors.

As a woman pioneering in a nontraditional field for women, she offers advice on how to deal with bias: "Shut it off and go on. If you let it in, it will overwhelm you. It's their problem. A high self-confidence level helps most of the time, enabling you to persevere." Where does she get her strength? "Greed and ambition," she says with a laugh, then answers seriously, "Mostly from the support of my family." She is married with two sons and serves on the boards of Phelps Dodge and Vastar Resources.

Career path:
Fluor Corporation: Supervisor, Analysis and Development
Atlantic Richfield:

ARCO Products Division: Senior Financial Analyst
   Manufacturing Controller
   Supervisor, Logistics and Economics, Crude and Product
      Supply
ARCO Corporate: Finance Manager, Treasury/Finance
   Manager, Investor Relations, Finance and Tax Division
   Managerial Positions in Corporate Treasury (Cash
      Management and Corporate Finance)
   Controller
ARCO Chemical, London: Vice President, Finance, Planning
   and Control
ARCO Corporate: Manager, Corporate Planning
   Assistant Treasurer, Banking
ARCO International Oil & Gas Company: Vice President,
   Finance, Planning and Control
ARCO Corporate: Vice President and Manager, Profit Plan-
   ning and Operations Analysis
ARCO Transportation Company: President
ARCO Corporate: Executive Vice President and CFO

GERALDINE LAYBOURNE, FOUNDER, CHAIR, AND CEO, OXYGEN MEDIA

Two principal causes have motivated Geraldine Laybourne's career: children and women, specifically "offering them something
they need and aren't getting." She revolutionized children's television at Nickelodeon and envisions doing the same for women
with her brainchild Oxygen Media, a multimedia company that
combines TV and the Internet. Known as an innovator, she attributes her success to knowing her market and to branding
what she's created.

With a background in elementary education and a brief teaching stint under her belt, she and her husband conceived a pilot
TV program for children and sold it to the new children's cable

network Nickelodeon. Two pilots later, it hired her and promoted her regularly until she reached program manager. Then her boss approached her to run the shop: "He said, 'I don't know what you can do, but I'm willing to just watch.' I jumped at it. It's a lot easier to take risks if you're driven to make a difference." She downsized to a core team and doubled the network's audience size in six months. "Quick success gave me great confidence I was right. Having kids as our mission—to develop creative, curious citizens—enabled us to develop a brand. Kids who were worried about growing up got a playground with Nickelodeon. If you get under the skin of consumers and meet a need, you have a business." She also founded Nick at Nite.

Laybourne left Nickelodeon "because I was forty-eight years old and felt I'd never do another thing in my life. I wanted to do something for women." Michael Eisner and Michael Ovitz convinced her to run Disney/ABC Cable, with responsibility for the Disney Channel, and Disney's share of Lifetime, A&E, the History Channel, and E! Entertainment channels. She was attracted particularly by Lifetime but soon found it already to be a successful brand "for women who want to emote. I was interested in the modern woman who's trying to figure out about balance, work, fulfillment, and not a victim, not trivial. Women have tremendous economic clout, feel more independent than ever, just have a feeling of well-being. And women are funny as hell. I wanted to build a positive brand on that." Entrepreneurial juices flowing, she launched Oxygen Media.

Among her greatest accomplishments, Laybourne counts helping other women: she brought the number of women into senior management at MTV up to 60 percent from just one woman.

Laybourne is married with two grown children.

Career path:
Concord Academy: Teacher
Early Bird Specials: Independent Producer

Nickelodeon: Program Manager
  Director, Acquisitions
  Director, Acquisitions and Scheduling
  Vice President, Acquisitions
  President, Nickelodeon, Nick at Nite
  Vice Chairman, MTV Networks, and President, Nickelodeon,
    Nick at Nite
Disney/ABC Cable Networks: President (oversaw Lifetime TV
    for Women)
Oxygen Media: Founder, Chair, and CEO

JOAN M. LEIMAN, EXECUTIVE DEPUTY VICE PRESIDENT FOR THE HEALTH SCIENCES AT COLUMBIA UNIVERSITY AND CLINICAL PROFESSOR OF PUBLIC HEALTH

Joan Leiman says she never meant to have a career at all—at least not in anything but the law. However, when she met with the assistant dean of Columbia Law School (it was in the sixties, just when they were thinking of letting women attend), he was "just very nasty and not nice. He acted as if I should be glad just to be in his presence."

Feeling rejected by the law, Leiman changed course. She "broke the gender barrier at the New York City Budget Bureau" during the John Lindsay administration. "I've never regretted making that choice," she says. The first woman had left a few months before: "They put her in a corner and no one ever talked to her." Leiman was determined to have a different kind of experience.

Mentors—all male—were very important to her. They helped her persist in an all-male environment. Her first big capital budget meeting was a case in point. "We did it on a Saturday morning. When it was time for lunch, one of the engineers went around and took everyone's lunch orders. When he came back, he collected money from everyone but me. I asked in a very little voice, 'Will you please let me pay for lunch?' He didn't respond, so I asked again. I asked a third time and he said, 'No woman will ever pay for lunch while I'm in the Budget Bureau.' Finally I turned to my boss (and his) and said, 'David, make Charlie let me pay for my lunch!' David said, 'Joan Leiman pays for her lunch and that's policy.' "

Leiman said networking became easier at the end of her years at the Budget Bureau. Her experiences there launched her long and rewarding career in the public sector and in academia. Comparing women's success in the public and private sectors today, she points out that leadership still makes all the difference, and leadership in the public sector has been quicker to respond to women's increasing numbers in the workplace. "Women's being hired and brought along has been more likely to happen in the public than the private sector. Government has been one of the most hospitable places for women. Here, as in nonprofits and in university administration, you find more women in senior positions than in the private sector." Now serving as chief administrative officer at Columbia's medical school, she sees a discrepancy between the situation for women in university administration and the faculty, pointing out that "you find lots of women in the entrance ranks of science, but women are still underrepresented as you go higher."

Work/life balance is a problem to which she sees no magic solution. "Sometimes one thing is out of kilter; sometimes another thing is. When you have small children, you cannot expect the same career trajectory as men have." She says you must react when demands of home and children are great, but understand and balance your priorities: "Knowing which is the path and which is the detour is the trick, but it's not always clear."

To her mind, you cannot get ahead without following these three steps: (1) maintain focus; (2) be sure you have lots of energy; (3) pace yourself. But of course that's not enough. You've got to be flexible about where you're going and what you need to get you there. "A lot of women in high places didn't exactly do it in a straight line," she says. "You've got to know yourself. And be yourself. Successful women do things their way; they don't press themselves into a mold."

Leiman, a Buffalo native who has lived most of her life in New York City, is married to a corporate lawyer with two grown children. She has three grandchildren with whom she is very involved.

Career path:

City of New York: Special Assistant to Major John V. Lindsay
    Deputy Commissioner for planning and evaluation,
        Addiction Services Agency
    Assistant Director, Bureau of the Budget, Health and
        Hospitals and Human Services
    Program Analyst, Bureau of the Budget
Ford Foundation: Fellow in Politics and Education
Manpower Demonstration Research Corporation: Vice
        President for program development and budget
Interfaith Medical Center: Vice President, Planning
The Commonwealth Fund Commission on Women's Health:
        Executive Director
Columbia University Medical School: Executive Deputy Vice
        President for health sciences; Chief Administrative
        Officer, Health Sciences Division and College of
        Physicians and Surgeons; and Clinical Professor of
        Public Health

REBECCA A. MCDONALD, CHAIR AND CEO, ENRON ASIA-PACIFIC, AFRICA, AND CHINA

Shortly after Rebecca McDonald joined a gas company, they asked her to start a sales and customer relations department. This opportunity placed her on the cutting edge of a changing industry, as she and "a couple of young people who are famous now" created one of the first nonregulated natural gas marketing companies, one that became a model for deregulation of the business. "Nobody knew it would be big, and no one wanted to mess with it. I moved up the ladder faster than I would have in the typical environment." She advises, "Don't go after the easy stuff. Go after the dirty stuff, and make it into something." With a laugh she says, "When others realized it was the wave of the future, they tried to take it over but couldn't because they weren't knowledgeable. That's the greatest compliment, when someone above you tries to take it over."

Getting to know all aspects of her business motivated her moves to Tenneco, where she learned some of the workings of headquarters, and to Amoco: "I knew about the energy business, but not about exploration and production. In a business with few women around, I needed to know a lot if I was going to be taken seriously." She looked at the big picture: "In a business that was becoming integrated quickly, there were still pieces that knew nothing about each other. I saw that if I understood all the pieces, that when the upstream piece became integrated, I'd have an edge." With her diverse experience, she has entertained changing to a more woman-friendly industry where she'd have a better shot at the top job. "But this is so interesting, and I'm having a good time helping shape a whole new industry. That may be more important than running something."

Married with one son, McDonald sits on the boards of Granite Construction Company and Eagle Global Logistics.

Career path:

Fluor Corporation: Expediter
   Assistant Buyer
   Buyer
   Project Procurement Buyer
   Negotiator
   Management Development Specialist

Consultant: Conflict resolution
Panhandle Eastern: Employee Development Coordinator
    Manager, Gas Sales and Customer Relations, Panhandle
        Eastern Pipeline and Truckline Gas
    Vice President, Sales Department, Panhandle Trading
        Company
    Vice President, General Manager, Panhandle Trading
        Company
Tenneco: Vice President, Strategic Planning, Tenneco Gas
        Company
    President, Tenneco Gas Marketing Company
Amoco: President, National Gas Group
    President and CEO, Amoco Energy Development Company
Enron: Executive Managing Director
    Chairman and CEO, Enron Asia-Pacific, Africa, and China

ANNE M. MULCAHY, PRESIDENT AND COO, XEROX CORPORATION

Having attained one of the highest offices held by women in a Fortune 500 corporation, Anne Mulcahy is a shining example of the well-rounded approach to getting ahead. Mulcahy began her career at Xerox in sales in 1976. "I wanted something that could be judged on absolute performance. Sales is line, core to the company, a totally tangible way to measure my success."

Fifteen years later, having risen to a senior management position with a solid career running field operations and operational groups, she switched from the line side to a staff job. "I decided I really needed to look at the company from a different perspective. This was a breakthrough experience in terms of coming out of the functional ladder approach to a much broader career."

The switch from line to staff can be tricky. How can you be sure you won't get stuck in a staff job ghetto? Mulcahy understood it all. "My experience and timing were important—if you have a line track record you won't get stuck." It only happens, she says, if you're switched by the company because you've failed at a line job. "Then you always have that black cloud hanging over you. I moved from a position of strength."

Mulcahy's position, of course, wasn't just any staff job. While she was responsible for human resources and several other areas, her title was chief of staff to CEO Paul Allaire. "I basically managed the management and organizational processes for the company. It was really about creating strategy for Xerox." It was from that job that she rose first to president of General Market Operations, a $6 billion business accounting for about 30 percent of Xerox's total revenue, then to her current high post.

Interestingly, Mulcahy says she is not much of a planner. She's of the "just enjoy your ice cream while it's on your plate" school, believing that if you focus too much on the future, you miss out on the present. "Many men and women get so obsessed with the next step that they miss opportunities that aren't in the plan they've built. That means you don't optimize your current job, either. I would focus on succeeding in and enjoying the current."

While she enjoys being a mentor, she wants to do it for "people who've earned" it. She's against formally orchestrated mentor programs. She advises looking for mentors all around you: "Good bosses make great mentors, but mentors don't have to be hierarchically ahead of you," she says.

As to work/life balance, "Kids come first" is her primary rule. "I always laugh when I have to write a résumé of any kind, in terms of hobbies and special interests. How does none sound? There's just no room. You can't do everything. Your ability to make some choices and stick with them allows you to have some peacefulness and be happy."

Mulcahy is married with two children.

Career path:

Xerox: Sales Representative
  Sales Operations Manager
  District Manager
  Marketing Operations Manager
  Region Sales Manager
  Operations Manager
  Vice President and Region Manager
  Vice President, Worldwide Marketing Planning
  Director, Human Resources Operations
  Vice President, Human Resources
  Vice President, Worldwide Customer Operations Staff
  Vice President and Chief Staff Officer
  President and COO

BARBARA PAUL ROBINSON, PARTNER, DEBEVOISE & PLIMPTON

When Barbara Paul Robinson asked the partners at her firm for the title of "Esq.," a title reserved for men, she might have surprised them, but she got it. She convinced the presiding partner to move the partners' lunch out of the all-male Racquets Club. When pregnant in 1967 with her first child, she asked for a "regular" five-day-per-week schedule, although she compromised by changing her specialty from litigation to trusts and estates. With her second child, she asked to go part-time. And when she asked to return to the partner track, she surprised the partners again. No woman at the firm ever had.

The first woman partner at Debevoise and the first woman president of the Association of the Bar of the City of New York, Robinson reports that when she was in law school, women couldn't use the reading room at the Yale University library, and when she entered a lounge where students hung out, "the entire room went drop-dead silent." She believes a law career to be somewhat easier for women today "because there's more acceptance and support, like institutionalized flextime or part-time programs," but she acknowledges the difficulty of succeeding as both a mother and a lawyer. She implores a discouraged woman not to drop out, as "she has already invested a lot in her own capacity, she's her own human capital. Whether she stays at a firm or not, she should make the most of the experience and reach out and grab what she wants."

Robinson wants to see firms work harder to retain women, and accordingly, she started a flextime program for Debevoise parents, one of the first of its kind in New York. Married with two children, she is a member of the Council on Foreign Relations.

Career path:
Debevoise & Plimpton: Associate
    Partner

JUDITH RODIN, PRESIDENT, UNIVERSITY OF PENNSYLVANIA

The first woman president of an Ivy League institution, Judith Rodin set out on a career of academic research and teaching armed with a Ph.D. in psychology from Columbia University. Winning the Early Career Award from the American Psychological Association for outstanding scientific contributions secured her reputation as a scholar; she's known for her research on aging, obesity, and jealousy. She pioneered as the first woman in all her medical school appointments. But she changed direction into administration after leading a multiuniversity, interdisciplinary network of scientists on research funded by the MacArthur Foundation, "which showed me you could do good science and administration and enable others to do what they do well. It was very gratifying."

She asked Yale's president for added responsibility and became the first woman chair of the Department of Psychology, knowing it would make her a candidate for a dean's position. Two years later, she became dean of the Graduate School of Arts and Sciences, and one year after that she was named provost. She continued "to keep my hand in research all my time at Yale, but I'm not able to do that now. Until I became president, I said I would return to full-time research and teaching. Now I realize how much I enjoy this work, and although I'm still thriving in my current position, it is preparing me for any next steps I choose to take. It's been a huge shift in my thinking."

Rodin's success strategies include asking for what she wants, taking risks, and what she calls "compulsive time management." She advises women to "be compulsive about organizing your time. Keep notes, figure out what you're going to do with all the minutes of your day to be productive." Rodin serves on the President's Committee of Advisors on Science and Technology, as well as on the boards of Aetna, EDS, AMR, Young & Rubicam, the Greater Philadelphia First Corporation, and the Brookings Institution. She is married with three children, two from her husband's previous marriage.

Career path:
New York University: Assistant Professor of Psychology
Yale University:
    Psychology Department: Assistant Professor
        Associate Professor
        Director of Graduate Studies
        Professor
        Professor of Medicine and Psychiatry
        Chair, Department of Psychology
    Graduate School of Arts and Sciences: Dean
        Provost
University of Pennsylvania: President and Professor of
        Psychology, Psychiatry, and Medicine

JUDY SPRIESER, CEO, TRANSORA

For the first fifteen years of her career, Judy Sprieser had no career plan: "I just made it up as I went; I caught waves." An English major on the job market "with no skills that would pay for an apartment and allow me to eat, I was fired as a secretary because I couldn't type well enough. I applied for a job at a commercial bank, as they'd hire anyone then. Harris Bank put me in a training program and paid for graduate school." The MBA led to her career in finance. "But," adds Sprieser, "I'm more savvy now: I try to create my own waves."

She changed her approach while at Sara Lee, going to her boss, the CFO, and asking what experience she needed to land his job. The answer was line experience, no easy avenue for a woman in a staff job. A doer by nature, she created her own "significant profit-generating project that nobody else wanted to do." To do so, she added to her work as CFO of a Sara Lee division and built a business in Mexico, "proving I could run something of significance." She takes naturally to risk and knows its importance to her rise, advising women, "You'll make it harder for yourself to get ahead if you don't take risks. It's the law of risk and reward." Her reward for the Mexican venture was being made president of the North American Bakery business; and on the basis of that success, she was named CFO of Sara Lee.

Having once accomplished the difficult switch from staff to line, she acknowledges that returning to staff to take the CFO job "was a difficult decision because I loved running the bakery operation, but it meant a significant rise in the corporate hierarchy." Today she feels she is "viewed as a finance person with line experience, rather than as a line person with finance experience" as she sets another line job as her goal. As a first woman in many of her positions, she finds that "so much of women's getting ahead is about role modeling and comfort levels. Part of my job is to be present at meetings where there haven't been women, so men stop thinking of women as outsiders, as anomalies." Sprieser serves on the boards of Sara Lee and USG Corporation and is married with two children.

Career path:
Harris Bank: Management trainee
  Commercial Banker
Esmark: Director of Treasury Operations
Naleo Chemical Company: Assistant Treasurer, International
Sara Lee: Assistant Treasurer, Corporate Finance
  Senior Vice President and CFO, Sara Lee Bakery North
    America
  President and CEO, Sara Lee Bakery North America
  Senior Vice President and CFO
Transora: CEO

CAROLE ST. MARK, FOUNDER AND PRESIDENT, GROWTH MANAGEMENT

What Carole St. Mark enjoys most is starting new businesses. At Pitney Bowes, she had the chance to do this on more than one occasion. One she grew into Pitney Bowes Management Services, with a half-billion dollars in annual revenue. "That was a risky move for the board," she says, "the way they threw me into the line job." She ran that business while serving as president and CEO of Pitney Bowes Business Services, then, after "having taken it beyond where I thought I could go, I wanted to do more of what I loved, so I started my own business." She now assists companies with the process of starting businesses.

In an uncommon career, St. Mark began in staff positions, earned her MBA over a ten-year period, and eventually crossed over to the line side. While she was in human resources at Pitney Bowes, her CEO selected her to overhaul strategic planning. Following on that success, the company added new-business development and mergers and acquisitions to her responsibilities, giving her a firm hold on profit and loss. She advises women who want to succeed "to find the biggest problem your company has—one that's important to the business, and especially one that no one wants to handle—and solve it. Take risks that expose you to decision makers, so you get noticed by people at the top."

St. Mark was always the first woman on the hall and found that "people didn't know how to act or treat me. I developed a style that was helpful, nonthreatening, collegial. I wasn't overtly competing, not raising my voice, but being firm, never emotional." She serves on the boards of SuperValu and Polaroid Corporation.

Career path:
General Foods: Personnel: Manager recruiting
St. Regis Paper: Personnel Manager
General Electric: Manager, Organization and Manpower
Pitney Bowes: Director, Human Resources Development
    Vice President, Strategic Planning
    Vice President, Corporate Planning and Development
    President, Pitney Bowes Business Units
    President and CEO, Pitney Bowes Business Services
Growth Management: Founder and President

LULU C. WANG, PARTNER AND CEO, TUPELO CAPITAL MANAGEMENT L.L.C.

As head of her own New York–based investment firm that has been described as among the largest woman-run hedge funds in the United States, Lulu Wang credits "making the right choices and setting priorities" as key to business success. She began her career in finance at the beginning of the 1970s, armed only with a Wellesley degree in English literature. Her first job was an editorial position in a Wall Street firm. "It took only a week or two before I realized that the real career path at an investment firm is in investing, not editing," she says. Accordingly, she shifted gears and began taking courses in accounting and securities analysis, becoming a Wall Street analyst by her "bootstraps." Within two years, she received an offer from one of the leading investment banking firms, Donaldson, Lufkin & Jenrette, followed by a post at Bankers Trust. Over the next two decades, Wang ascended the ranks of professional money management. After ten years at Equitable Capital Management and another ten at Jennison Associates Capital Corporation, where she managed assets of more than $4 billion, Wang founded Tupelo Capital Management.

"I learned to prioritize, both professionally and personally, early in my career. It was one of the most important lessons I learned," Wang says. "Fairly early on in my career, I had an attractive offer to go into investment banking. Choosing that career path rather than staying with securities investment would have meant working 24-7, it would have meant neglecting every other part of my life. In investment management, I knew I would have more flexibility to build a name and track record without losing the important balance in my work and personal life. Within investment management, I've been able to be a 'whole' but still very competitive person."

Based on her experience, Wang's advice to young women hoping to succeed in business is to choose your priorities and stick with them. "When you are young, hopefully full of fire and with some talent, you can move in many directions. Frankly, when I was a young analyst, there were many different things that I wanted to do, and I probably tried to do more than I should have." She also emphasizes the importance—particularly for women—of building your credentials with a view toward your future goals: "I started with a clear view to having my own firm someday. I started with a five- to ten-year plan and built up valuable investment experience. But you also need to build up other credentials. I started on Wall Street without an MBA. In 1980, I determined that if I wanted my own firm, having the credentials on paper was also important. In a service industry, that matters a lot, and perhaps still more so for women than for men."

Despite her responsibilities as CEO and general partner of one of the most successful start-ups in the investment industry, Wang still finds time for a range of activities outside of work, including collecting American art and vintage cars. She is married with one son and serves on several nonprofit boards, among them WNYC, New York's public radio, and the New York Community Trust, where she heads the finance committee. She is also a trustee of Wellesley College and chairs the board's Investment Committee.

Career path:

Donaldson, Lufkin & Jenrette: Analyst
Bankers Trust: Trust Officer, Analyst
Equitable Capital Management: Senior Vice President and
     Managing Director
Jennison Associates Capital Corporation: Director and
     Executive Vice President
Tupelo Capital Management L.L.C.: CEO and General Partner

RITA P. WILSON, PRESIDENT, ALLSTATE INDEMNITY COMPANY

As president of Allstate Indemnity, Rita Wilson has responsibility for the $3.1 billion nonstandard insurance operation. She began her professional career as a teacher in the Department of Defense Overseas schools, then decided to tackle the corporate world, beginning at the "desk level" in preparation for a supervisory position. She gained visibility, both within and outside the company, by capitalizing on the opportunity to represent the company in their advocacy of air bags in cars in the early 1980s. This visibility led to her being placed on the company's management rotation program, designed to fast-track high-potential leaders. There, her experiences included sales (a booth at a Sears store), claims, and other assignments where "I got to experience and understand the organization from the ground up."

In 1983, Wilson became the company's first woman regional vice president (although not the first African American), based in Milwaukee and responsible for operations in four states. "That was a big stretch, warp speed from a fifth-grade teacher eight years earlier. On my first day in the job, I had so much anxiety, I stayed in my office most of the day, doing busy work from setting up my desk to reviewing color charts for a company car." That night, she determined "to go to my strengths . . . my belief in the frontline employee and our ability, together, to read our business goals and objectives. I spent the next day on the floor and began to learn what was going on in the region. I never lost sight, from that day forward, of how the best leaders never forget what they are privileged to lead—the people." Wilson says she "has depended on this time and again throughout my career: to go directly to the front line, clearly articulate the direction and goals of the organization, and ask for their commitment, support, input, and ownership."

Wilson briefly left Allstate for Ameritech, "the smartest and dumbest thing I've done. Smart because I learned so much during that time and dumb because I left an environment I flourished in." She finds that "often, it was not difficult to exceed the expectations others have of you as a woman or minority. If you get trapped in that heady experience of being satisfied with reaching others' expectations, it's unlikely you'll grow and be of ultimate value to the organization. Set your own standards and definition of what success looks like for you and don't stop until you can look at yourself and know you succeeded." Her mentor of twenty years, the CEO of Allstate, invited her back "to help him with corporate relations, and I returned where I felt I had the opportunity to make a contribution, one that would be satisfying for me professionally." Before retiring, the CEO promoted her to her current line position. She is married with a son.

Career path:

Allstate: Operations Supervisor trainee
  Public Affairs Manager
  Assistant Regional Manager
  Regional Vice President, Milwaukee
  Regional Vice President, Houston
  Regional Vice President, Illinois
  Territorial Vice President
  Senior Vice President, Corporate Relations
Ameritech: Senior Vice President, Corporate Communications
Allstate: Senior Vice President, Corporate Relations
  President, Allstate Indemnity Company

Notes

Introduction

1. *Women of Color in Corporate Management: Dynamics of Career Advancement* (New York: Catalyst, 1998).
2. U.S. Bureau of Labor Statistics, *Employment and Earnings,* January 2000, p. 78, and *20 Facts on Women Workers,* U.S. Department of Labor, Women's Bureau, March 2000.

Chapter 1: Wise Up

1. "Cracks in the Glass Ceiling [Editorial]," *The New York Times,* July 21, 1999, p. A22.
2. Jennifer K. Glass and Lisa Riley, "Family Responsive Policies and Employee Retention Following Childbirth," *Social Forces* (vol. 76, no. 4), pp. 1401–36.
3. *Women Entrepreneurs: Why Companies Lose Female Talent and What They Can Do About It* (New York: Catalyst, 1998).
4. *Closing the Gap: Women's Advancement in Corporate and Professional Canada* (New York: The Conference Board of Canada

and Catalyst, 1998), and *Women in Corporate Leadership: Progress and Prospects* (New York: Catalyst, 1996).

Chapter 2: You Can If You Plan

1. *Internet Board Index* (New York: Spencer Stuart, 1999).
2. Donald O. Parsons, *Poverty Dynamics Among Mature Women: Evidence from the NLS, 1967–1989,* National Longitudinal Surveys, U.S. Department of Labor, Bureau of Labor Statistics, NLS 95-25, January 1995, p. 4.

Chapter 3: Get-Ahead Basics

1. *20 Facts on Women Workers,* U.S. Department of Labor, Women's Bureau, March 2000.
2. *Women of Color in Corporate Management: Opportunities and Barriers* (New York: Catalyst, 1999).
3. Cheryl Thompson-Stacy and Gregory Pogue, "Run Silent, Run Cheap: The High Price of Not Asking for Salary Equity," *Black Issues in Higher Education* (vol. 2, no. 9), pp. 24–25. This study looked at women in academia, but Catalyst found that the same holds true for women throughout the working world, although the statistics vary. Eighty percent of the top women administrators had not negotiated for their salaries when offered current and past positions, and 60 percent were paid less than their male counterparts. Some institutions saved 25 to 30 percent in salary costs by hiring women executive managers over men, according to the study.
4. If the time arrives when you need flexibility in your work schedule, it might be possible to trade money for time out. Negotiate so when you return, you're back on track.

Chapter 4: Style Matters

1. *Women in Corporate Leadership: Progress and Prospects* (New York: Catalyst, 1996) and *Closing the Gap: Women's Advancement in Corporate and Professional Canada* (New York: The Conference Board of Canada and Catalyst, 1998).
2. Deborah Tannen, *Talking from 9 to 5: How Women's and Men's Conversational Styles Affect Who Gets Heard, Who Gets Credit, and What Gets Done at Work* (New York: Morrow, 1994), p. 112.

3. *The CPA Journal* (New York: New York State Society of Certified Public Accountants, January 2000).
4. Stephen Gandel, "New Ideas Getting Exchanged Among NYSE Floor Brokers," *Crain's New York Business*, March 20, 2000.
5. Vicki Schultz, "Reconceptualizing Sexual Harassment," *Yale Law Journal* (vol. 107, no. 6 [April 1998]), pp. 1683–1805.

Chapter 5: Become Known

1. Catalyst conference, "Perception and Reality: The Status of Women in Corporate America," New York, June 5, 1997.
2. Ibid. At the time, Hancock was Executive Vice President, Apple Computer, previously at National Semiconductor and the first female senior vice president at IBM.
3. Carol Jenkins, The Benenson Lecture, 92nd Street Y, New York, May 11, 2000. Carol Jenkins and Company.
4. Catalyst conference, "Perception and Reality: The Status of Women in Corporate America," New York, June 5, 1997.

Chapter 6: Your Number One Success Strategy: Networking

1. *Women in Corporate Leadership: Progress and Prospects* (New York: Catalyst, 1996).
2. *Closing the Gap: Women's Advancement in Corporate and Professional Canada* (New York: The Conference Board of Canada and Catalyst, 1998).
3. *Women of Color in Corporate Management: Opportunities and Barriers* (New York: Catalyst, 1999).

Chapter 7: Making Your Life Work

1. Maggie Mahar, "A Change of Place," *Barron's*, March 21, 1994, p. 33.
2. Howard Hayghe, "Married Mothers' Work Patterns: The Job-Family Compromise," *Monthly Labor Review*, June 1994, p. 30.

Chapter 8: Find a Mentor/Be a Mentor

1. F. J. Lunding, G. E. Clements, and D. S. Perkins, "Everyone Who Makes It Has a Mentor," *Harvard Business Review*, July–August 1978, pp. 89, 100.

2. *Korn/Ferry International's Executive Profile: A Decade of Change in Corporate Leadership* (New York: Korn/Ferry International and UCLA Anderson Graduate School of Management, 1990).
3. *Women of Color in Corporate Management: A Statistical Picture* (New York: Catalyst, 1997).
4. "Everyone Who Makes It Has a Mentor," p. 89.

Chapter 9: Conduits to Top Leadership

1. *Knowing the Territory: Women in Sales* (New York: Catalyst, 1995).

Chapter 10: What to Expect at a Firm

1. Nancy Ballard, "Equal Engagement: Observations on Career Success and Meaning in the Lives of Women Lawyers," Center for Research on Women, Wellesley College, no. 292, 1998, p. 18.
2. See *A New Approach to Flexibility: Managing the Work/Time Equation* (New York: Catalyst, 1998).
3. See Catalyst's book on creating and sustaining successful networks, *Creating Women's Networks* (San Francisco: Jossey-Bass, 1999).

Chapter 11: Wisdom from the Pioneers

1. U.S. Department of Education, National Center for Education Statistics, Higher Education General Survey (HEGIS), *Degrees and Other Formal Awards Conferred,* Surveys and Integrated Postsecondary Education Data.

Index

SHEILA WELLINGTON has served as president of Catalyst since 1993, arriving after a pioneering term as the first woman secretary at Yale University. She worked in the public health arena for more than twenty years as director of two psychiatric facilities serving the mentally ill poor.

Catalyst is the nonprofit research and advisory organization that works to advance women in business. Its dual mission is to enable professional women to achieve their maximum potential and to help employers capitalize fully on the talents of their female employees.

ABOUT THE TYPE

This book was set in Sabon, a typeface designed by the well-known German typographer Jan Tschichold (1902–74). Sabon's design is based upon the original letterforms of Claude Garamond and was created specifically to be used for three sources: foundry type for hand composition, Linotype, and Monotype. Tschichold named his typeface for the famous Frankfurt typefounder Jacques Sabon, who died in 1580.